UNDERWATER

SOCIETY AND THE ENVIRONMENT

SOCIETY AND THE ENVIRONMENT

The impact of humans on the natural environment is one of the most pressing issues of the twenty-first century. Key topics of concern include mounting natural resource pressures, accelerating environmental degradation, and the rising frequency and intensity of disasters. Governmental and nongovernmental actors have responded to these challenges through increasing environmental action and advocacy, expanding the scope of environmental policy and governance, and encouraging the development of the so-called green economy. Society and the Environment encompasses a range of social science research, aiming to unify perspectives and advance scholarship. Books in the series focus on cutting-edge global issues at the nexus of society and the environment.

Series Editors
Dana R. Fisher
Lori Peek
Evan Schofer

Super Polluters: Tackling the World's Largest Sources of Climate-Disrupting Emissions,
Don Grant, Andrew Jorgenson, and Wesley Longhofer

Underwater

LOSS, FLOOD INSURANCE, AND THE MORAL ECONOMY OF CLIMATE CHANGE IN THE UNITED STATES

Rebecca Elliott

Columbia University Press
New York

Columbia University Press
Publishers Since 1893
New York   Chichester, West Sussex
cup.columbia.edu

Library of Congress Cataloging-in-Publication Data

Names: Elliott, Rebecca, 1984– author.
Title: Underwater : loss, flood insurance, and the moral economy of climate
change in the United States / Rebecca Elliott.
Description: New York : Columbia University Press, [2021] | Series: Society
and the environment | Includes bibliographical references and index.
Identifiers: LCCN 2020020518 (print) | LCCN 2020020519 (ebook) |
ISBN 9780231190268 (hardback) | ISBN 9780231190275 (trade paperback) |
ISBN 9780231548816 (ebook)
Subjects: LCSH: National Flood Insurance Program (U.S.) | Flood
insurance—Government policy—United States. | Flood insurance—Social
aspects—United States. | Flood insurance—Moral and ethical
aspects—United States. | Flood damage—Economic aspects—United States. |
Flood damage—Social aspects—United States. | Liability for
environmental damages—United States. | Climatic changes—
Economic aspects—United States.
Classification: LCC HG9983.3 .E54 2021 (print) | LCC HG9983.3 (ebook) |
DDC 368.1/22200973—dc23
LC record available at https://lccn.loc.gov/2020020518
LC ebook record available at https://lccn.loc.gov/2020020519

Columbia University Press books are printed on permanent and durable acid-free paper.
Printed in the United States of America

Cover design: Julia Kushnirsky
Cover photo: ©iStockphoto

CONTENTS

CONTENTS

ACKNOWLEDGMENTS

Writing a book is in many ways an unavoidably solitary task, but for me it has not been a lonely one. Any faults you may find with the book are my responsibility, but my work has benefited immeasurably from the assistance, support, feedback, and patience of so many people, and finishing this book gives me the opportunity to thank them.

First, I owe my deepest gratitude to the many people in New York City, New Jersey, Washington, DC, and elsewhere, who shared their stories, expertise, opinions, and feelings as I pursued answers to my research questions. I thank them for their time, candor, and trust. To those I met who were recovering from Hurricane Sandy, I am so humbled and grateful for the invitations into your homes. Even though those homes may not have lived up to your standards, or yet felt presentable for guests, they were spaces of such kindness and care to me. I owe special thanks to Joseph Pupello and David Gaul of Zone A New York, Amy Bach of United Policyholders, and Carolyn Nagy and Matthew Hassett of the Center for New York City Neighborhoods, who invited me to turn my research findings into materials that might help Hurricane Sandy–affected residents, exposing me to the power and importance of public sociology. I also thank Katherine Greig, with the New York City Mayor's Office of Recovery and Resiliency, who was always keen to share ideas and to discuss really complex questions about the future of New York City.

This book began as my PhD dissertation at the University of California, Berkeley. There I benefited from the tremendous intellectual firepower of my faculty advisors and fellow graduate students. Marion Fourcade provided indispensable guidance and encouragement as not only the chair of my dissertation committee, but as a mentor through the entirety of graduate school and beyond. She showed incredible trust and patience when I would come into her office to riff about my semiformed ideas and she believed in the project, and in me, the whole way. My intellectual development generally, and this project specifically, have benefited enormously from her ability to be simultaneously demanding and kind. Neil Fligstein kept me tethered to the big questions when I went wading into the weeds of flood insurance history and administration, helping me always to think about the more broadly sociological significance of my research. I am grateful for his attention and interest. Cal Morrill taught me how to do qualitative research. He let fifteen-minute meetings stretch to take up the better part of an hour and provided careful feedback on drafts, which was precious to me. He helped me to distill my sprawling ideas, and his creativity inspired me at every turn. I always left his office excited to keep working. I am also grateful to Arlie Hochschild, who took me on as a research assistant on her own project about environmental peril, but who always took time out of our meetings to ask about how my work was going. Working for her was a master class in conducting and writing up research from a place of earnest curiosity and empathy. At Berkeley, I was also helped along through my participation in several workshops with faculty members and my fellow graduate students. Heather Haveman, Anne Swidler, and Cihan Tugal provided comments on work in progress, as well as valuable advice, in those settings. I am grateful to Alex Roehrkasse, Ben Shestakofsky, Roi Livne, Katherine Hood, Beth Pearson, Jonah Stuart Brundage, Jacob Habinek, Daniel Kluttz, Sarah Macdonald, Herbert Docena, Sunmin Kim, Gowri Vijayakumar, Carter Koppelman, Ryan Calder, Carlos Bustamante, Megan Peppel, Peter Ekman, and Caleb Scoville. All of them read and responded to early drafts, or listened to me present them, and they were wonderful friends to me besides.

If I left an intellectually supportive community behind at Berkeley, it was only to join another at the London School of Economics, where the project of writing this book began. I have been privileged to have as mentors Bridget Hutter and Nigel Dodd, who were excited about this book and gave me useful guidance as I worked on it. In our departmental writing group and in conversations over coffee, I received indispensable feedback and advice on the book proposal, chapter drafts, and revisions from Fabien Accominotti, Carrie Friese, Sam Friedman, Liene Ozolina-Fitzgerald, Monika Krause, Sara Salem, Jeremy Brice, Alexander Dobeson, Jonathan Mijs, Ioanna Gouseti, and Leon Wansleben, along with a fabulous crew of our PhD students. I have also learned by the example of my colleagues, as I've engaged with their research and seen their own projects come to fruition. I am also thankful for the support I've received from my affiliations with the LSE's Grantham Research Institute on Climate Change and the Environment, the LSE US Centre, and the Centre for the Analysis of Risk and Regulation. All of these research centers gave me opportunities to share my work in progress.

I never anticipated when I began this project that I would find so many wonderful fellow travelers in the world of floods, disasters, risk, finance, insurance, and climate change. It has been a privilege of my life just to be around these people, to talk to them about this project, and to think through its various dimensions in dialogue with their own work. Karen O'Neill sought me out at the first American Sociological Association meeting where I presented some of this research and encouraged me from the very start. Through ASA I also met Rachael Shwom, who provided valuable advice and encouragement on some early drafts. I have been lucky to be a part of a group of scholars writing about the intersections of insurance and climate change: Turo-Kimmo Lehtonen, Stephen Collier, Savannah Cox, Zac Taylor, Leigh Johnson, Kevin Grove, and Ian Gray. Conversations with them about shared interests have helped me enormously in articulating the stakes of my own research. My work has also improved thanks to the interventions of the critical disaster studies researchers convened by Andy Horowitz, Jacob Remes, and Elizabeth Angell; Ryan Hagen and Scott Knowles read carefully and responded constructively to my work in that context. It was also a joy and privilege to collaborate with environmental writer Elizabeth Rush along the way.

I owe incredible debts to Kasia Paprocki, Liz Koslov, and Daniel Aldana Cohen, my most generous and consistent interlocutors and collaborators on all things related to the social life of climate change. So many of the moments of clarity in writing this book came out of their reading parts of it. I am routinely awed by their own powers of insight and analysis and have been so fortunate to benefit from their respective expertise and collective wisdom. Kasia in particular, as my colleague at the LSE and dear friend, has been the wind in my sails throughout this process. It is no exaggeration to say I could not have done it without her.

If I could thank by name everyone who attended one of my talks about chapters of this book or who asked a penetrating question, I would. But suffice it to say that I am very grateful to audiences and copanelists at various professional conferences and workshops over the years. In these settings, I owe particular thanks to Asa Maron, Daniel Hirschman, Ann Orloff, Isaac Martin, Miriam Greenberg, Emanuel Ubert, Liz McFall, Ine Van Hoyweghen, Mikell Hyman, Marie Piganiol, Sebastian Kohl, Brett Christophers, and Debbie Becher for their generative comments as discussants and organizers.

Sections of this book have appeared in journal articles and I thank those publishers for allowing me to reuse my previously published material in some of the chapters in this book. Parts of chapter 2 appeared in "Scarier than Another Storm: Values at Risk in the Mapping and Insuring of U.S. Floodplains," in the *British Journal of Sociology* 70, no. 3 (2019): 1067–1090, published by Wiley. Chapter 4 expands on "Who Pays for the Next Wave? The American Welfare State and Responsibility for Flood Risk," in *Politics & Society* 45, no. 3 (2017): 415–440, published by SAGE.

I thank the Department of Sociology at the University of California, Berkeley; the Mellon Foundation and American Council of Learned Societies; and Phi Beta Kappa for the financial support that made this research possible.

My thanks to Eric Schwartz, my editor at Columbia University Press, for his support, expert advice, and critical eye, and to Bridget Flannery-McCoy, who first mentioned me to Eric. Thanks also to series editors Lori Peek, Dana Fisher, and Evan Schofer, who saw the potential of this book before it was written and who cheered me on along the way. The anonymous reviewers of both the proposal and the full manuscript also did me and this project a huge service; thank you for the thorough and thoughtful feedback, which guided my revisions. I am thankful also to Lowell Frye, Kathryn Jorge, Anne Sanow, and the entire production team at Columbia University Press for the time and care they have put into preparing this manuscript for production.

ACKNOWLEDGMENTS

Finally, I thank the friends and family who have sustained me these last several years. I thank my parents, Beth and John Elliott, and my grandmother, Bernice Karp, a wonderful New Yorker who passed away while I was finalizing this manuscript, for urging me to follow my bliss. I thank my brother, Peter Elliott, for his wit and lessons in heterodox economics. The extended Duncan family has surrounded me with warmth. I thank my friends in New York City, who gave me reasons beyond research to want to spend so much time there, especially Jessie Katz, Adrienne Trinka, Lauren Trinka, Libby Burton, Matt Sherrill, John Wunderlin, Chris Boulos, Chris and Alexandra Wrobel, and Leslie and Steve Goldrich, who housed me for parts of my fieldwork. Emily Timberlake and Katharine Blake, both wonderful writers and friends, commiserated when it was hard to get words on the page and when it was hard to let them go. Anders Bjornberg quite literally nourished me through the writing of the book, with home-cooked meals and freshly baked loaves of bread. Finally, I thank my partner, Andrew Duncan, whose unflinching faith in me has propelled me through moments of doubt and whose love enriches the celebration of every achievement.

Three weeks after I submitted the draft of this manuscript to Eric, I gave birth to Ruth Elliott Duncan. I have been able to follow every difficult day of revising with her infectious laughs and irresistible smiles. She makes everything worth doing and a more humane future worth fighting for. I dedicate this book to her.

TIMELINE OF EVENTS

1917   Flood Control Act of 1917. Congress takes on federal responsibility for flood control, with the Army Corps of Engineers authorized to oversee flood-control improvements.

1927   Great Mississippi Flood of 1927. Floods 16.5 million acres of land. Prompts private insurance companies to cease flood risk underwriting by 1929.

1928   Flood Control Act of 1928. Commits federal government to pay for construction of protective measures.

1936   Flood Control Act of 1936. Provides funding for construction, examinations, and surveys of flood control projects. Establishes a national approach to reducing flood damages through engineering projects.

1938   Flood Control Act of 1938. Authorizes new dams, levees, dikes, and other control measures.

1945   *Human Adjustment to Floods: A Geographical Approach to the Flood Problem in the United States*, geographer Gilbert White's dissertation, argues for nonstructural approaches to reducing flood losses.

1950   Disaster Relief Act of 1950. Establishes first permanent system for disaster relief without need for congressional action.

1952   President Truman pursues flood insurance program. Truman calls for enactment of a federal flood insurance program and proposes legislation to establish a national system of flood disaster insurance.

1956   Federal Flood Insurance Act of 1956. Establishes a direct federal flood insurance program, a federal reinsurance program, and a federal loan contract program covering flood losses, to be run by a new Federal Flood Indemnity Administration (FFIA). These initiatives go unfunded and are eventually abandoned.

1960   Flood Control Act of 1960. Assigns responsibility for producing flood information studies to the Army Corps of Engineers; the Corps is now promoting the use of nonstructural measures.

1965   Southeast Hurricane Disaster Relief Act. Passes in the wake of Hurricane Betsy, which hit the Gulf Coast in September 1965. Mandates that the Department of Housing and Urban Development (HUD) study "alternative permanent programs which could be established to help provide financial assistance in the future to those suffering property losses in floods and other natural disasters, including but not limited to disaster insurance or reinsurance."

1966   Two reports that inform the design of a federal flood insurance program delivered to Congress: *Insurance and Other Programs for Financial Assistance to Flood Victims*, by HUD, and *A Unified National Program for Managing Flood Losses*, by a Bureau of the Budget Task Force headed up by Gilbert White.

1968 (AUGUST)   National Flood Insurance Act of 1968 (Title XIII of the Housing and Urban Development Act of 1968). Authorizes the National Flood Insurance Program (NFIP), a national program to make flood insurance available to occupants of flood-prone areas through cooperation of the federal government and private insurance industry.

1968 (DECEMBER)   National Flood Insurers Association (NFIA) created. Industry flood insurance pool is formed to sell and service NFIP policies.

1969 (JANUARY)	NFIP begins operations.
1969 (JUNE–AUGUST)	First communities join the NFIP. Communities in Louisiana, Alaska, Virginia, and Mississippi enter the program.
1969 (AUGUST)	Hurricane Camille hits the Gulf Coast. None of the affected communities are covered by the NFIP.
1969 (DECEMBER)	Housing and Urban Development Act. Authorizes the NFIP to start an emergency program that would provide limited amounts of subsidized insurance to communities before completion of their flood information studies and flood insurance rate maps (FIRMs). Extends deadline for when communities have to comply with floodplain management measures. Extends flood insurance coverage to small businesses.
1970	Disaster Relief Act of 1970. With subsequent amendments, codifies and expands disaster assistance to individuals.
1972	Risk rating changes. The NFIP replaces community risk zones with nationwide risk zones, used for new insurance rate tables.
1973	Flood Disaster Protection Act of 1973. First NFIP reauthorization. Makes the NFIP compulsory for majority of homeowners through addition of mandatory purchase requirement. Provides for grandfathering of subsidized rates. Repeals a provision of the authorizing legislation that had denied disaster relief to persons who could have purchased flood insurance for a year or more but did not do so.
1977	NFIA terminated. Following disagreements between HUD and NFIA, private insurers exit risk-bearing pool in the NFIP. Federal government assumes full operational responsibility for the NFIP.
1979	Federal Emergency Management Agency established. FEMA takes over administration of the NFIP from HUD.
1983	Write-Your-Own program established. Private insurers brought back into the NFIP as fiscal agents of the federal government, marketing, selling, and writing flood insurance policies but bearing no risk. WYO companies receive a commission for this work.

1983   First FIRMs published for New York City.

1994   National Flood Insurance Reform Act of 1994. Tightens mandatory purchase requirement; codifies Community Rating System; requires review of FIRMs every five years; establishes a Technical Mapping Advisory Council.

2005   Hurricane Katrina. NFIP $16.1 billion in debt to U.S. Treasury.

2007   PlaNYC launch. New York City mayor Michael Bloomberg launches coordinated effort to make the city "greener" and "greater." Reports in the following years call on FEMA to update New York City's FIRMs.

2009   FEMA Region II receives funding for FIRM updates in New York and New Jersey.

2011   FEMA Region II begins remapping work.

2012 (JULY)   Biggert-Waters Flood Insurance Reform Act. Mandates gradual phase out of subsidized rates; immediate end of grandfathering; updates to flood insurance rate maps; reconvening of Technical Mapping Advisory Council to advise on incorporating future conditions into maps.

2012 (OCTOBER)   Hurricane Sandy. NFIP is $24 billion in debt.

2013 (JANUARY–FEBRUARY)   Advisory Base Flood Elevations delivered to Sandy-affected areas. Summarizes available information about flood risk so that residents have best available information for rebuilding.

2013 (FEBRUARY)   Stop FEMA Now founded by George Kasimos in Toms River, New Jersey.

2013 (JUNE)   Preliminary Work Maps delivered to New York City. Maps incorporate more refined wave modeling.

2013 (SEPTEMBER)   Stop FEMA Now rallies. Protests across ten states on the eve of rate increases mandated by Biggert-Waters.

2013 (DECEMBER)   Preliminary Flood Insurance Rate Maps (pFIRMs) delivered to New York City. Release of the version of the FIRMs that would enter formal adoption phase. Maps show expanded flood zones and higher base flood elevations; almost 400,000 New Yorkers live in the redrawn high-risk flood zones; number of structures inside the zones doubles from around 35,000 to 71,500.

TIMELINE OF EVENTS

2014 (MARCH)	Homeowner Flood Insurance Affordability Act passed. Maintains commitment to updated flood risk assessment and mapping; reinstates grandfathering; limits annual rate increases to 18 percent for most homeowners (severe repetitive loss properties can continue to see up to 25 percent increases).
2014 (SEPTEMBER)	Technical Mapping Advisory Council begins meeting.
2015 (JUNE)	New York City pFIRM appeal filed. City argues, on basis of its own risk assessment, that FEMA's models have overestimated water levels by over two feet and unnecessarily mapped 26,000 buildings and 170,000 residents into high-risk zones.
2016 (FEBRUARY)	Technical Mapping Advisory Council reports published. Indicate that information about future conditions, including conditions related to climate change, should be delivered for advisory purposes.
2016 (OCTOBER)	FEMA and New York City announce two-map solution. One map will show current risk and be used for flood insurance premium rating. The other map of future risk will help the city plan for climate change.
2018 (APRIL)	*An Affordability Framework for the National Flood Insurance Program* report published. Outlines different flood insurance affordability program design options.

INTRODUCTION

Insurance and the Problem of Loss in a Climate-Changed United States

Palmer Doyle is a retired firefighter who lives in a modest home in Rockaway, Queens. In early 2013 he found out that his flood insurance premiums would be changing, due to proposed updates to New York City's flood maps and to new flood insurance rating rules passed by Congress the previous summer. His and his neighbors' insurance premiums were set to increase from hundreds to thousands of dollars per year. When he received this news, Palmer was finishing repairs on his home, which had taken on eight and a half feet of water during Hurricane Sandy a few months before. That water was covered in a slick of heating oil from a tank that had ruptured in one of the beachfront homes during the storm. The oil left behind a gray line that still stretches along the length of his house a year after the storm, when I first met him, a reminder of those days spent underwater.

Because Palmer lives in an official high-risk flood zone, according to the government's maps, and has a mortgage, he is required by law to have a flood insurance policy in place, as are most of his neighbors. He's worried about a wave of foreclosures if he and his neighbors can't afford to pay the new rates. And who would buy their risky homes, with huge flood insurance premiums attached to them? His house is no longer physically underwater but could soon be financially underwater. Palmer contemplates a bewildering set of options, available to him according to the terms of his insurance policy. He can try to find $100,000 for home elevation, turning his home back into a construction site in order to mitigate his risk and lower his premiums. Or he can get his family out of harm's way and off the hook for flood insurance by abandoning his neighborhood altogether—leaving behind family, friends, and a lifetime of memories. In the meantime, he has already used claims money from his existing flood policy, as well as his own savings, to repair his house back to livable condition, leaving him vulnerable to the next catastrophic flood, which government officials, scientists, and journalists keep saying is coming—though he's not sure he's convinced. Sandy was, he tells me repeatedly, exceptional in its destructive strength. It seems to Palmer there are no good options here, even though he wants to protect his house and his family. They are losing too much. What was happening to them just wasn't fair. He barely survived the flood. Now he's not sure he'll survive the increase in flood insurance rates.[1]

At around the same time that Palmer learned about the changes to flood maps and insurance premiums, a man named George Kasimos in Toms River, New Jersey, assembled a small group of his neighbors at a local deli. Like Palmer, George had survived Hurricane Sandy. Like Palmer, new flood maps showed he was now in a riskier flood zone and his premiums would be increasing. Like Palmer, he felt his community was getting a bad deal. With premiums going up, property values would fall, local tax bases would disintegrate, and neighborhoods would be economically destroyed, even after surviving the storm. "How many of your neighbors have the same issue, they just don't know what to do?" he asked the group. "I see this young lady here—she's ready to cry. We've all been there. I got up at 3 o'clock in the morning; I can't sleep right now." Murmurs of agreement followed. "We gotta get together . . . We need to get the word out," George urged. Reach out to homeowners in flood zones in New York, in Louisiana, he told the group. "This is grassroots." These were national problems and members of Congress needed to hear from them.[2]

In a few short months, what started in that New Jersey deli would grow to become "Stop FEMA Now," a nationwide network of homeowners—in blue states and red states, in working-class neighborhoods and beachfront vacation areas—mobilized to fight federal efforts to make flood insurance rates reflect "real risk" (FEMA, the Federal Emergency Management Agency, was singled out because it now administers flood insurance). Ultimately, Stop FEMA Now would face off against taxpayer and libertarian groups, who argued that subsidized flood insurance had allowed flood zone homeowners to shirk responsibility for their own losses, passing them off to taxpayers who lived nowhere near the water. Insurance and reinsurance lobbyists and trade associations would also get involved in the fight, advocating for adjustments to flood insurance regulations that would protect and potentially even grow their own lines of business. Those groups would form an unlikely coalition with environmentalists, who argued that in a world shaped by climate change, risk-based insurance rates premised on accurate, up-to-date maps of flood risk were necessary to adapt to rising seas and shifting precipitation patterns, in large measure by keeping people from building, or rebuilding, in vulnerable areas. Changes to flood insurance would help people to see that some parts of the country were simply too risky—and too expensive to protect and rebuild—and would have to be lost to human habitation, "returned to nature."

This is a book about loss in a climate-changed United States. It is by now obvious that climate change devastates, damages, and destroys. Atlantic Coast cities are laid low by severe hurricanes, the way New York City was in Hurricane Sandy. Mobile homes in California burn to ash in hotter and longer wildfires. Louisiana wetlands disappear into the Gulf of Mexico as seas rise and storms accelerate erosion. Streets in Miami, New York City, and Charleston are submerged even on sunny days, as tidal "nuisance" flooding becomes more common, making the normal routines of life impossible. However, this book is *not* about these moments of acute and conspicuous destruction and loss. Such moments tend to occupy the focus of the public and the press; the disasters themselves attract our attention and seem emblematic of how climate change will disrupt and transform the world. Instead, this book is about the before and after, about the institution that manages loss and losses, inscribing disasters into the everyday reality of residents, communities, and governments, even in times of relative calm: insurance. Insurance connects disasters and losses in the past to expectations for losses in the future and requires action—the payment of a premium, the zoning of an area, the adoption of a building standard—in the present.

Insurance links loss, lives, and landscapes. For Palmer, cumulative changes to the natural environment, wrought by already-observed sea level rise, as well as by population growth and real estate development, were reassessed, turned into a risk classification on a map, and priced into his individual policy. This is a transformation that economic sociologists recognize as one of *economization*: a dynamic, contingent, and often unstable process of rendering diverse objects, actors, processes, and practices "economic." In other words, flood hazards, and decisions regarding what to do about them, do not have an inherent economic character that simply needs to be revealed and acted upon. Rather, hazards and decision-making have to be *rendered* economic, formatted in ways that make things calculable and people calculative. Insurance transforms and defines things *as* economic problems.[3] Flood insurance incorporates and builds on techniques from environmental science, which have framed water as a manageable natural resource and floods as probabilistic hazards that can be assessed on the basis of data and models. Flood risks can then be assigned insurance prices. This, in turn, makes decision-making about exposure to flood hazards a matter of calculating dollars and cents. If we are interested in how climate change affects individual lives and shapes communities, we need to examine how people develop, use, and contest economic arrangements like insurance, premised on quantification, pricing, and calculation, in the management of environmental threats. As Palmer's experience suggests, once a storm, fire, or flood becomes a distant memory, its incorporation into economizing institutions continues to shape the trajectories of lives for a long time.

Economic sociologists have also shown that processes of economization are disputable. Michel Callon writes that for the groups they affect, such processes spawn "matters of concern" about the way calculations are framed: what is included, what is excluded, and what seems to defy (or "overflow," in Callon's terms) calculation altogether.[4] Wendy Espeland also shows how commensuration—the comparison of different entities according to a common metric (like risk or price) and constitutive of economization—can be a terrain of struggle where different modes of valuing something conflict.[5] In the domain of insurance, processes of economization may result in issues appearing or being treated as "merely" administrative or technical, but they can also ignite controversies over who ought to do what, how, and at what cost—questions George and his neighbors were turning over in that New Jersey deli. The terms of insurance format different kinds of responsibility, on the basis of economic considerations. In the case of flood insurance, individualized policies made Palmer's calculated exposure to risk something he in a sense "owned" and would have to manage, through a set of ostensibly rational strategies (elevate or relocate) that would reduce the likelihood of future losses and save him money on his premiums. At the same time, the very provision of flood insurance creates other kinds of responsibilities for governments and private industry: for studying flood risk and producing up-to-date maps of it, for forging a pool of insureds that would share the risk and establishing the terms of that risk-sharing, for managing overall solvency, for selling policies and administering claims. The nature and distribution of such responsibilities can change and shift over time, as the result of disputes between people and groups over the terms, uses, and effects of economization.

By extending compensation and incentivizing risk mitigation, flood insurance was meant to protect Palmer from loss: from the destruction of his asset. This reflects the technical and rather narrow understanding of loss that is operative when insurance is viewed through the lens of finance and economics—the dominant frames brought to bear on analyses of insurance institutions. Those frames tend to dominate the policy discourse about climate change, as well.[6] And yet in his interactions with flood insurance, Palmer felt he was poised to lose a great deal. George and his neighbors in New Jersey shared this sentiment and it eventually became their rallying cry for preserving the economic viability of floodplain communities and protecting investments in homes and property as seas and insurance premiums rise. The slogan printed on Stop FEMA Now's fliers, protest signs, and bumper stickers was "Save Our Homes." The stakes were enormous, as the other political actors who got involved in flood insurance debates also appreciated. Flood insurance became a way to address threats to public finances, private profitmaking in real estate development, coastal and riverine ecologies, housing markets, and ways of life, a way to negotiate who could live where, for how long, and on what terms. The dilemmas surrounding what to do about flood insurance are not simply math problems of how to price risk or how to make premiums-in balance claims-out. They are political and moral dilemmas of how to manage destabilizing losses that can ruin individuals and communities—losses that some will resist and mourn, losses that are not only financial but also social and emotional.

This book examines the politics of loss as they manifest on the terrain of interactions with, and contestations over, flood insurance. How do people understand loss? Whose or which losses are made to matter? What constituencies and coalitions, discourses and claims, are created around loss?

Who is or ought to be responsible for loss? What constitutes "rational" or "prudent" action in anticipation of future loss? How are risks estimated and losses predicted? What places, ways of life, and communities will, must, or should be lost, and what role will insurance play?

As these questions imply, I am taking a broader view of the concept of loss, as both object and process, than is conventionally deployed in academic and public policy discussions of insurance.[7] For my purposes, loss has both a quantitative and qualitative character. It encapsulates the version of loss that prevails in insurance discussions, specifying things that people deem measurable and countable, like buildings destroyed and property values diminished. But it also encompasses the things that are not so easily accounted for with numbers, like a sense of security, a rhythm of life, connections to a community or a history, and the stable meanings that frame our lives and that root our senses of identity and belonging.[8] Some losses can be commensurated and compensated in dollar terms, while some cannot.[9] Loss, like climate change, is real, made so through the intersection of social processes with ecological conditions. It is physical and material: land disappears beneath the waves; economic value is destroyed. "Loss" is also discursively potent, a concept that people use to motivate and justify action; things are done *in the name of* loss. It can give rise to what Kasia Paprocki calls "anticipatory ruination": destruction in anticipation of real or perceived threats, as when expectations of future losses in the floodplain motivate real estate devaluations or relocation in the present, transforming the physical and social landscape before waters reach the doorstep.[10] In the story told here, people contend with the ways that insurance is implicated in the physical and economic reshaping of a landscape in the present in relation to plural and contested visions for floodplain futures.

The thematic of loss also reframes questions about and understandings of climate change, which are more typically motivated instead by an interest in what can be *sustained*. Social science has taken up sustainability as a research area and a paradigm, which necessarily comes with a focus on what can be preserved and reproduced, which elements of the status quo can be maintained, even as ecological conditions imply or demand certain kinds of social and economic change. Focusing instead on what does, will, or is made to disappear—and how people both actively shape and respond to those disappearances—brings into view new dynamics, underscoring that climate politics in the United States is in large part a politics of those who have something to lose. People mobilize to defend their financial, social, and emotional investments in homes and communities when they are threatened not only by disasters and hazards, but also by the institutions, like insurance, that manage their relations to them.[11]

I argue that as the climate continues to change, insurance acts as a platform through which people negotiate issues of loss: what is fair and valuable, what needs protecting and what should be let go, who deserves assistance and on what terms, and whose expectations of future losses are used to govern the present. This is best understood as a set of dilemmas related to the moral economy of climate change, composed of three interrelated dimensions that define what is at stake in dealing with the losses that climate change involves. The first is *responsibility for loss*, where responsibility encompasses both *causality* and *accountability*.[12] Debates about insurance involve disputes over who or what is to blame, who or what is "responsible" for causing the loss. Is it the result of an act of God? The recklessness or ignorance of individuals? The malfeasance of industry? The ineptitude of government? The limitations of science? Insurance provides a terrain for people to figure out how, and with what effects, this thing we call "climate change"—a bundle of various impacts that will be felt differently at different times and places—should interact with other perceived causes of loss. Insurance also specifies responsibility in the sense of designating who has to *do* something about loss and what that something is, who is accountable for responding to a loss and preventing further losses. The terms of insurance arrangements assign tasks to different actors and stipulate, explicitly and implicitly, what virtuous behavior vis-à-vis a natural hazard consists of, for example, flood-proofing a home or moving away. These arrangements are expressed in the technologies of insurance and create a kind of ethics, a set of practices for governing the self in a time of climate change.

The second dimension is *justification of loss*. Debates about insurance often involve discussion of whether or under what conditions losses are justified or deserved. For instance, some believe that if insurance pressures work to price people out of risky neighborhoods, this is justified if those areas are, or soon will be, no longer fit for human habitation, in a world of more intense flooding. However painful it may be in the near term, this is good for people and good for coastal and riverine ecologies over the long term. Others disagree: retreat from the water's edge is a sacrifice (of land, of economic value, of historic communities and ways of life) that is neither necessary nor acceptable, and the terms of insurance should continue to underwrite human habitation there. Negotiations over the design and reform of insurance institutions, practices, and technologies can effectively work out, in provisional fashion, how concern for "the greater good," future generations, or environmental stewardship stacks up against the rights or needs of existing communities and homeowners. In these discussions, who stands to lose also comes to matter a great deal; at issue is which people, if anyone, deserve to lose. Do homeowners who ought to have "known better" than to buy in a floodplain deserve sympathy and redress when there are consequences of that "choice"? Do they if the homes they own are vacation homes on the shore and are not their primary residences? How people feel about insurance, and the changes they fight for, reflects in part the imagined beneficiaries and the rhetorical figures mobilized in political contestation.

The third dimension is *compensation for loss*. Insurance promises a payout of claims money for policyholders who meet the terms of the insurance contract. But with catastrophic losses increasing, this obligation to compensate, in public insurance contexts, can run into budgetary constraints, public liabilities, and taxpayer obligations. This broadens the question of compensation from being one about individual contracts to being one about collective resources. The question of "fair" compensation then involves examining what policyholders ought to expect, what broader publics are willing to support, and whether those two things conflict. More generally, public and private insurance provides monetary compensation for things that can be assessed in monetary terms, like the cost of replacing a heating system or drywall, or of rebuilding a room. This helps people recover and resume the normal rhythms of life. But money cannot compensate for the loss of many things that matter. A flood may also take with it a sense of security, and dealing with the financial pressures of flood insurance may threaten someone with the loss of treasured connections to homes and places. Experiences with insurance prompt people to reflect on what it means to be "made whole" where money is an inadequate or only partially adequate response. These experiences involve people in contemplating whether, for some kinds of losses, compensation is even possible.

In all these ways, flood insurance participates in constructing a moral economy of climate change in the United States. In the domain of insurance, the interaction of moral issues with economic arrangements shapes how people understand, experience, and respond to problems of loss associated with climate change. There are, of course, many other domains in which climate change, and particularly economic understandings of it, are subjected to moral debate, within the United States and beyond. At the level of international governance, for instance, proceedings of the annual Conference of the Parties of the United Nations Framework Convention on Climate Change inevitably involve contentious discussions about how the costs of climate change mitigation and adaptation should be distributed between wealthy, developed countries, who are responsible for the lion's share of global emissions, and poorer, less developed countries who have historically emitted relatively little. Within countries, policymakers must decide how to allocate economic resources today, for climate change mitigation or adaptation, that will benefit future citizens, or what intergenerational justice requires. Some countries face pressing decisions about how to deal with the rights of migrants from denuded environments, as well as with how to support workers in agriculture, fishing, and other industries that depend on particular climatic conditions. Policy experts develop recommendations about what governments ought to do through efforts to measure, quantify, price, and plan for the risks that climate change poses to national economies at large. Governments that are undertaking steps toward greener economies create the possibility for new winners and losers. Through social action within all these arenas (and others), at a variety of scales, people and institutions enact contestable and dynamic moral economies of climate change that have significant consequences for the way benefits and burdens are distributed in a warming world. The moral economy of climate change is a big, complex, and changing picture, even within the United States. Flood insurance can't tell us everything about the shape it does or will take, but it shows us the contours of part of it—specifically illuminating the intersection of climate change with moralized and moralizing economic arrangements for managing loss.

This book explores issues of moral economy through an in-depth historical and sociological examination of the U.S. National Flood Insurance Program (NFIP), the financial institution the United States has long been using to manage flood risk and loss. Indeed, the NFIP was in place decades before climate change became a public policy issue. But the issues of moral economy that the NFIP has revealed throughout its history provide a window into the moral controversies, political obligations, and economic realities that the upheavals of climate change confront. In this story, climate change appears in and recedes from view at different points. People vary in the kinds of connections—if any—they draw between flood risk, insurance, and climate change at different moments in time. Climate change gets enrolled in different kinds of political claims-making. But whether or not flood insurance politics are climate politics in an explicit way, the various actors involved in flood insurance constitute a kind of "climate public": a constituency created by the public policies and economic arrangements that transmit changing hazards into daily life and its governance. As Daniel Aldana Cohen argues, though such actors may not "complain in everyday life about the atmosphere's concentration of carbon dioxide," everyone's actions have ecological consequences and we should thus understand everyone as an ecological actor.[13] In working to solve problems of housing, investment, risk management, and economic security, as they understand them, homeowners, as well as insurers, federal officials, elected politicians, risk experts, and others involved in flood insurance issues, produce ecologically, socially, and morally consequential outcomes for a climate-changed United States.

Floods are already the costliest natural disaster in the United States and are poised to do even worse damage to American lives and landscapes in the years to come.[14] In the context of this threat, academics, insurance professionals, policymakers, global civil society actors, and other observers have begun to reflect on the role that insurance and reinsurance might play in helping societies to adapt to climate change, through their traditional functions of unlocking recovery funds after catastrophic losses and incentivizing risk mitigation, as well as through novel scientific and commercial products that offer new tools for risk management. Insurers and reinsurers today promise social change on the basis of quantification, modeling, economization, and commercialization—promises that are very similar to those made by the architects of the NFIP in the mid-twentieth century. My intention therefore is not only to excavate and examine the conflicts and contradictions that have shaped the NFIP, and how Americans are exposed to, negotiate, and deal with loss as a result, but also to draw lessons for how the elegant solutions newly on offer from insurers and other risk industry actors will inevitably strike upon political and moral fault lines.

EXAMINING FLOOD INSURANCE

I began this study in the aftermath of Hurricane Sandy, which devastated the greater New York City area, and affected two dozen U.S. states as well as several Caribbean islands, in the autumn of 2012. In addition to the news stories about recovery and rebuilding that tend to appear after any disaster, I started seeing articles about homeowners, like Palmer, who were facing a distinct problem: as they were beginning to repair their homes, to "get back to normal," they were finding out that they may no longer be able to afford to insure them. Flood maps in New York and New Jersey had changed, as had some of the rules governing flood insurance. The price of insurance was going up, in order to cover higher expected future losses and to put the NFIP, which was, I learned, billions of dollars in debt to the U.S. Treasury, on a path to solvency. I set out for New York City to find out how people there were experiencing and responding to the increasing risk and its cost. I wanted to seize this unique opportunity to study a crucial period of transition following a major catastrophe, in the nation's most populous floodplain and one of its most valuable and dynamic real estate markets. This was a site where the economic impacts of flood damage, and of the political efforts to respond to it, could be felt in all of their magnitude. New York City has also historically been a pioneering site for efforts to rationalize urban governance through quantification and calculation, and here too it was the first major metropolitan area to undergo changes that would be spreading nationwide.[15] If flood hazards were indeed increasing in much of the country, and if national reforms to flood insurance meant everyone would be dealing with new maps and insurance premiums at some point, it seemed to me that New York City was in some ways a bellwether for issues that many Americans would soon be confronting. Inspired by C. Wright Mills's "sociological imagination," my objective at this early stage was to examine the role of insurance in transforming the "public issue" of flooding into the "personal trouble" of what to do about it.[16]

Although I shouldn't have been, I was surprised when during one of my first interviews, someone cried. This happened more than once. Sometimes they were tears of sorrow, sometimes tears of anger or frustration. It turned out that talking to residents about things as arcane and technical as flood maps and insurance premiums got them talking also about economic insecurity, their hopes and fears for the future, their attachments to their

neighbors and local gathering places, their family histories, and their feelings about the political actors and economic institutions that govern and
shape their lives. I also found that local and federal officials, lawyers, insurance brokers, city planners, architects, housing counselors, and other
expert professionals on the ground were emotionally attuned to these issues,
often understanding themselves as working in a situation that offered no
good, only less bad, options. I didn't find experts, typically presumed to be
"rational," always opposed to laypeople, typically presumed to be "emotional," as is so common in many studies of risk.[17] Instead, I found a lot of
confusion and ambiguity, and also a sense of shared struggles. The central
conflicts, it seemed to me, were really reflecting *conflictedness*: not necessarily picking a side, not "doing something" about flood risk or ignoring it,
but rather a recognition that there were competing principles and commitments at play here, a lot at stake, and a lot of ambivalent outcomes for
individuals and for the city as a whole.

I was able to see this because the study began by situating the NFIP in
social life and tracing its operations and effects on the ground. Largely in
New York, but also in New Jersey, I followed ethnographically how people
understood and responded to the changes to flood insurance, in a variety
of sites: public meetings and government hearings related to flood insurance; flood insurance "help desks" organized by local housing organizations; professional meetings of architects, planners, and construction
managers; Sandy recovery events for residents and disaster case managers;
door-to-door canvassing by FEMA and local nonprofit organizations in
flood zone neighborhoods; and meetings of legal clinics and housing organizations. Drawing on this ethnographic data, as well as on interviews with
the many different actors who interacted with flood insurance on the
ground, I learned that the rational calculus at the center of flood insurance
in fact generated tremendous social and political uncertainty.

I then sought to understand the national-level changes that produced the
tough circumstances facing New Yorkers—circumstances that would face
floodplain communities nationwide as new maps and insurance premiums
later rolled out around the country. Three months before Sandy, Congress
had passed the most substantive overhaul of the NFIP since its founding
in the late 1960s. This reform changed the NFIP in ways that would have
many floodplain homeowners paying more for flood insurance. This was
the moment that spawned Stop FEMA Now. I collected and analyzed

congressional debate and hearing transcripts, interviewed supporters and opponents of reform, and observed and followed the activities of experts working on flood insurance affordability studies, in order to assess how the reform was initiated, passed, and eventually, partially, rolled back and slowed down.

My next task was to set these events in their historical context in order to understand how the NFIP had reached a point of financial crisis, the stakes of contemporary political struggles over its future, as well as the role flood insurance had played in the broader federal approach to flood loss. I went into the National Archives in Washington, DC, to unearth the transcripts of 1950s and 1960s congressional floor debates, federal agency and task force reports, and records of the Department of Housing and Urban Development (HUD) and FEMA. These documents authorized and outlined the basic structure for this ambitious new program.

It was clear to me from both my historical investigation and fieldwork that the flood maps, and the insurance premiums they made possible, were central objects of political contestation. I began to examine the production of these tools in detail. At the time, New York City was preparing to make an official "appeal" of its newest flood maps. This provided an opportunity to witness the complex considerations and negotiations that underpin the production of scientific estimates of risk and its price—and, as a result, the challenges attendant on constructing collective imaginaries of the future. Drawing on scientific and government reports, the proceedings of FEMA's Technical Mapping Advisory Council meetings as well as their meeting minutes, and interviews with flood risk experts, I was able to get underneath the procedural rationality of the NFIP's key risk instruments.

Assembling this variety of qualitative data allowed me to follow processes unfolding over time; the accounts, understandings, and experiences of key actors; and the collective production of the NFIP's "problems" and "solutions" under complicated and changing circumstances. Throughout the book, I supplement the data I collected with evidence from documents, including: media accounts; official and technical documents related to risk assessment and insurance rating; reports authored by think tanks, nonprofits, government agencies, insurance trade organizations, and regulatory bodies; engineering and flood management studies; planning documents; and political materials (emails, tweets, fliers, websites, and Facebook posts) created in the controversies surrounding flood insurance. More detail about my methodological choices and strategies can be found in the methodological appendix at the end of the book.

HIGH FLOOD PRESSURE: NFIP FUNCTIONS AND FAILURES

The NFIP is a public, federal program of insurance—which may seem a rather strange creature in the context of a general American ideological preference for private markets (even if, as political sociologists have observed, many seemingly "stateless" markets are anyway profoundly structured to act as indirect policy tools of the U.S. government).[18] The NFIP writes flood insurance for homes and small businesses in the United States. There are NFIP policies in every state, but currently the largest numbers of them are in Florida, Texas, Louisiana, California, New Jersey, South Carolina, New York, North Carolina, and Virginia, states that combine large populations with significant lengths of vulnerable waterfront. Like any program of insurance, the NFIP compensates policyholders when they suffer a flood loss; the payment of annual premiums entitles the policyholder to claims payment in the event that their property is damaged, which they can use to finance their recovery. The NFIP is also designed to prevent or minimize future losses, reflecting economic thinking about the ways that prices should provide both information and incentives. This preventative function depends on a risk-based, or "actuarial," rate for insurance. An actuarial rate is meant to provide a "price signal" of the underlying risk: higher premiums reflect higher risk. That risk is assessed in terms of probabilities. In this imagining, insurance acts as a relay of information to policyholders and the public. "Rational" economic action here involves actors internalizing this information to avoid (re)building in the riskiest—that is, the most expensive—areas, or to build differently, in ways that reduce risk and its cost. For actors already located in a flood zone, or mapped into one when risks change and their classifications are updated, the premium provides an incentive to take risk-mitigating action. As Palmer learned, a policyholder can bring down the cost of his premiums by relocating—getting out of the flood zone—or by elevating the building structure above the expected flood height, called the "base flood elevation" or BFE. These individual-level calculations help the property owner to save money and avoid loss. In addition, when these individual-level calculations are aggregated together, if everyone is calculating rationally and acting on that basis, they lower the overall pressure on the risk pool and, in catastrophic circumstances, on the U.S. Treasury, which backs up the program.

In brief, the NFIP is a public policy instrument that is meant to rationalize our relationship to a volatile world, turning on the notion that "one can, in principle, master all things by calculation," as Max Weber characterized fitful and contingent social and historical processes of rationalization.[19] By taming some of the uncertainty of living with flood hazards, or at least appearing to, insurance allows individuals and communities to build, plan, and live with greater confidence. The application of probabilities, as Ian Hacking notes, brings order to chaos; floods become, if not precisely predictable, at least patterned in ways that humans can understand and anticipate.[20]

This rationale constituted a significant pillar of the support among policymakers for establishing the NFIP in the late 1960s. Rising flood losses were a huge public policy problem even then. Policymakers and flood experts believed that an actuarial program of flood insurance would stem these losses through the provision of information and incentives. Rather than the federal government outright prohibiting all kinds of development in vulnerable areas, insurance would work through the calculative decisions of local decision-makers to shift land use away from risky uses over time.[21] To facilitate this, the federal government would commit to a hugely ambitious—and, as we will see, highly contentious—project of mapping the country's floodplains. These "flood insurance rate maps," or FIRMs, are central technologies of the NFIP. State-produced maps like these, in the words of James C. Scott, make space "legible from above and outside," making it possible for state actors to treat the floodplain, which is actually a complex and changing ecology, as flood *zones*: simplified, stable, discrete areas of higher and lower risk that can be administered uniformly.[22] The flood zones and BFEs on the maps would form the basis of risk-based insurance rating.

At the time of its establishment, members of Congress regarded the NFIP as boldly "experimental."[23] But the hopes and expectations of policymakers and experts in the 1960s have not been realized. Today, there are more people and more properties at risk than ever before. From 1970—coinciding with the early days of the NFIP's operation—until 2010, the population in coastal counties increased by 40 percent.[24] From 1996 to 2010, 24,000 acres along the U.S. shoreline changed from wetlands—which provide natural protection from flooding—to developed land.[25] New York University's

Furman Center estimates that there are now nearly 13 million housing units and 30.2 million people in the combined 100-year and 500-year flood zones, designations used by FEMA when it produces the NFIP's flood maps and establishes insurance requirements.[26] Over recent years, the number of policies-in-force, across the NFIP's 22,000 participating communities, has hovered around just 5 million, despite the fact that flood insurance is legally required for many homeowners in high-risk flood zones.[27] The NFIP has also paid to rebuild some of the most flood-prone homes again and again. Across the United States, more than 30,000 NFIP properties are now classified as "severe repetitive loss properties."[28] Though these homes represent less than 1 percent of insured properties, they have accounted for a disproportionate 9.6 percent of all damages paid, as of 2015.[29] Coastal counties are dense not only with homes, but also with jobs: they produce more than $8.3 trillion in goods and services each year.[30] The total insured value of exposed residential and commercial properties in coastal counties now tops $13 trillion.[31]

This is the landscape of human settlement that is now facing intensified climate change. As the population continues to grow, more and more people will be exposed to worse and worse hazards. A 2016 Congressional Budget Office (CBO) report concluded that the costs associated with hurricane damage will increase more rapidly than the economy will grow.[32] But this isn't just a coastal problem in places where hurricanes produce storm surge: riverine flood zones around the country are also projected to expand.[33] Already-observed sea level rise means that even without a storm and on otherwise sunny days, high tides are flooding cities—and at an accelerating rate. The National Oceanic and Atmospheric Administration (NOAA) estimates that, assuming only intermediate forecasts of future sea level rise (from 1.5 to 3 feet by 2100), cities on the Atlantic coast will see high-tide flooding 25 to 130 times per year by 2050. By 2100, this could happen almost daily.[34] These forecasts are themselves developing in ways that suggest climate change is occurring earlier and more rapidly than we have long expected. And as with so many things, poorer Americans are most vulnerable to these threats. According to FEMA, generally, incomes are higher outside the flood zones than they are inside. The Furman Center also compared poverty in census tracts inside and outside the nation's floodplains and found that a higher share of the population lives in a moderate- or high-poverty census tract inside the floodplains than outside.[35] According to a report by the Union of Concerned Scientists (UCS), 40 percent of the 175 communities nationwide that will see significant chronic flooding by 2045 already have poverty rates above the national average. Many of these same communities are what the UCS calls "hotspots of risk": places where relatively high rates of poverty intersect with concentrations of historically underserved groups, African Americans, Hispanic Americans, and tribal communities. In addition, of the roughly 400 U.S. communities with at least 50 homes at risk of chronic inundation in 2030, about 60 percent currently have large populations of elderly people. For elderly residents who live on fixed incomes, own their homes outright (i.e., have paid off their mortgages), or have a large share of their personal wealth tied up in their property, a drop in property values caused by chronic flooding cannot be recouped through future income.[36]

Even as floodplain development continued apace, for many decades, the NFIP was financially solvent, able to cover claims out of the premiums it collected, relying on help from the Treasury in especially bad years but able to repay its debts.[37] Then Hurricane Katrina in 2005 generated massive damages and claims in the Gulf Coast region and plunged the program $16.1 billion into debt, seeming to inaugurate a new period of catastrophes on immense scale. The NFIP has not been able to claw its way out of debt ever since. After subsequent catastrophic storms and floods, its debt eventually ballooned to $30 billion, reaching the program's maximum borrowing authority with the U.S. Treasury.[38] To many observers, the financial strain on the program suggests it is today manifestly unequipped to deal with the kinds of catastrophes we associate with climate change. Regular audits of the NFIP by the Government Accountability Office (GAO) and the CBO have found persistent operational challenges that have compromised FEMA's ability to produce maps, set premiums, resolve claims, and even keep appropriate data about the NFIP's scope and condition. As a result of its "substantial financial exposure and management and operations challenges," the NFIP has been on the GAO's "High Risk List," a list of programs and operations that are vulnerable to fraud, waste, abuse, and mismanagement, or that need transformation, since 2006.[39]

As a result, this is a program that is today most commonly discussed as a failure. A 2016 academic article published in a policy studies journal begins with: "The National Flood Insurance Program (NFIP) has a history of failure, ineffectiveness, and costliness."[40] A 2017 popular press book on climate change and sea level rise characterizes the NFIP this way: "NFIP was a good idea at the time. But it has grown into a bureaucratic, outdated, mismanaged program . . . Whatever its virtues, the program has encouraged building in flood-prone areas and conditioned a generation of American homeowners into thinking that a cheap rate for flood insurance is their natural-born right as US citizens."[41]

Everyone seems to agree that the NFIP has and is worsening a problem it was intended to solve. But ideas for fixing it differ substantially, and they reflect different understandings of both the roots of the NFIP's problems specifically and the character of insurance more generally. From an economics point of view, which we will see has been influential on the design and reform of the NFIP, two central issues are the limits of individual cognition and moral hazard. First, people are bad at processing risk information and using it to make rational decisions. Laypeople overestimate or underestimate "real" risks, when compared to experts relying on probabilistic assessments. We use lots of different heuristics to make judgments instead. As a result, we ignore, misinterpret, or deny the information coming to us on flood maps and via insurance premiums, and continue building and living in harm's way.[42] Second, there are pervasive problems of what economists call "moral hazard." Moral hazard is the idea that having insurance, or not paying the full cost of insurance (because of a subsidy, for instance), causes individual insureds to expend less effort to avoid losses or even to cause losses intentionally—because they know they are indemnified (i.e., they will receive a payment should a loss occur). This is not necessarily a mark of bad, virtue-deficient character, which was how early insurance actors used the term "moral hazard" at the dawn of the private industry in the nineteenth century.[43] In the economics of insurance, it is instead a rational response to a subsidized price—and the NFIP, for reasons discussed in subsequent chapters, has long offered subsidized or otherwise "below-risk" premiums to many policyholders. Many believe this also encourages floodplain development. In offering this account of the NFIP's problems, this perspective emphasizes the decision-making of individual economic actors.

Other observers, who take what we might call a political economy view of risk, emphasize instead the interaction of insurance with powerful interests in the context of local "growth machine" politics, and within capitalism more broadly. In the United States, local politicians rely heavily on tax revenue based on property values in order to provide services to constituents. As such, their interests often align with real estate and finance industries that want to profit from the continued commodification and development of land. This produces an imperative to keep growing via real estate, with other important considerations—like whether such development takes place in hazardous areas—left by the wayside. The NFIP forms part of the policy backdrop that makes that possible. In the pursuit of growth, local authorities bend or outright ignore land-use regulations, which are meant to be a condition of participation in the NFIP. Local growth machine coalitions sell growth as a public good, obscuring the fact that the benefits accrue largely to developers and their political allies, while risks fall to residents, who must insure themselves and will likely face a flood at some point. This helps us to understand why, at the national level, organizations like the National Association of Home Builders, the National Association of Realtors, the American Bankers Association, and the U.S. Chamber of Commerce lobby intensely for NFIP reforms that maintain the viability of mortgage lending, property transactions, and construction in flood zones. In offering this account of the NFIP's problems, a political economy perspective emphasizes structural conditions and the short-sightedness, opportunism, and inequities they make possible.[44]

Some sociologists of risk might understand the NFIP's challenges as a feature, not a bug. From this perspective, there is a kind of internal logic at play whereby risk assessment, management, and governance inevitably give rise to contradictions, unintended consequences, and the proliferation of new and different risks and uncertainties—which then seem to call forth even more risk assessment, management, and governance.[45] This is a key dynamic of what Ulrich Beck called "risk society," his epochal designation of our modernity as one in which we are preoccupied with predicting and controlling the future, with using science to exterminate uncertainty through its rationalization.[46] Our efforts to do so, however, break down in the face of new "uncontrollable threats" and "unbounded" risks, such as catastrophic ecological disaster and climate change, which elude existing forms of expert assessment and cannot be distributed over a population. In other words, these new risks are "uninsurable"—at least through the conventional actuarial techniques of insurance.[47] Viewed through this lens, the recent breakdowns in the NFIP perhaps signal the inherent brittleness of traditional scientific and actuarial techniques and the essential hubris of human attempts to calculate and rationalize immense uncertainties.

Each of these perspectives informed my own thinking as I embarked on this study. However, none of them could fully explain or help me to analyze the kinds of outcomes and dilemmas I was observing on the ground. Economic notions of rationality and moral hazard were too simplistic to describe how people actually understood and made decisions about flood risk, loss, and insurance—and such notions, it seemed to me, were precisely part of what warranted explication. Their methodological individualism also did not satisfy me as a sociologist interested in collective action, institutions, and political culture. Political economy approaches helped me to contextualize the NFIP in broader structures and to take seriously questions of power and inequality. But that left a relatively unexamined layer of emotive and affective dimensions of loss, and to the ambivalence and uneasy compromises, in lives and in policy, to which those dimensions gave rise. I was interested too in what James C. Scott calls "the normative roots" of politics, in "what makes [people] angry" and what can generate explosive situations.[48] Critical risk scholarship provided a way to examine expert-led processes of risk calculation and pricing, but its deterministic bent didn't leave space for the contingent, negotiated, and creative ways in which actors sought to resolve the NFIP's problems as they emerged. I needed a different framework. In order to understand both what makes the NFIP so complex and hard to manage, as well as the significance of that complexity for Americans facing climate change, I needed to think in terms of moral economies.

INSURANCE AND MORAL ECONOMIES

Coming to understand loss, framed more broadly than denoting simply a quantitative estimation of damage, as central to struggles over flood insurance necessarily took me onto a different analytical plane. The various actors I encountered, both those subject to the requirements of flood insurance and those involved in creating or enforcing those requirements, could not talk about what was wrong with the NFIP, or what needed to be made right, without talking about what was fair, prudent, just, deserved, or equitable. Claims about flood maps, risk classifications, and the price of premiums, even when couched in a language of scientific "accuracy," as they typically were, also always drew upon an unremarked backdrop of normative commitments about what states, markets, and individuals can or ought to do. Notions of what fails—and what functions—about flood insurance as it confronts climate change are powerfully shaped by these competing understandings and commitments. In brief, contestation and settlements of insurance arrangements reflect and enact particular moral economies, which in turn result in (re)distributions of risk and responsibility, setting the terms upon which we are willing to live together and to face the uncertainties of life.

The British historian E. P. Thompson first wrote about "moral economy" as a way to understand how eighteenth-century peasants, rioting over the price of bread, asserted moral scruples about "just" prices in order to place certain limits on commerce. For Thompson, the idea of the moral economy solved an empirical problem of determining when the free market came to supersede tradition and custom in the conduct of economic life. (His answer: we find roots of the free market economy in the seventeenth and eighteenth centuries, but commitments to the "doctrine of the fair price" extended also into the nineteenth and twentieth). But a key element of Thompson's historical story, one essential to the legacy of the concept, was the larger argument that moral life is always shaping economic decisions and relations. Old (i.e., premodern) customs gave way, but new norms and solidarities formed, in interaction with new economic arrangements and systems.[49] For sociologists and anthropologists who have taken up and developed ideas about moral economy, the implication here is that the moral economy is empirically emergent and dynamic, varying across time and place and reflecting the observable diversity in human culture and social relations. They are also, therefore, plural: there are moral *economies* rather than a singular moral economy. When we talk about "the" moral economy, we are really talking about *a* moral economy, and the relations that prevail at particular times and places, among particular ideas and actors.[50]

To analyze operative moral economies and understand their social effects, we have to proceed with Émile Durkheim's orientation to morality. That is to say, we have to consider what the implicated actors, groups, and societies themselves consider to be good or bad, right or wrong, deserving or undeserving, valuable or worthless, when it comes to settling the economic arrangements that govern their lives.[51] For my purposes, this means excavating and examining the claims that different actors make—about how flood insurance does or should operate, who should be responsible for what, who or what is to blame for floods and flood losses, and what fair insurance arrangements look like—without suggesting that any one group is on the side of virtue.

A robust Durkheimian sensibility has two important implications. First, in contrast to early deployments of the term, when we use "moral economy" we are not positing some separate, ethical realm where people behave "better" toward one another according to some universal principles. The moral economy is not a realm standing in antinomous relationship to the "real" (i.e., market or capitalist) economy.[52] As James McCarthy has noted, a moral economy need not necessarily be about resisting commodification per se, or other (capitalist market) processes that social researchers and moral philosophers have characterized as corrosive to social life. Rather, a moral economy can advance claims and arguments that justify *particular* property relations, entitlements, costs, and benefits. For example, in McCarthy's case study, the Wise Use movement in the rural American West of the 1980s and 1990s made claims to defend commodity production on federal lands, while also insisting that such lands should not be fully marketized or privatized. Though oriented against deepening capitalist relations, the demands were not progressive so much as they were about securing and reproducing perquisites that inured to the benefit of a few at the expense of broader environmentalist agendas.[53] This can be uncomfortable for some analysts, but apprises us to the empirical complexity of actually existing coalitions, to the competing ideas and commitments people are capable of living with and fighting for, and to the simple fact that in many actual social dramas, there may not be clear heroes or villains.

Second, and relatedly, those social actors most closely associated with "real" economic phenomena or the market do not operate within an "amoral" economy, that is, in a realm purified of social constraints, customs, and norms. As Marion Fourcade puts it:

The sentiments that circulate within the economy interact with its operations. Rules, beliefs and emotions about appropriate and inappropriate relations, fair or unfair transactions, just or exploitative practices, the worthy and the undeserving, shape whether economic exchange occurs at all, and the terms under which it takes place ... Morality and sentiments are not a postscript to our more serious scholarly work, to be treated separately from economic processes. They do a lot of economic work, too.[54]

For instance, when economists talk about economically "rational" action, as they do in the context of the NFIP, they are espousing a particular value about human behavior, how it should be governed, and the criteria against which it should be judged—namely, that it be based on quantitative calculation, accounting, and deliberate planning.[55] Such meritorious behavior defines the "prudential subject," in Pat O'Malley's terms, who engages in a form of active citizenship that involves taking responsibility for their own risk.[56] In addition, in the economics of insurance, risk-based pricing is regarded as not only efficient (itself a normative objective), but is also described in overtly normative language as "actuarial fairness": higher premiums for higher risk, lower premiums for lower risk. Higher-risk insureds are more likely to file claims, so they should pay more; this way, everyone pays their "fair share." This particular conception of fairness is premised, in turn, on a faith in objective risk assessment, which yields individualized prices that are equitable, and legitimate, for being quantified, dispassionate, and standardized: everyone is subjected to technical processes of risk assessment and economization.[57] Insurance and the other economic institutions that govern our lives come larded with all kinds of these (often implicit) moral commitments and they depend upon the legitimacy of those commitments in order to continue functioning smoothly.[58]

Studies of insurance provide unique purchase for examining moral economies. It is no coincidence that Viviana Zelizer's classic 1979 book *Morals and Markets* was a case study of life insurance. As she showed, in its early days, commercial life insurance related death, money, and profit in ways that were morally troublesome for political authorities and prospective customers. These moral scruples circumscribed the expansion and deployment of novel technologies of risk calculation and were eventually themselves transformed as sales techniques and other practices promulgated new discourses about the ethical legitimacy of putting dollar values on human lives. From Zelizer we learned how insurance participates not only in the social construction of risk,[59] its raw material, but also in the social and cultural definition of a broader array of human events, activities, and artifacts (death and dying, but also gambling, mourning and grief, and money).[60] As a result, insurance transforms ideas about the legitimate relations between them. Similarly, flood insurance mobilizes particular conceptions not only of floods as a "risk object,"[61] but also of homeownership and its responsibilities, planning and security, and the worthiness of a given place for different kinds of activities.

Insurance is also conspicuously implicated in questions of moral economy because it is a technology of distribution.[62] It establishes how the benefits and burdens of social interdependence will be shared. When we create insurance for a given peril, we agree to share the risk. As members of a risk pool, we each contribute something to indemnify the losses faced by any one of our members. Principles of *solidarity* have been foundational to the very idea of insurance and have governed the design of particular insurance institutions throughout history.[63] But insurers can forge this solidarity in different ways, and to a greater or lesser extent, which they adjudicate through the way risks are classified, premiums established, and terms of contracts specified.[64] Insurance pools necessarily include some people and risks while excluding others. In the words of Tom Baker,

Our insurance arrangements form a material constitution, one that operates through routine, mundane transactions that nevertheless define the contours of individual and social responsibility. For that reason, studying who is eligible to receive what insurance benefits, and who pays for them, is as good a guide to the social compact as any combination of Supreme Court opinions.[65]

We see this in the ways that the "boundary classifications" of insurance—who is in the risk pool and who is out—reflect and enact social belonging and moral designations of worthiness. In the example of insurance redlining in U.S. cities, urban areas with high concentrations of African American residents were long deemed too "risky" to insure, making it nearly impossible for residents to secure mortgages or gain access to smaller loans for the maintenance of property and thereby reproducing exclusion and discrimination in housing markets.[66]

Insurance also produces effects on the ways moral and political concepts are perceived, establishing and organizing relations of responsibility as a result.[67] As Francois Ewald has shown, developing a Foucauldian tradition, insurance as a technique provided the philosophical and legal foundation for Western welfare systems, in which states can manage populations probabilistically and ascribe values to centrally managed individuals.[68] Risk is a characteristic of the population, which each individual bears differently.[69] The modern welfare state is really an "insurance state," in the view of David

Garland, one that particularly benefits the middle classes and the employed, as well as employers and corporations. Programs of social insurance, which are central pillars of welfare state governance, socialize or collectivize activities, requiring contributions from participants to enable the provision of state protection against economic risks. Insurance provides a contractual template for how citizens relate to each other and to the state. It therefore serves as a terrain of moral struggle over the contours and limitations of mutual aid, compassion, and membership.[70]

For these reasons, studies of insurance that address the distributional implications of moral economies tend to focus on those government programs of social insurance that address health, injury, employment, and old age, such as Social Security, Medicare, workers' compensation, and pension programs. In these empirical contexts, scholars are well aware that debates over deservingness, choice, and fairness have significant consequences for the kinds of access different groups are given to resources and risk-sharing, as well as for the conditions of their participation.[71] The elderly, for instance, cannot help getting old and thereby becoming less able to provide for themselves through continued employment. They are perceived to be blameless for their precarity and therefore "deserving." We are more willing to devote some of our collective economic resources to sustain them—in the United States, through Social Security. Many U.S. social programs reflect this moral economy of redistribution based on fault: Are you to blame for the losses you face or not?[72] These distinctions have always been entangled with moral assumptions about gender, race, citizenship, and work that have consigned women, racial and ethnic minorities, immigrants, and the able-bodied poor to less generous public assistance.[73]

Natural hazards policy and programs of disaster insurance—like the NFIP—are not conventionally considered to fall under the umbrella of American social protection. They are more commonly analyzed as environmental or disaster policies, with foremost interest in their consequences for land use, ecologies, infrastructure, and budgets. Yet as Michele Landis Dauber has shown, disaster policy was central to the very development of the American welfare state, with disaster relief providing the earliest and most muscular exercises of federal power to make direct transfer payments from the Treasury to those "in need." Indeed, natural disaster policy provided discursive and constitutional precedent for the architects of the New Deal. President Franklin D. Roosevelt likened the "disaster" of the Great Depression to the Dust Bowl, tornadoes, and floods, the kinds of disasters to which the federal government had by that point long been responding in some fashion.[74] Today, like other kinds of social programs, disaster relief and flood insurance commit federal expenditures to respond to those in need. Policymakers may not design such policy as a form of anti-poverty welfare, but flood insurance nevertheless shares risk and compensates individuals for loss and suffering.[75] It provides for the economic security of those who have something to lose: a house.[76] Like many social policies, the NFIP sustains and promotes the American dream of home-ownership, forming part of a larger policy infrastructure that situates home-ownership at the center of American citizenship, economic security, and wealth creation. This dream is unequally realized, with a huge and persistent racial homeownership gap showing that it is has been much more easily within reach for white homeowners like Palmer and George. In the United States, the politics of property and land use are deeply imbricated with a racialized politics of social provision.[77]

All of this suggests that extending an analysis of moral economies to flood insurance can help explain designations of how much, or what kinds of, responsibility individuals and local communities are expected to assume to protect themselves. Just as there was more at stake than simply grain prices for E. P. Thompson's peasants, there is more at stake in flood insurance than simply economic losses due to flood damage. Using moral economy as an analytical framework gives purchase on the broader meanings of loss that are operative here and implicated in insurance generally. I grant the economists that people are generally bad at handling risk probabilities. We tend not to think that bad things will happen; if they do happen, we tend not to think they'll happen to us; and if they do happen to us, we tend not to think they'll be that bad. But I part ways with them in identifying this human frailty as the major driver of the NFIP's fate. In addition, the moral economic dimensions analyzed here unfold in interaction with the political economy of flood insurance that many scholars, journalists, and policy experts have identified. Conflicts and struggles between political groups over interests, resources, profit, and power are centrally important. But those moral economic dimensions are crucial for helping us to understand the terms of what people and political groups believe to be possible, preferable, and legitimate, as well as how those actors mobilize opposing commitments and connect them to specific policy changes. Attention to moral economies also helps to characterize and analyze the significance of shared sentiments that unite groups on different sides of a given flood insurance issue and allow for certain kinds of political settlements. The story of flood insurance is also a story about expertise, technology, and rationalization, as the sociology of risk would emphasize. But it is too a story about social interdependence and mutual obligation, in which the problems people are trying to solve relate not only to the adequacy of economization and scientific measurement and prediction, but also to how these activities align, or don't, with vernacular understandings of value, risk, and loss, as well as with political moralities of responsibility. What I offer with a moral economies framework is an alternative way of seeing flood insurance and its social significance.

This book also resituates questions about climate change within sociology. Environmental sociology, for its part, has produced revealing findings and important insights about the anthropogenic driving forces of climate change; climate politics, climate justice, and inequality; adaptation and mitigation; public opinion and denialism; and the social theory of climate change.[78] Environmental sociologists and other critical scholars of disaster have also done much to show how so-called natural disasters, of the kind we now associate with climate change, have eminently human and social causes and produce highly uneven effects. The "disaster," the designation of which is itself an act of interpretation, can be located as much in the organizations and sociotechnical systems that societies use to manage and respond to hazards and harms, as it can in any given event.[79] This book builds on two key insights from this body of work. First, climate change is not a narrowly "environmental" problem, nor should it be studied as such. Second, a lot of the socially significant action takes place before and after the flood events occur. Taken together, these two insights motivate my objective of expanding sociological engagement with climate change beyond environmental sociology and disaster studies. In the chapters that follow, I use tools from economic sociology in order to understand the character and consequences of economic "styles of reasoning" and policy devices for managing risk and loss.[80] I draw on the traditions of political sociology to situate such approaches in broader contexts of social provision and public policy and to analyze political claims-making around them. And I bring to bear insights from sociologies of science, technology, and knowledge to denaturalize underlying assumptions in processes of risk assessment and economization and to explain how problems, objects of intervention, and solutions are constituted.

UNDERWATER

We begin at the beginning of the NFIP. Chapter 1, "Transforming the Management of Loss: The Origins of the National Flood Insurance Program," explains how a public insurance program became for federal policymakers a solution to the problem of rising flood losses—but proved to be a problematic solution. The chapter examines how moral claims shaped the NFIP's technical and economic arrangements. In this policymaking moment, we see how insurance constructs new risk objects for which individuals and governments are made responsible in new ways. With the stroke of a pen, national politicians transformed floods from an uninsurable "act of God" into—at least in theory—a measurable, quantifiable, manageable peril, something that the government would scientifically assess and map, and that individuals could account and prepare for financially. The establishment of the NFIP also shows how the design of insurance systems articulates specific visions of virtuous behavior, aligning economic calculation with actions that mitigate risk and lower demands on collective resources to respond to loss. At the same time, policymakers grappled with precisely where and how the NFIP should redraw the limits of "personal responsibility." Concerns of moral economy have been just as central to the NFIP's design and operation as have objectives related to land use and environmental management. They help to explain the particular compromises policymakers forged in the NFIP's earliest years. More fundamentally, from the NFIP's history, we can appreciate that natural hazards insurance is not simply a rational, technocratic tool for managing risk, but is a site for moral claims-making about loss: the reasons for it, how best to manage and avoid it, and how to respond to the needs of those who face it.

In chapter 2, "Losing Ground: Values at Risk in an American Floodplain," we follow the NFIP out of the halls of Congress in the 1960s and onto the streets and waterfronts of New York City in the wake of Hurricane Sandy over forty years later, in order to examine everyday encounters with insurance. There, New Yorkers navigated a new official landscape of risk and its cost, enacted through an updated flood insurance rate map and grafted onto the physical and social realities of a place. In the previous chapter, policymakers reconfigured responsibilities for flood loss, operating with conventional understandings of loss as pertaining to property destroyed and money spent in response. But in practice people on the ground confront a more complex picture of loss, one in which the loss of their property can also mean the loss of social ties and emotional connections. Though the insurance map frames calculative decision-making about loss as a matter of protecting property "value at risk" of flooding, we can see the relevance of this broader set of losses by observing *values at risk*. In other words, local understandings of loss that encompassed other kinds of "values" imbued in a home and a place, as well as other perceived "risks" beyond floodwaters, together shaped decisions of what to do and when. Far from producing clear strategies of action, the flood map produced ambivalent actors and outcomes—in part, because people felt that compensation for some kinds of losses wouldn't be fair or even possible in this context. In addition, even when people took steps to reduce their flood risk, they often did not feel that they were better off or more secure for having done so. However "prudent" or "rational" such actions might be, their exposure to other kinds of losses as a result did not seem wholly justifiable. In the experiences of flood insurance in New York City, we see that questions of compensation for and justification of loss are unsettled and unsettling as communities confront further effects of climate change.

With so much at stake, estimations of flood risk and their depiction on FEMA's flood maps are highly consequential. In chapter 3, "Visions of Loss: Knowing and Pricing Flood Risk," we look squarely at the production of scientific and economic knowledge about flood risk and its actuarial price. How does FEMA determine an area's flood risk? How does the NFIP know how to price it? The chapter provides a fine-grained account of the central instruments that make flood insurance possible—FEMA's flood insurance rate maps and actuarial premiums—as they have developed over time and as experts and policymakers attempt to incorporate climate change as a potential contributor to risk and a source of future losses. The chapter shows how the "accuracy" of a risk assessment, its depiction on a map, and its cost are matters of political agreement, forged in practice through often contentious negotiations between multiple stakeholders. The result is a particular vision of the problem of flood loss that can be accepted as *reasonable* for the actors involved. The chapter tells the story of New York City's appeal of its new flood insurance rate maps, initiated once the difficulties facing the city's residents, described in the previous chapter, became clear. The city had to navigate a complex techno-political dilemma in its appeal, forging a strategy that would signal a readiness to adapt the city to climate change, while also responding to moral economy pressures related to the legitimate distribution of responsibility. Fights over whose version of a risk map will be used to govern what, or who, are fights over who should pay the costs of climate change and when.

Local-level dilemmas in New York City reverberated up to national-level policymaking. Stop FEMA Now, the grassroots network of homeowners, began in the remapped flood zones of New York and New Jersey before spreading to twenty other U.S. states. It became the face of a nationwide backlash to the Biggert-Waters Flood Insurance Reform Act, which passed with bipartisan support in July 2012 and phased out long-standing flood insurance subsidies; ended the grandfathering of older, lower rates; and mandated that FEMA assess how to incorporate climate science into its flood maps. Chapter 4, "Shifting Responsibilities for Loss: National Reform of Flood Insurance," examines this reform in greater detail, tracing the political and moral claims made both to secure its passage in 2012 and then to retreat on several of its key provisions just eighteen months later. The debate that ensued exposed the ongoing relevance of the moral economy dilemmas at the heart of flood insurance, wherein stakeholders articulated commitments to ideas about choice, responsibility, fairness, and deservingness in order to advocate for different distributions of individual versus collective responsibility today and into the future.

Next, we turn to floodplain futures. The NFIP is still in a fragile state and its recent controversies raise larger existential questions about the physical and financial futures of America's floodplain communities. How should insurance operate to govern human activity and decision-making in the present, in light of expectations for a future in which the ground beneath our feet literally disappears? What role, if any, will or should insurance play in determining how and when retreat from the coasts takes place? How will evolving understandings of climate risk, shaped in large part by instruments like flood maps and insurance premiums, depreciate property values and erode the economic prosperity of individuals and communities in the nation's floodplains? Is insurance actually working to camouflage a climate change bubble in the housing market that, once recognized, could suddenly collapse the value of real estate investments and set off another financial crisis tied to housing? Chapter 5, "Floodplain Futures: Trajectories of Loss," assembles and synthesizes the available evidence of where climate-related economic losses are starting to appear and who is beginning to feel the financial pressure. On the basis of this emerging evidence, the chapter outlines different trajectories for floodplain futures. Each trajectory reflects different orientations to loss: the extent to which it is viewed as inevitable, manageable, or acceptable. Each involves a vision of the role insurance does or should play in organizing those losses.

In the conclusion, "What Do We Have to Lose?," I synthesize some of the lessons of the NFIP for thinking about insurance and the moral economy of climate change, which can help us to grapple with the real effects and stakes of our economizing institutions going forward. I conclude with a discussion of the "moral opportunity" of insurance, addressing what we might lose—or more precisely, what we might *let go*—as Americans have a harder time keeping their heads above water.

Chapter One

TRANSFORMING THE MANAGEMENT OF LOSS

The Origins of the National Flood
Insurance Program

As President Lyndon B. Johnson walked through the crowded and darkened corridors of George Washington High School in New Orleans, Louisiana, on September 10, 1965, he was stopped by refugees of Hurricane Betsy, begging for water.[1] The storm had slammed into the Gulf Coast the day before, driving a storm surge that overwhelmed the Industrial Canal levees and flooded thousands of homes.[2] As Louisiana senator Russell Long described it in a phone call to the president, "Hurricane Betsy picked up [Lake Pontchartrain] and put it inside New Orleans and Jefferson Parish . . . Mr. President, we have really had it down there, and we need your help."[3] The Louisianans who met Johnson that night were just some of the 250,000 people displaced by the flood and sent to makeshift refugee centers like the high school. The floodwaters, which reached the eaves of many homes in the mostly below-sea-level city, did not recede for weeks.[4] According to the *New York Times*, Johnson was "shocked by the sight of death and destruction."[5] Betsy was the first natural disaster to generate more than $1 billion in damages (1965 USD).[6]

During that visit, Johnson promised Betsy's victims that federal help was on the way. The president soon dispatched the Army Corps of Engineers, the Navy, and the Coast Guard to clean up the debris and mobilized several federal agencies to help people put their lives back together. But beyond this show of solidarity in the storm's immediate aftermath, Hurricane Betsy would have a more lasting legacy. In his statement upon the signing of the Southeast Hurricane Disaster Relief Act of 1965, two months after Betsy, President Johnson indicated that the United States had a problem of flood loss and that insurance needed to be a bigger part of its solution. "Thousands of families have had their homes severely damaged or destroyed by floods or other water-caused damages against which they could not purchase insurance protection, because insurance for this type of risk was not available for them to buy," his statement read. The act would therefore mandate "the immediate initiation of a study by the Secretary of Housing and Urban Development of alternative permanent programs which could be established to help provide financial assistance in the future to those suffering property losses in floods and other natural disasters, including but not limited to disaster insurance or reinsurance." Such a study was "long overdue" and would be the act's "most significant potential contribution."[7] That study would ultimately outline the contours of the National Flood Insurance Program (NFIP).

Forty years later, in the wake of another devastating hurricane in New Orleans, that solution to the problem of flood losses would prove, in dramatic fashion, to be a problematic solution. Claims related to Hurricane Katrina in 2005 plunged the NFIP $16.1 billion in debt to the U.S. Treasury.[8] J. Robert Hunter, an administrator of the NFIP in the 1970s, told Congress in hearings after Katrina that "political pressure" and "program error" over several decades had threatened "the overall viability and effectiveness of the flood insurance program."[9] The crisis presented by Katrina was only the latest episode in a history of challenges to this beleaguered program. The NFIP had grown slowly, was difficult to implement, and had proven nearly impossible to reform. A major reason for establishing flood insurance was to reduce flood losses, but more people and property were located in hazardous floodplains than ever before.

Many accounts of the NFIP's history aim to explain the program's various failures and come to conclusions about technical incompetence, bureaucratic mismanagement, venal meddling from interest groups, and short-sighted governance. This account has different aims. From a twenty-first-century vantage point the NFIP looks like a failed land use program, a misapplied environmental policy. Its operations seem, to many, to defy common sense. In the mid-twentieth century, however, when poli-cymakers, administrators, and flood experts were debating its merits, a flood insurance program represented an ambitious and experimental reconfiguration of responsibilities for flood loss. It was discussed in highly moralized terms, explicitly related to broader goals of social protection and premised on, and itself enacting, changing understandings of not only floods (discussed, if inconsistently, in terms of *risks*), but also disasters more generally, victimhood, and blame. The NFIP's continued operation—in spite of its manifest challenges—reflects also normative commitments to the American dream of homeownership and the role of the federal govern-ment in facilitating and protecting that dream. It reflects the by now taken-for-granted legitimacy of science and economic analysis as a basis for policy-making and administration, the manifestation of a shared confidence in our ability not just to control or tame nature, but to *know* it—to use scien-tific and economic techniques to assess, predict, visualize, and price the consequences of our interactions with natural events. And it embodies an impulse to govern indirectly, through incentivizing and subsidizing private actors, rather than outright regulating or redistributing for the public good.

For all of these reasons, then, this chapter provides a historical account of the origins and early implementation of the NFIP that pays particular attention to how moral claims shaped technical and economic arrange-ments. Doing so helps us to understand how various actors framed the problem of loss: its causes, consequences, and who ought to be responsible for it. It fills out the picture of what makes the NFIP such a complex and beleaguered program as it confronts climate change, uncovering the unin-tended consequences of well-intentioned efforts. But more fundamentally, a moral economic history of flood insurance clarifies how it came to reflect and enact a kind of common sense about not only how to best manage human relationships to water, but also cross-cutting relationships between governments, local communities, and households. Following the approach taken by David Moss in his history of American risk management policy, this chapter focuses on the problems policymakers were trying to solve and the ideas and values they drew on to do so.[10] Government officials, mem-bers of Congress, and the experts they relied upon assessed trade-offs and forged compromises in order to pursue multiple and sometimes competing objectives, in light of beliefs about what was right, fair, and prudent. I also derive inspiration from Wendy Espeland's study of bureaucratic culture and a problem of water—in her case, scarcity rather than abundance—and trace how a particular rational form changes the interpretations and meanings of activities, actors, and events.[11]

To appreciate the NFIP's ambition and significance, we need to begin with an account of flood loss before flood insurance. What kind of problem was a flood, who was expected to respond to it, and how? How had the moral economy of disaster and redistribution in response to flood loss developed up to the point of the NFIP's establishment?

FLOODS BEFORE FLOOD INSURANCE

The flood damage from Hurricane Betsy was catastrophic, but it was in fact the last in a longer series of devastating floods, most caused by hurricanes, in seven of the twelve years from 1954 to 1965. Together, these floods resulted in several billion dollars in property damage. Federal disaster assistance ballooned from $52 million in 1952 to $374 million in 1966.[12] By 1965, when Johnson put flood insurance on the national agenda, floods had become very expensive calamities for the federal government. For this to be the case, two important things had to be true. First, there had to be economic value in place that could be destroyed: private homes, commercial properties, and public infrastructure, all located within reach of the floodwaters. Second, for floods to become expensive *for the federal government*, a particular liability of the public purse, there had to be by the 1960s a shared presumption that the federal government *should* and *could* deploy resources to rebuild communities in the wake of disaster. In other words, the state had to have the willingness and capacity to prevent and respond to natural disasters. It had to become a "sympathetic state," as Michele Landis Dauber puts it in her history of disaster relief and social welfare. In the history of the federal government's response to flood loss, we can identify the appearance and significance of new ideas about "the nation's obligation to citizens in distress," as well as about humans' relationship to nature, which have informed the ways in which government involves itself in the lives of ordinary Americans. What counts as a disaster and who represents a disaster victim are matters of moral claims-making, argument, and judgment, shifting over time and often contested in the context of specific catastrophes.[13]

For much of American history, from the founding to around the turn of the twentieth century, floods and other natural disasters were often understood as local problems, demanding a local and private response to deal with resulting losses. The federal government would provide resources from the national treasury, if "sufferers" could make a successful application to Congress that they were "victims of circumstance," but only in episodic fashion. According to the historian Gareth Davies, Congress "much more commonly did nothing." This reflected in part logistical obstacles related to communications and transportation over this period; it was hard to get information about disasters or to send help in a timely fashion. But this reticence can also be attributed to the particular way Americans made sense of sudden, unanticipated catastrophe. In his study of disaster response in early American history, Davies notes a lack of any sense that people are, or can expect to be, masters of their environment. The hazards of daily life were great and could not be predicted. Furthermore, many religious Americans took the notion of an "act of God" seriously and as more than just figurative; disasters had at some level unknowable origins and purposes. They were themselves morality tales, meted out by a just God. Penitent "fast days" were a common response to natural disaster in the early national period. Davies also notes "boosterish narratives" that celebrated the optimism of the afflicted and the voluntarism of local communities (narratives that stay with us today). For these reasons, in many cases, Americans did not expect relief from the government and therefore did not ask for it. The flood-affected understood themselves as subject to "bad luck" or "divine will," but did not always understand their status as victims to be a legitimate basis for making claims on collective resources. Nevertheless, over this period, Congress increasingly often allocated funds for disaster relief; by 1822, this largely took the form of general relief bills.[14]

Over the course of the early twentieth century, there was still no federal policy or program for responding to natural disasters after they struck, but governments at all levels began to play a bigger role in preventing and preparing for them. Natural disasters were still understood as "individual, isolated, and random acts of God,"[15] though this was by now predominately figurative; "nature trumped God and man in the metaphysics of causation," as the historian Ted Steinberg explains.[16] Yet over this period, growing federal resources were devoted to natural hazard management—even if *individuals* were still not expected to exert control over, or reasonably prepare for, floods and other disasters, the federal government might and ought to. In the case of floods, at the time, this intervention relied primarily on infrastructure: levees, dams, and other structures that would redirect the water so that it served people and settlements without imperiling them.

The federal government had been financing and constructing "river improvements" since the Supreme Court authorized such activities in *Gibbons v. Ogden* in 1824. However, it was the early twentieth century that saw a series of "Flood Control Acts" in 1917, 1928, 1936, and 1938, which explicitly made flood control a national problem and federal responsibility.[17] As the names of the measures convey, floods were now framed as "controllable"—not by ordinary people certainly, but by experts, the professional engineers and planners who increasingly populated government agencies. The Flood Control Acts codified and expanded the Army Corps of Engineers' purview, creating a multibillion-dollar program to survey, tame, and redirect the nation's rivers. By midcentury, federal expenditures for dams and levees under construction or authorized since the Flood Control Act of 1936 had surpassed the prior total federal spending for such structures since 1776.[18] Major flood security infrastructure projects also constituted important sources of employment as President Franklin D. Roosevelt tried to steer the country out of the Great Depression. The largest of them, the Hoover Dam, was built by the Public Works Administration, which employed 10,000 people in the effort. At its dedication, Secretary of the Interior Harold Ickes said of the achievement: "Pridefully, man acclaims his conquest of nature."[19] New Deal agencies were central in responding to floods in 1936 and 1937, and to the New England Hurricane of 1938. Disaster relief was also added to the mandates of several New Deal agencies, including the Reconstruction Finance Corporation and the Bureau of Public Roads.[20]

In the early twentieth century, the locus of federal control over disaster prevention and relief also shifted from Congress to the executive branch, where it would stay. Whereas in the earlier period, supplication to and debate in Congress drove federal action after disasters, with the rise of the modern presidency, the president began to use executive power to direct the bureaus and agencies of the executive branch to engage in disaster relief, as President Theodore Roosevelt did following the San Francisco earthquake of 1906.[21] With enhancements in communications technologies and the emergence of national media, natural disasters became national issues to which the president felt compelled to respond. This enhanced public expectations of aid to the disaster-afflicted, usually funded by the federal government and carried out by the executive branch, the military, and a few nonprofits. Individuals also began to receive their first direct forms of federal relief, then in the form of low-interest loans, the terms of which were repeatedly liberalized after World War II.[22] The Disaster Relief Act of 1950 replaced these ad hoc, case-by-case aid packages with the first general and comprehensive law governing disaster relief. The act formally authorized the federal government to assist state and local government disaster response efforts and enshrined the central position of the president in disaster relief by establishing presidential discretion to declare national disasters.[23]

Governments also shouldered the majority of rising flood relief costs alone. The extraordinary Great Mississippi Flood of 1927, which submerged 16.5 million acres of land, had financially devastated the several dozen private fire insurance companies that also sold flood insurance policies at the time. Individual flood hazards were highly correlated in specific regions, and the Great Mississippi Flood, followed by further flooding around the country in 1928, led private insurers to decide that the prospect of catastrophic flooding rendered this particular risk "uninsurable": one extremely bad flood could bankrupt the insurers doing business in the area. The private insurance sector abandoned the flood market by 1929.[24] From the perspective of the flooded, this state of affairs meant that, unable to insure their structures or belongings on the private market, American property owners were left to hope for disaster relief after the flood. Though these kinds of outlays to flooded communities had indeed become more likely, they were not guaranteed. If a flood event failed to rise to the level of disaster for the purposes of disbursing federal relief, local communities and individuals bore full financial responsibility for rebuilding and replacing their homes and property.

FROM FLOOD CONTROL'S PROBLEM WITH WATER TO FLOODPLAIN MANAGEMENT'S PROBLEM WITH PEOPLE

By the time Hurricane Betsy crashed into New Orleans in 1965, a number of important features of American political culture and institutions had been established. The federal government had, to a significant extent, nationalized policy responses to natural disasters. It had taken on more responsibility both for building structures that would ostensibly protect residents and property from floods and for coming to their assistance if and when those structures failed. Flood disaster relief costs had come to constitute a huge and unpredictable drain on public resources. And flood losses were uninsured. With the private market out, recovery was difficult to finance. Especially confounding to policymakers, floods continued to devastate American communities *despite* the proliferation of all those ambitious structural flood control projects: the dams, dunes, and levees built across the country (with over $8 billion spent between 1936 and 1967).[25] Policy actors began looking for alternatives to conventional, structural forms of flood security.

The central protagonist in building a case for those alternatives was the geographer Gilbert Fowler White, regarded by many as "the father of floodplain management." White graduated from the University of Chicago in 1934 and spent the first eight years of his career in Roosevelt's New Deal administration. His first professional assignment took him to the Missouri and lower Mississippi river valleys, where he first encountered the Army Corps of Engineers as part of a flood mitigation effort. This early experience laid the foundation for a philosophy that would consolidate in opposition to the Corps' "levees-only" approach to flood security and provide the intellectual basis for a national program of flood insurance.

White came to regard the major infrastructure projects designed and built by the Corps with increasingly strong skepticism.[26] These projects, in his view, actually generated a *social* dynamic that explained the increase in flood losses. Protected from routine nuisance flooding by these structures, the vulnerable areas behind them appeared newly safe for human habitation, encouraging families and businesses to move in. Indeed, in the context of the increasing suburbanization of the United States, facilitating further development of floodplains was eventually quantified as a benefit in the cost-benefit analyses underlying Army Corps of Engineers projects.[27] But when major catastrophic flooding events inevitably overwhelmed dams, dunes, and levees, they now generated exorbitant losses, as more people and property were exposed than likely would have been in the absence of such structural protection. In his 1942 doctoral dissertation, White dubbed this the "levee effect."[28]

It thus appeared to White that the primary federal strategy for flood security was exacerbating a problem it was meant to solve by putting more property and people in harm's way.[29] Again, this was happening in a context in which local communities and states had become more empowered to seek federal relief following these catastrophic floods.[30] White argued in his dissertation: "On the whole, present policy fosters an increasing dependence by individuals and local governments upon the federal government for leadership and financial support in dealing with the flood problem."[31] The federal government had saddled itself with financing both structural flood protection works *and* the relief that followed when that flood protection failed. The better approach, in White's view, was to adjust human occupancy in and uses of land near the water's edge. He did not dispute the role of the federal government in providing flood security, nor did he think all infrastructure projects were counterproductive. But his argument against an overweening focus on flood control structures like dams and levees reflected his particular causal theory about how people responded to a false sense of security provided by dams and levees.[32] Given this causal theory, White believed, it simply made more sense to keep people away from the flood, rather than keep the flood away from the people. The puzzle was then how to inculcate a new ethics of living with water, for both individuals and governing authorities. White argued that federal activity should instead emphasize a "non-structural" approach to flood control—namely, better land-use planning and building codes. Specifically, this could rely on some mix of flood-proofing, relocation, insurance, and regulation: measures that, taken together, could change human behavior rather than change the course of the water.[33]

At the start of his career, White's ideas were unconventional, even "un-American" in the view of the California congressional delegation, which began an investigation into White following his suggestion at a national planning conference that no further funds for constructing dams in California should be spent unless legislation was enacted to control encroachment into floodplains. But after his dissertation was published in 1945 as a University of Chicago research paper titled "Human Adjustment to Floods: A Geographical Approach to the Flood Problem in the United States," White's ideas grew in popularity as they were picked up and elaborated by other scholars, in both the social and physical sciences, elevating his stature and influence in domestic flood security policy. Though White would never again enter direct government service after leaving Roosevelt's administration, he held highly influential committee and advisory positions in each of the subsequent twelve federal administrations.[34]

White's nonstructural approach would, in turn, require the resolution of a host of technical issues related to defining local flood problems. If the problem of flooding was to be governed not on the basis of controlling the events themselves, but rather on the basis of managing the areas and people most exposed to them, experts and authorities would have to arrive at some shared understanding of which areas were indeed hazardous and in need of nonstructural intervention. This implied a commitment to scientific floodplain studies that included accurate, regularly updated maps of at-risk areas. Floods were not sudden, unpredictable, and unfortunate "acts of God" that could befall *anyone*. Rather, they were foreseeable and knowable, if not precisely predictable, meaning that their attendant losses were preventable—so long as decision-makers possessed and acted upon the right information. But producing such maps and studies would depend on some agreement as to the magnitude of flooding upon which to base such maps; in other words, what were the acceptable thresholds within which to allow development and what were the levels of projected water rise that would determine how to manage structures in those areas? White spent much of the 1950s convening his contacts in the Army Corps and the Tennessee Valley Authority (TVA) in order to develop and collate the data, hydraulic expertise, and mapping techniques that could form a credible set of standards and guidelines for floodplain management.[35]

The catastrophic Kansas–Missouri floods of 1951 renewed attention to flood disasters after an extended period of relative quiet. In response to those floods, which had again produced immense uninsured losses, President Harry S. Truman sent a message to Congress asking for funds to finance a federal insurance program. Truman was keenly interested in the compensatory function of insurance: the way insurance speeds the disbursement of funds to the policyholder who has suffered a loss, allowing them to recover more quickly than they would if they were reliant on politically capricious disaster relief, private charity, or their own resources. He recommended the creation of a "national system of flood disaster insurance, similar to the war damage insurance of World War II." Floods might be scientifically foreseeable, but they were experientially like wars: traumatic, destructive, produced by forces stronger than any individual, and demanding solidarity from citizens facing a shared adversary. He wrote, "The lack of a national system of flood disaster insurance is now a major gap in the means by which a man can make his home, his farm, or his business secure against events beyond his control."[36] Truman proposed a system of flood insurance based on private insurance with reinsurance by the federal government. Reinsurance is essentially insurance for insurers; it allows the primary insurer to pass on some of its own liabilities to another entity. In this case, the idea was that the federal government would step in to limit the losses faced by private insurers in the event of a catastrophic event. No action was taken in direct response, but flood insurance ended up on the agenda of the Senate Committee on Banking and Currency for the next five years. In 1955, the chairman of that committee directed the staff to undertake a study of the feasibility of a federal flood insurance program, which identified the general problems that would have to be overcome in order to get such a program off the ground. In 1956, President Dwight D. Eisenhower requested a flood insurance program in one of his State of the Union addresses. The Senate Subcommittee on Securities organized a series of hearings around the country on the subject, ultimately eliciting sufficient congressional support to secure passage of the Federal Flood Insurance Act of 1956.[37] The act established three new federal programs: a direct federal flood insurance program, a federal reinsurance program, and a federal loan contract program covering flood losses.

The 1956 Act also created the Federal Flood Indemnity Administration (FFIA) as a unit of the Housing and Home Finance Agency.[38] However, when the FFIA submitted its request for program funds to Congress, the House Appropriations Committee denied it.[39] According to HUD Under Secretary Robert C. Wood, recounting this earlier failure during congressional hearings ten years later, at the time, the FFIA had made no presentation of what the insurance rates in insured areas would have to be and the Appropriations Committee concluded that there was no way of measuring the government's contingent liability.[40] In other words, even in the 1950s there were concerns that federal flood insurance could become an excessively costly program. In addition, officials expected that to sufficiently cover the estimated losses, flood insurance rates would be prohibitively expensive for those most at risk. The system proposed by the FFIA appeared more like a social insurance program, a mechanism simply to socialize the risk of flooding.[41] Advocates who favored expanded government relief supported it anyway, and on precisely these grounds, making early connections between flood insurance and other forms of social welfare. The federal government wrote social insurance against unemployment and old age without calculation of differences in risk and, by analogy, flood insurance could and should be underwritten the same way.[42] But without the necessary funds, the program went dormant before ultimately being abolished.

The final report to Congress on the activities of the nascent FFIA indicated a need for a more thorough study of flood insurance feasibility.[43] These early legislative efforts did not have the support of the private insurance industry, which contributed to their failure.[44] At the time, the industry believed the technical challenges associated with estimating flood hazards, combined with the commercial challenges of getting people to buy what would likely be an expensive product, made flood insurance uninsurable— not only for the private market, but also for the state. An insurance industry study of flood insurance concluded: "There is no reason to believe that the Government would encounter fewer obstacles to such an undertaking than private insurers."[45] But White, now a geography professor at the University of Chicago, continued to convene academics and his allies in the Army Corps and TVA, who were interested in closing the technical gaps that would make science-based floodplain management, including insurance, possible. He succeeded in convincing the Council of State Governments to recommend that Congress direct federal agencies to produce evaluations and maps providing basic data on flood magnitude and frequency for flood risk areas. Congress took up this recommendation in the Flood Control Act of 1960, which assigned coordinating responsibility for this effort to the Army Corps. The Corps would produce these "Flood Information Studies" to inform state and local efforts to reduce damage and mitigate flood hazards through local regulation, land-use planning, and other means, including some structural projects.[46]

However, floodplain management involved more than just an understanding of hydrology, hydraulics, and topography. The other major piece of the puzzle was human behavior. After all, keeping people away from the floods was, fundamentally, about shaping decision-making.[47] Specifically, it was about encouraging different, wiser uses of the floodplain. Here was where insurance could potentially intervene, acting as one plank of a comprehensive floodplain management strategy targeting land use. Through creating a risk-based (actuarial) price—not for the federal government building dams and levees, but for individual decision-makers deciding whether or not to build or buy homes—insurance would offer and incentivize economically rational choices. All those economically rational choices, taken together, would reduce flood losses over time by transforming where and how people lived in relation to the water. As Stephen Collier has observed, flood insurance would treat individuals as "different kinds of political subjects: calculating agents who could take into account—would, indeed, be forced to take into account—the costs of living in a floodplain."[48] As White and colleagues would explain to policymakers, an actuarial insurance scheme would provide a kind of behavioral engineering, altering the calculation and distribution of costs and benefits of occupying the floodplain, and thereby making it clear that some uses of the floodplain were uneconomical and therefore imprudent.

DESIGNING FEDERAL FLOOD INSURANCE

By the time Hurricane Betsy hit, flood insurance, it had started to seem, might solve several problems at once. With disaster relief ballooning, the compensatory function of insurance had growing appeal. Flood insurance promised to ease the demand for such relief, which disaster victims and their local representatives appeared increasingly emboldened to seek. Through the payment of annual premiums, residents in floodplains would in a sense "prefund" their own disaster relief in their relatively more likely event of a loss. To policymakers, including President Johnson, compensation via premiums rather than relief also signaled a different and enhanced kind of solidarity with disaster victims. The provision of insurance would transform the flood victim into an insurance customer. The customer would thereby have a contractual right to claims payments, as a result of paying yearly premiums, which would be a more reliable source of recovery funds than the beneficence of government aid, access to low-interest loans,[49] and assistance from nonprofits like the Red Cross. It would turn the postevent, ad hoc nature of compensating the victims of acts of God into a consistent, nationally standardized response to flood loss.

The federal government could set up flood insurance to step in where the private market had failed, coming to the assistance of homeowners facing otherwise uninsurable risk while at the same time managing aggregate financial pressures. By establishing national flood insurance, the federal government would make flood, by definition, insurable. In the process, turning floods into a risk object would have the effect of normalizing disaster; floods were not best approached as exceptional events, but rather as regular ones, with varying probabilities of occurrence.[50] Policymakers and experts expected that a federal insurance program could operate on geographic and time scales that individuals and the private market could not, making it possible to socialize this risk more broadly. No one's share of that risk would be "too bad" to be covered. In private industry parlance, the government would not "defensively underwrite" by excluding or dropping the riskiest policies; the safety net would catch everyone with a policy, which is to say, the largely white homeowners for whom previous decades of housing policy had facilitated access to property ownership. At the same time that policymakers were extending insurance support to these homeowners, insurance redlining and other racist discrimination in real estate practices continued to exclude African Americans and other people of color from property ownership.[51]

The next step in establishing flood insurance was a new flood insurance feasibility report, with responsibility assigned to HUD in the Southeast Hurricane Disaster Relief Bill of 1965. At the time, technocrats and experts had become influential policy actors, as the (nonpartisan) quantification, engineering, and planning skills they offered seemed to rationalize public policy choices on the basis of scientific objectivity.[52] The report, headed up by Resources for the Future[53] president and economist Marion Clawson and titled *Insurance and Other Programs for Financial Assistance to Flood Victims*, was delivered by the Secretary of HUD to the president and Congress in August 1966. Concurrently with the production of Clawson's HUD report, the Bureau of the Budget commissioned a second report, under the auspices of a Task Force on Federal Flood Control Policy, which White agreed to convene and chair. Though sought for technocratic guidance, these two reports set out the rationale for flood insurance in moral terms, as well, evaluating different options in light of how they would reapportion responsibilities across the state, taxpayers, and at-risk residents. The recommendations from the reports would strongly inform subsequent congressional debates over authorizing a flood insurance program.

For its part, the HUD report faulted the federal government's historical preference for structural flood protection, which had counterproductively increased flood exposure and losses. Echoing White, the report explained, people had moved into coastal and riverine areas *because of* flood protection works. Structural flood protection sent the wrong signal to prospective floodplain occupants about the risk by misplacing the price of protection—often only the federal government knew it, and often only, or mostly, the federal government paid it. Many factors were driving the development of flood-prone areas, including population growth and rising incomes, but: "It is also clear that the substantial separation of costs from benefits—whereby the general public bears most of the costs of flood protection works while individual members primarily receive the gains—has been a major factor encouraging such development."[54] Here was a causal story about flood loss, where the actions of people in response to prevailing government approaches, rather than the disasters themselves, were to blame. This was only compounded by more generous disaster relief, which was showing an upward trend. The report offered a ponderous contemplation of the effect that more generous relief was having on personal responsibility:

If there should be a trend toward greatly more generous treatment of the victims of natural disasters, certainly one of the major restraining influences on location in highly flood hazardous areas will have been reduced. If one knows that the Federal government will make good his losses when they occur, then gambling on gains exceeding such losses offers less chance of loss and equal chance of gain, compared with the past. Risk of life and some risk of property may still remain, but the costs of location in highly hazardous areas are cut sharply.[55]

Yet this did not mean that federal relief after floods could or should disappear. The report argued that flood insurance would necessarily coexist with relief. But advancements in risk assessment meant that floods were now reasonably foreseeable; they did not strike communities completely unawares. Their risk could be classified and priced, and therefore planned for. In light of this, insurance provided an alternative and preferable institution for formatting responsibility in the face of flood loss—one that had proven workable for other "risks inherent in social life" in ways that "reduced [them] to a size that the individual can cope with," as the HUD report put it.[56] Rather than the federal government using risk assessment to engage in cost-benefit analysis for each dam, levee, floodwall, or canal, this responsibility would now be devolved to individuals, who would undertake the calculation and bear its consequences:

Knowing what the cost of insurance would be, any prospective occupant could decide if the advantages outweighed those costs. If he did so, he would know the cost of locating in a flood-prone area; if he did not, it would be because the cost was a deterrent [*sic*]. For this rational choosing process to be effective, it is essential that the person making the choice both reap the advantages and bear the costs that would follow a decision to locate in the flood hazard area; he should pay the full premiums on actuarially sound flood insurance. Flood insurance would be particularly valuable to those prospective occupants of flood hazard areas who make rational choices based upon weighing advantages against costs.[57]

Through taking on this responsibility of rational calculation, individuals would effectively pursue the collective aim of increased security from flood loss. Better yet, this would happen without the state determining or enforcing the same orientation toward the value of land on everyone; individuals were now free to decide if floodplain occupancy was an economically appealing proposition.[58] In the HUD report, this had a certain moral superiority:

Independence and self-reliance are deep-seated American traits, dating back to the extended pioneer period when such traits were not only highly valued but essential for survival and success. Most people in this country today prefer to manage their own affairs, to receive the gains—if any—from their actions, and to take the consequences if things turn out badly.[59]

Assuming proper design, the report concluded, "Flood insurance is both feasible and can promote the public interest." As Collier observes, this articulation of the benefits of flood insurance shows what we now recognize as a neoliberal preference for using public policy to constitute individual citizens as risk-taking agents, responsible for their own security— decades before the ideological transformations of the late 1970s and 1980s emphasized in many accounts of American political development. Yet at the same time, this was not sought in order to enable the retreat of the state, but rather to create a new role for the state in providing "a more reliable and complete form of security."[60]

We can see this in the HUD report's emphasis on the need for broad participation that would socialize the risk widely; the authors observed that the success of a flood insurance program would depend on it. This would in turn depend on the willingness and ability of potential policyholders to join the risk pool. In already-developed high-risk floodplains, the actuarial cost of insurance—a risk-based premium—would presumably be quite high. And floodplains contained within them a considerable measure of variation in ability to pay premiums of any size; rich and poor might end up living near the water, but the HUD authors believed that "many property owners in flood-prone areas could not afford the high premiums which a full-cost rate structure would entail." As a result, they suggested, "it may be necessary to subsidize flood insurance premiums for existing property owners in the highest risk zones."[61] This was not only practical, enhancing the acceptability and therefore feasibility of introducing flood insurance, it was also morally justifiable. "The persons who occupy these areas and built houses there did not understand the risks they were accepting by their acts," the report argued, in some cases having even been "completely misled" as to the extent of the flood hazard. This could reflect ignorance or malfeasance on the part of local authorities, home-builders, and real estate developers; "outright fraud in some areas is not impossible." Or the flood hazard may have increased since the occupants located in the floodplain, as a result of factors beyond their control, such as developments elsewhere in the floodplain or watershed. Property owners would also be justified in pointing out that there was no "effective public safeguard" against their occupancy. These areas were zoned for development; building permits were made available from public bodies; and information about flood hazard was in many cases unavailable even if it was sought.[62] For all these reasons, individual homeowners could not easily be blamed for their exposure to risk or the event of a loss, making it more difficult to lay full financial responsibility at their feet.

In addition, the HUD authors recognized that pricing people out of the floodplains could be economically catastrophic for them. Their investments had been made, and the federal government ought to do something to protect them. Property owners might regard "failure to provide insurance protection at reasonable rates on their past investment in such area [sic] as inequitable."[63] Homeownership was (and is) central to U.S. housing policy and to social welfare more generally. As Keeanga-Yamahtta Taylor notes, the homeowning boom of the 1950s "creat[ed] a bedrock of middle-class prosperity" for ordinary white people, whose prerogatives housing policy has historically been designed to protect. Through tax policy, interventions in housing markets, and reconfigurations of housing finance, the federal government has shown a longstanding interest in promoting and facilitating home buying, on deeply unequal terms for white and black Americans, and, relatedly, in fostering the continued prosperity of the private real estate industry that would produce the supply, even in hazardous areas. At the time of the HUD report's writing, homeownership was already symbolically as well as materially important to a sense of citizenship, security, and upward mobility.[64] And for those in the floodplains whose homeownership was most precarious—people who were just managing to make their mortgage payments as it was—an additional yearly insurance premium would be a nontrivial addition to tight household budgets. For all these reasons, subsidies were defensible and perhaps even necessary, though it would mean sacrificing, for some portion of policyholders, the actuarial principles that promised to make flood insurance a public policy instrument for land use. A subsidized flood insurance policy was not, after all, one that straightforwardly signaled the risk to the insured. How to design such subsidies—the price at which they should begin, the properties that would be eligible, the degree of the discount—were matters that would need careful consideration. The HUD report included a figure meant to depict the importance of this balancing act in quite literal form (see figure 1.1). Ultimately, the HUD authors recommended, for all existing properties in officially designated special flood hazard areas, that insurance should be offered at unspecified

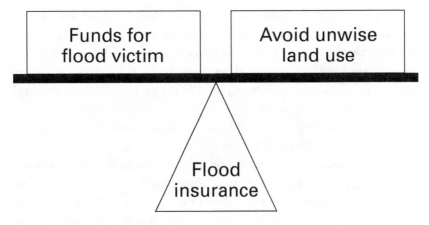

FIGURE 1.1 Graphic from the U.S. Department of Housing and Urban Development, *Insurance and Other Programs for Financial Assistance to Flood Victims* (Washington, DC: HUD, 1966), 2.

"reasonable" premiums, "with Federal payments to cover the difference if and when such reasonable premiums are less than full actuarial cost."[65]

White's task force at the Bureau of the Budget was markedly more cautious than HUD on many of the questions surrounding flood insurance. His team brought together senior leaders from the Army Corps, the TVA, the U.S. Geological Survey, HUD, and the Department of Agriculture, along with Resources for the Future economist John Krutilla[66] and a representative of state government from Pennsylvania.[67] White was himself concerned that the focus of policymakers had overly narrowed on flood insurance, reflected even in the title of the HUD report (*Insurance and Other Programs for Financial Assistance to Flood Victims*), at the expense of a broader view of floodplains that treated them as ecosystems requiring unified, national management. In the White task force report, *A Unified National Program for Managing Flood Losses*, insurance was one recommendation out of sixteen, one part of his more holistic vision, which included a strong emphasis on state and local land-use regulations. Only such a vision, "based on the best use of our knowledge of hydrology and economics," could disrupt the "dismal cycle of losses, partial protection, further induced (though submarginal) development, and more unnecessary losses."[68]

White's task force explained the role flood insurance could play in a larger public policy regime targeting wiser land use, emphasizing insurance's preventive function over its compensatory one, in contrast to many politicians. The report asserted that private individuals and corporations made most of the decisions affecting new development. This had to be addressed in light of a clear normative commitment: "Those who occupy the flood plain should be responsible for the results of their actions." Yet as the report also observed, these decisions and actions occurred within limits set by state and local plans and regulations, as well as federal investment and policy. The overall policy response to the problem of flood damages needed to achieve a more "equitable apportionment of responsibilities" in ways that would bring "the moral, legal, and fiscal responsibilities of all parties involved into effective alinement."[69]

In this context, fostering more individual responsibility was not a matter of exposing people to market forces: "Free market solutions alone cannot provide an appropriate incentive structure to cope effectively with flood problems." Instead, "Collective action, through appropriate public policies, is required." The state should use public policy to create the conditions that "alter the price signals received by potential flood plain developers."[70] Insurance was "a theoretically ideal procedure for using economic incentives to adjust flood plain use optimally in taking into account the hazards imposed by nature." If each new development were required to pay an annual charge—that is, an insurance premium in proportion to its hazard—then in the long run (1) "society would be assured that occupants of new developments were assuming appropriate responsibility for locational decisions"; (2) "new development in the flood plain would be precluded unless the advantages were expected to equal or exceed the total social (public and private) cost"; (3) "there would be incentive to undertake . . . flood damage reduction measures"; and (4) "there would be support for appropriate regulation of flood plains to help, where possible, reduce the costs of flood plain occupance."[71] Like the HUD report, the task force sketched out the logic of the state governing *through* incentives, providing information rather than infrastructure and, in the event individuals did not respond to those incentives rationally, absolving the state from doing more when the flood came.

However "theoretically ideal," White's task force strongly urged further study of flood insurance, as "design and management of a national flood insurance fund involves many unknowns." The report advocated that any flood insurance program be piloted on a limited, trial basis in select locations, particularly because the task force, like the HUD authors, recognized the high likelihood that some degree of premium subsidization would be required at the outset. But the benefits of flood insurance in the long run depended on risk-based insurance rating, making subsidization a very delicate matter of policy design. The report warned that flood insurance, if not "used expertly," could suffer the same fate as dams and levees, insofar as it could end up worsening the very problem it was meant to solve—this time by encouraging flood-prone development through insurance subsidization, rather than through structural protection: "Incorrectly applied, [a flood insurance program] could exacerbate the whole problem of flood losses. For the Federal Government to subsidize low premium disaster insurance or provide insurance in which premiums are not proportionate to risk would be to invite economic waste of great magnitude." The authorization for the HUD study did not permit adequate time for investigation. White's report warned: "An incomplete study would raise false hopes, invite hasty decisions, and perhaps subvert the long-range potential of the insurance concept."[72]

If we view the two reports together, the anxiety at the center of the insurance design question is what economists and insurers call "moral hazard": the idea that when people are separated from the costs of their actions, they take less care. Structural flood protection and disaster relief were faulted for doing precisely that; however noble the sentiment, efforts to protect people from loss encouraged them to take actions that caused greater loss. To the authors of the studies, it was important that insurance not replicate the mistake by offering unduly or permanently subsidized prices. Counterintuitively, then, doing *less* to help people would help them to be better off.[73] As Tom Baker lays out in his genealogy of moral hazard, in the years immediately prior to the release of these two reports, economists had discovered (from private insurers) and debated the concept, specifically, whether the problem of moral hazard had anything to do with virtue. Were people who took less care, once provided insurance, willfully negligent and ethically derelict with respect to the collective that bore the costs? Or were they simply responding rationally to a set of incentives? In the 1960s, the view that won out among economists was that moral hazard was about the rational calculation of costs and benefits in a given context of incentives, to which anyone, "good" or "bad," would respond. This does, nevertheless, assert a particular vision of virtuous behavior, one in which decision-makers are responsible for having, accurately interpreting, and acting upon certain kinds of information. It also assumes that people do have meaningful control over themselves and their property; they are capable risk-bearing subjects who can shape their own outcomes. If individual homeowners can *know* their flood risk, as floodplain experts then believed they could, then they can and ought to be able to control their exposure to it; insurance premiums are "actuarially fair" when individuals assume the costs of the risk they then bring into the risk pool. Concern about moral hazard often reflects a particular worry about the costs of social (i.e., collective) responsibility for facing adverse events, treating such risk-sharing as a kind of redistribution that is not under all circumstances normatively legitimate (for instance, when people seem to blame for their loss), if helping people has harmful consequences (to the insurer). There are hazards to compensating people, in other words, which implicitly override any hazards of *not* compensating people. The economics of moral hazard provides a scientific basis for withdrawing certain kinds of support, legitimating that withdrawal, in Baker's words, "as the result of a search for truth, not an exercise in power."[74]

DEBATING FLOOD INSURANCE: THE PLANS GO TO CONGRESS

The HUD and Bureau of the Budget Task Force reports were quickly taken up in congressional hearings and floor debates. Despite the caution urged by White's task force, a legislative proposal to establish federal flood insurance went to Congress in 1967, outlining a program that followed the recommendations of the HUD report. Policymakers echoed the virtues of greater individual responsibility articulated in both reports, asserting that Americans were indeed eager for such an opportunity. In the words of Representative Carl Albert (D-OK), "Our people want the opportunity to protect themselves. They do not want to rely on relief agencies, Government largesse, or charity. They want to protect themselves and it is up to us to help them do it."[75] Yet members of Congress frequently invoked a quite different justification for starting the NFIP: that flood insurance was about the federal government helping the flood-afflicted, showing solidarity with those who found themselves victims of acts of God. In other words, while the reports made an intellectual case for insurance largely on the basis of its preventative function, assuming risk-based insurance rating and rational calculation on the basis of knowable probabilities, policymakers made political arguments on the basis of its perceived advantages for compensation. Insurance would replace unreliable and politically motivated aid with the guarantee of claims money owed to a policyholder. During House and Senate floor debates on establishing the NFIP, members of Congress typically justified flood insurance as better than relief for the purposes of the flood victim, whose "rights" should be protected; in the words of Senator Harrison "Pete" Williams (D-NJ): "Congress should not legislate on a case-by-case basis by passing specific relief measures following each major disaster. Rather, it is preferable to adopt a consistent and comprehensive program of flood insurance to provide relief to flood victims as a matter of right."[76] Like social insurance programs, flood insurance would reduce the economic and social effects of hardship and loss, expanding the social safety net in new ways.

In congressional debate, the participants in a potential flood insurance program were discussed not as calculating agents making choices about foreseeable natural hazards, but rather as innocent victims, who deserved financial protection from events they could neither anticipate nor control. Ignoring the language of flood experts, policymakers described floods as fundamentally unpredictable calamities. In early congressional discussions about starting a national flood insurance program, Representative Hale Boggs (D-LA) said:

As you know, I represent an area which two years ago was horribly battered by Hurricane Betsy. But hurricanes and floods are not district or regional problems. They are national problems. No one knows where they will strike. And they require national solutions before thousands more are hit without adequate protection.[77]

Floods were inevitable but unpredictable; in the words of Representative Claude Pepper (D-FL): "Floods may occur at any time and at any place. It is certain that they will continue to cause damage in the future, may even cause further loss of human life, and will occur again and again, without warning."[78] Representative Peter Rodino (D-NJ) described floods as an "evil stroke of nature" that could completely destroy "the future security of many individuals."[79] As Andy Horowitz has observed, ascribing disasters like floods and hurricanes to "nature" also had the effect of absolving the government and other powerful actors from responsibility for causing any resulting losses. In this narrative, relief, in whatever form, is framed not as "restitution for damages wrought by human action," but rather as "charity for an unlucky few in the wake of a blameless accident."[80] Insurance was then a particularly compassionate response.

Though they would be more active participants in their own financial preservation under an insurance system, floodplain residents who had been or would become flood victims were still understood as unlucky, not willfully irresponsible, uninformed, irrational, or neglectful. They were, in the words of Representative John Young (D-TX) during the 1967 House debate, "subject to catastrophic flood losses beyond the control of humankind."[81] In the estimation of Representative Albert (D-OK), they deserved greater protection than "ad hoc disaster relief" could afford; such relief provided "neither security nor dignity."[82] Even while raising objections about the unspecified costs of the new program, Representative Garry Brown (R-MI) nevertheless acknowledged: "Who can deny that the Federal

Government has a responsibility to the victims of floods and other natural disasters?"[83]

Members of Congress framed flood insurance as something that would preserve the dignity owed to innocent victims of catastrophes they could not reasonably be expected to foresee or prevent. This can be read as mere political posturing, a way for policymakers to make what was, in effect, an attempt to shift costs back to households appear politically palatable. However, all this talk of victimhood had the effect of introducing notions of social protection and deservingness into the discourse surrounding the NFIP's specifications. The imagined flood insurance policyholder, over the long term, was the rational decision-maker calculating the most economical course of action with flood risk assessments, maps, and insurance in place. But the imagined beneficiary of flood insurance in the near term, the people who would be buying flood insurance next month or next year, would be the people who were already in the floodplain, likely people who had been victims of floods before. As the HUD report had stressed, the actuarial price for them would presumably be quite high. If flood insurance was centrally about the state providing greater financial security for blameless victims, what sense would it make to saddle these victims with even more burdensome new costs? And as the HUD report had also explained, for an unknown but potentially large number of property owners, the risk was not in any meaningful sense knowable or actionable at the time they purchased and built. From the perspective of actuarial fairness in the economics of insurance, none of that was relevant; it was as if NFIP policyholders stood outside of history. For policymakers, however, it mattered a great deal. Expecting existing floodplain residents to take personal responsibility on the basis of an actuarial price thus seemed both unrealistic and unfair.

It was also unworkable. The plans at this stage conceived the program as a voluntary one, and high rates would discourage participation among those in the floodplain who were most in need of insurance. The program needed to be affordable in order to be broadly accessible. The solution policymakers came up with, following recommendations made in the HUD report and echoed more cautiously by White's task force, was subsidization. The NFIP would indeed include subsidies for existing properties in high-risk areas. Picking up on language used by HUD, members of Congress

repeatedly used the word "reasonable" to describe what this group of policyholders should pay. The subsidy would be the difference between the calculated actuarial rate and this unspecified, to-be-determined reasonable
rate. These below-risk rates promised no penalty for having a property in
the floodplain before it was mapped, or for experiencing previous flood
losses.

Policymakers and officials justified the subsidies in part by noting that
even subsidized premiums would nevertheless lower *overall* burdens of
compensation for loss on the public treasury: the policyholder would be car-
rying at least *some* portion of the costs of his flood risk, reducing the
amount of relief that might be requested or required. More importantly, the
subsidies were expected to be temporary, a short-term "interim" strategy
to grow the program. Experts at HUD urged that subsidization not interfere with "long range readjustments in land use," one of the central public
policy objectives of flood insurance, which they believed depended on risk-
based insurance rating.[84] Policymakers and federal officials expected that
there would be "natural attrition" of subsidized policies over time as the
number of properties in floodplains gradually diminished following damage. These were homes in the floodplain, after all; they would flood, aging
them quickly if not completely destroying them, at which point they would
presumably be abandoned. The task force estimated that the subsidies for
existing high-risk properties would be required for approximately twenty-
five years.[85]

With the passage of the National Flood Insurance Act in 1968, Congress
established the NFIP, creating at the same time a Federal Insurance Administration (FIA) to run it, both under the purview of HUD. The NFIP would
socialize the risk of flooding, while at the same time acting as a nonstructural mechanism for reducing flood losses over time. This would happen
not only through risk-based rating for new construction, but also through
state and local zoning ordinances.[86] Policymakers designed in an essential
quid pro quo: in exchange for access to a subsidized program of flood insurance, participating communities would have to commit to and implement
actions to mitigate flood hazards, such as land-use controls. Congress
wanted the program up and running quickly, but in deference to the caution urged by the likes of White and his task force, included a "sunset clause"
in the legislation that required the NFIP to be reauthorized every five years,

providing regular policymaking junctures at which the design and implementation of the program could be revisited.

IMPLEMENTING THE NFIP: OBSTACLES TO
NEW AND SHIFTING RESPONSIBILITIES

The elegant logic of insurance imagined by geographers, economists, federal agency officials, and members of Congress proved almost immediately to be exceedingly difficult to realize on the ground. The new NFIP faced a host of technical and political obstacles. Perhaps most fundamentally, the federal government struggled to fulfill the new roles and responsibilities it had set for itself in terms of risk mapping and assessment. The provision of flood insurance to floodplain communities required first the mapping of those communities' risks, which turned out to be a resource- and time-intensive process, exceeding experts' estimates. NFIP administrators needed those maps, first, in order to figure out which communities should be offered flood insurance and, second, to calculate insurance premiums for individual policyholders. This mapping work was, at the time, done by the Army Corps of Engineers, based on a nationally uniform "100-year flood" standard, which is still used today.[87] The 100-year flood is the flood with a one percent chance of happening in any year. The areas with a one-percent-annual chance of flood were official high-risk flood zones, or "special flood hazard areas." In many cases, the local information needed to produce the maps was not available. Furthermore, HUD's FIA had not arrived at a rate-setting method that could connect risk information, where it could be delivered, to insurance pricing.[88]

Because these flood insurance rate maps (or FIRMs) took such a long time and turned out to be more costly than anticipated to produce, the NFIP was getting off to a slow start admitting communities to the program—which soon proved unacceptable to policymakers once Hurricane Camille hit the Gulf Coast in August 1969, devastating several communities, none of which were yet covered by the NFIP. With rapid coastal and suburban/exurban development ongoing throughout the 1970s, "it was clear that being 'done' assessing flood-prone communities was a fantasy."[89] As of December 1969, only four communities in the country had joined the NFIP and only sixteen policies had been sold. That month, the Housing and Urban

Development Act authorized the NFIP to start an "emergency program" that would provide limited amounts of subsidized insurance to participating communities *before* the completion of their detailed flood insurance studies and FIRMs. Once the studies and FIRMs were done, the community could be moved into the "regular" program, when premiums would shift to actuarial rates.[90]

The 1969 Act also provided the first of several deadline extensions for when communities had to comply with floodplain management measures, as well as extended coverage to small businesses. The growth of the program nevertheless remained sluggish, such that less than one percent of insurable damages were covered when Tropical Storm Agnes hit the east coast in June 1972. A month later, the NFIP lowered subsidized rates by another 37.5 percent to encourage participation in the program.[91] Shortly thereafter, the Federal Insurance Administrator estimated that there were approximately 10,000 flood-prone communities in the United States, about twice as many as had been estimated in 1968, all of which would eventually need FIRMs.[92] In place of some portion of direct outlays of resources to compensate loss or build flood protection, the state had set for itself the responsibility of producing risk information, to govern on the basis of incentives. Though this was an indirect and somewhat inconspicuous form of administration, it had proven nevertheless to be a large, slow, expensive, and complicated undertaking. In the meantime, more and more communities were entering the program, and new construction was taking place, insurable at subsidized rates.[93] By 1978, only 2,818 of a total 16,116 participating communities had actually moved from the emergency program into the regular program. At that point in the life of the NFIP, only about eight percent of premiums were based on actuarial rates; the rest were subsidized.[94]

Despite its early challenges, policymakers voted to continue the NFIP at its first reauthorization in 1973. Representative J. Wright Patman (D-TX) said on the House floor that the NFIP "represented a new and untried venture involving concepts of insurance and actuarial science, concepts of government-private organizational cooperation, concepts of local responsibility and Federal encouragement that were frankly untried and experimental."[95] But it was an experiment worth continuing, because flood victims still deserved the financial protection provided by insurance:

I am sure there are many in this body who share my opinion that financial protection against the damages wrought by floods is a prime necessity for many property owners. All of us are familiar with heartrending accounts of individuals who have scrimped and saved over the years in order to have a home or a business they can call their own, only to see those years of labor and dedication swept away overnight in a disastrous flood. Federal relief after a disaster, although welcome, can never substitute for the repayment of losses that is available through flood insurance. Disaster relief, even at its most generous, cannot begin to repay the tremendous physical and psychological losses which unfortunate flood victims suffer every year.[96]

Representative William Moorhead (D-PA) also rose in support of the reauthorization, citing his personal experience of witnessing disaster aftermath: "We have met and talked with thousands of constituents and dealt first hand with those innocent victims who must piece together their lives following one of these catastrophes."[97]

However, it was clear that financial protection, even at subsidized reasonable rates, was not enticing enough to draw people to the program. Part of the issue may have been framing the risk in terms of the 100-year flood, which did not communicate the risk to prospective policyholders and local officials in a way that made insurance seem necessary or worthwhile.[98] Policymakers intervened with legislation to reform the young program: the Flood Disaster Protection Act of 1973. The act transformed the NFIP from a voluntary program to a compulsory program for the vast majority of floodplain homeowners, via the addition of a "mandatory purchase requirement," over the objections of the National League of Cities, the National Savings and Loan Association, and the National Associations of Bankers, Realtors, and Home Builders.[99] The requirement mandated that all property owners in the high-risk flood zones with federally provided or backed mortgages *must* carry flood insurance; the federal government would refine its strategy for governing individuals, this time by altering the mortgage market conditions they faced. To make the program work, it turned out, individuals would have to be *compelled* to make these risk and insurance calculations. The new requirement would target the issue of low participation (or "take-up") rates, bringing more revenue into the program and increasing the coverage of insurable property. This was followed by two decreases in rates, program-wide, first in January 1974 and again in July 1974, to fend off political resistance to the mandatory purchase requirement.[100] At the time, Federal Insurance Administrator George K. Bernstein told the *New York Times*, "The purpose of these requirements is that we want communities to prepare for floods . . . We don't want them to expect Uncle Sam to bail them out."[101] He had earlier described the voluntary nature of coverage as "the principal defect of the program."[102]

At the same time, policymakers remained concerned about existing floodplain occupants. To ease the financial burden facing them, the new law also provided for "grandfathering," meaning that "pre-FIRM" structures (built in high-risk areas before they were officially identified as such) could maintain their subsidized rates after they were mapped.[103] Eventually, the grandfathering rule also came to apply to property owners who had an effective flood insurance policy, but saw their maps revised in a way that would increase their premiums; these property owners could maintain their "favorable rate treatment," even transferring this older, lower rate to new owners when the property was sold.[104] Grandfathered rates were also made available for structures built outside of the flood zones and later "mapped into" a high-risk zone; these policyholders were eligible to purchase insurance based on an average cross-subsidized rate. In addition, the 1973 law repealed a provision of the authorizing legislation that had denied disaster relief to persons who could have purchased flood insurance for a year or more but did not do so. The federal government would now require insurance, not only through the mandatory purchase requirement but also by making it a condition of receiving any federal disaster assistance for acquisition, construction, or improvement of floodplain properties. However, it would not penalize property owners for not having insurance in place at the time of disaster, because doing so was believed to discourage communities from joining the program.[105]

Even though reducing the overall costs of flood relief constituted a key motivator for establishing flood insurance, at the same time, the federal government also put in place increasingly generous disaster relief programs. In the 1960s and the 1970s, the federal government began extending aid (rather than just loans) directly to afflicted individuals instead of only funneling aid through state and local governments; this arrangement was codified in the Disaster Relief Act of 1970, a "watershed in the federal role" in disaster relief.[106] Following the act, disaster relief and assistance continued to grow as a kind of "right" of citizenship that the federal government was obligated to respect. Congress also expanded the types of support that went into disaster relief, adding funding for temporary housing, unemployment compensation, legal and mental health services, food coupons, and payments to communities to offset lost tax revenue.[107] The new law meant that individuals could now anticipate, at least in the case of severe disasters, that the federal government "would weave a tighter safety net that would treat all disaster victims equitably and would help them back on their feet more quickly than the previous patchwork of state, local, and voluntary resources."[108] In practice, in the decades since, sociologists have shown that disaster assistance often has inequitable effects, intensifying racialized wealth disparities.[109] But the commitment in principle was that in the context of any given flood, individual risk-bearing and calculation, enacted via flood insurance, would coexist with collectively funded disaster relief.

The promise that premium subsidies would be temporary, so as not to compromise the land-use function of flood insurance, had been key to securing the NFIP's establishment. In fact, these subsidized policies did not disappear from the program. Even after experiencing flood losses, people tended to want to rebuild where and back to the way they were before. Indeed, as policymakers had hoped, flood insurance would disburse claims money to policyholders relatively speedily compared to the vagaries of federal aid, which helped them to get back to normal—and normal rarely meant relocating. "Severe repetitive loss" properties—properties that have been repeatedly flooded and repeatedly rebuilt in place—became a recognized and costly segment of the NFIP policies in force. Federal officials also found that once subsidies were in place, they were hard to undo. The winners in such a move would be diffuse—taxpayers at large—whereas the losers were a targeted group of people who had become accustomed to this particular benefit and who could punish policymakers for any backtracking. These dynamics are similar to those of welfare state politics more generally, in which the constituencies created by the beneficiaries of particular public policies create high political costs of change for elected officials.[110] In this case, people and local communities adapted to this version of a (subsidized) insurance program, set expectations with subsidies in place, and mobilized to defend them.

In his 2005 Senate testimony, former flood insurance administrator J. Robert Hunter said he nearly lost his job on more than one occasion for trying to implement a subsidy phase-out during his tenure in the 1970s. He learned that:

Congress was not fully committed to the implementation of the program they designed. I once took a lot of heat from a congressional delegation when I priced the cost of flood insurance for a well-connected individual's $200,000 home at $50,000 a year because it was built outside of the dunes on a beach and was therefore far more vulnerable to flooding.[111]

Powerful people and interests—realtors, real estate developers, and politically influential landowners—were able to interfere with actuarial pricing. Subsidies, in practice, provided relief to homeowners, but the benefits of relatively cheap flood insurance also accrued to the financial and real estate sectors, whose profit-making capabilities were protected or even enhanced. In this way, the NFIP functions like a great deal of U.S. housing policy in its use of state power to underwrite the risks of the private real estate industry.[112] New construction continued apace in flood hazard zones and, with subsidies and grandfathering in place, home and business owners continued to buy properties at flood insurance rates that were not actuarially derived. State governments, planning authorities, and local regulators "struggled to place the principles of flood mitigation above the politically vital ethos of development," despite warnings from experts.[113]

In the same Senate testimony, former NFIP administrator Hunter also reflected on the difficulty of enforcing land-use and building codes connected to accessing the NFIP: "On another occasion, I almost lost my job as Administrator because I refused to bend in my determination to fully implement the land-use provisions that one powerful senator felt were harmful to some special interests (developers and land owners) in his state."[114] In 1976, the General Accounting Office (GAO, now the Government Accountability Office) released *Formidable Administrative Problems Challenge Achieving National Flood Insurance Program Objectives*, which concluded that the FIA still had "not established an effective system for monitoring community efforts to adopt and enforce required flood plain management regulations." The federal government, "though heavily subsidizing the flood insurance program . . . had no assurance that the communities' flood-prone lands were being developed wisely to prevent or minimize future flood losses." The GAO routinely echoed these findings and admonitions in subsequent reports.[115]

Environmental historian Ted Steinberg captures how this tension between safe land use and local real estate development played out in St. Charles, Missouri, which was developed largely below the base flood elevation as specified in the Army Corps' maps. For St. Charles and communities like it, "the federal flood insurance program amounted to a death sentence"; compliance with stricter land-use regulations and building codes as a condition of the NFIP "threatened to regulate the town out of existence."[116] Given the high stakes, local officials avoided enforcing the regulations. In a 1982 investigation, FEMA, which took over responsibility for the NFIP from HUD upon its establishment in 1979, found that St. Charles County's board granted lots of building variances, ignoring the Army Corps' survey of land at-risk and allowing developers to continue building below the base flood elevation.[117] It was the poor who often ended up living in the riskiest, and cheapest, areas. This reflects a more general condition of social vulnerability to disaster in the United States, identified by many researchers. Floodplains (and other hazardous areas) are often the cheapest available sites for development. Marginalized groups, particularly people of color facing cumulative discrimination, disadvantage, and deprivation related to unequal access to jobs and housing, often end up concentrated in them.[118] In St. Charles, mobile home developments were located in areas that flooded in 1978 and again in 1986. As Steinberg puts it, the NFIP helped to "underwrite life among the disadvantaged . . . flood insurance helped to sustain what little material life they had."[119] Following the 1986 flood, FEMA tried to pass a new rule for mobile homes that would make it more difficult to rebuild without elevating above the base flood elevation, but coalitions of landlords and the National Manufactured Housing Federation succeeded in getting Congress to suspend the regulation. The same year, the Reagan administration, which had also tried but failed to get FEMA to relax the 100-year flood standard, made the requirement that state and local authorities adopt substantive floodplain regulations "the preferred approach."[120] Rather than hold communities like St. Charles to the bargain of access to flood insurance in exchange for stricter land-use regulations, the federal government progressively watered down its standards, such that by 1994 "the Clinton administration simply required that 'positive attitudes' with respect to floodplain management be 'encouraged.'"[121]

Though implementation of the NFIP had been shaky from its earliest days, the program became the target of sustained criticism beginning in the 1980s. Members of Congress faulted the program for its continued subsidization and its failure to gradually transfer the costs of flooding from taxpayers to NFIP policyholders, as was initially promised when the NFIP was established.[122] In bad flood years during the 1970s, when the National Flood Insurance Fund ran into the red, it would regularly borrow from the U.S. Treasury to pay out claims; it had borrowed $854 million by 1980. Aligned with the prevailing rhetoric of the Reagan administration, these deficits were by then interpreted as a sign of government overreach and the folly of subsidies, rather than an acceptable cost for socializing risk and spreading the burdens of flood losses. From this particular ideological perspective, the subsidies represented irresponsible and unjustifiable federal meddling in what should work more like a true market for flood risk. Insurance premiums should instead reflect market rates. In 1981, the FIA under the Reagan administration sought for the first time to make the NFIP "self-sustaining," meaning it would have to cover its own costs for the "average loss year."[123] To meet this goal, the FIA increased premiums by 45 percent in 1981 and a total of 120 percent over the next seven years. The FIA might have done more, but these moves quickly earned the attention and ire of property owners, who prevailed upon their elected representatives in Congress to hem in the NFIP's ability to increase premiums. Congress first froze premium increases in 1983 so that the government could study them and, when the freeze was lifted, prohibited increases in premiums of greater than 10 percent per year for any risk classification. With the premium-increase route curtailed, the FIA turned instead to reducing the scope of insurance coverage—in other words, chipping away at the protections offered by the NFIP product so as to reduce the government's liability. This took the form of several exclusions, such as limits to coverage for basements and detached garages so that the policy would not pay for repairing or replacing finished walls, floors, furniture, or other personal items. The exclusions were added to NFIP policies and maintained even in the face of litigation brought by policyholders and criticism from Congress. These combined changes allowed the program to achieve a limited measure of financial sustainability: it was indeed funded solely by premiums from the mid-1980s to 2005, but it was never able to generate a reserve for a catastrophic flood year.[124]

The Reagan administration also revised the relationship between private insurance companies and the NFIP, which continues to this day, through the establishment of the Write-Your-Own (WYO) program. The authorizing legislation for the NFIP had actually set out two versions of this relationship vis-à-vis risk-bearing. Part A, which policymakers were convinced would be the viable, long-term operating mode of the program, had private insurance companies forming and capitalizing a risk-bearing pool. The federal government would provide financial assistance, covering the pool's claims only in the event of catastrophic losses.[125] However, this relationship fell apart within just ten years of the NFIP's operation due to disputes between HUD and the private insurers over issues of authority, costs, and oversight.[126] The program then took the form outlined in part B of the authorizing legislation: the federal government's full assumption of operational responsibility.[127] In other words, the private companies were kicked out and all NFIP policies became direct obligations of the United States; the federal government was the lone risk-bearer.

For a few years, insurance policies were issued directly by the FIA, which actually cut the costs of administering the program.[128] But without the commercial network and customer service capabilities of the private companies, policy growth stagnated and consumer dissatisfaction grew. In September 1981, the FIA opened discussions with representatives of the private insurance industry about re-involvement in the NFIP.[129] The resulting WYO program began in 1983. Under this program, private insurance companies act as "fiscal agents" of the federal government; they sell and service policies and receive a commission on each policy (estimated at about 30 percent today). Write-Your-Own refers to the fact that participating insurance companies could write flood insurance policies on their own paper or policy forms. With this structure, from the perspective of policyholders and in its routine functioning, flood insurance looks like a private market, with the state submerged and governing out of view, as is the case with much of American housing policy.[130] Many homeowners assume that flood insurance is part of their general homeowner's insurance, because they buy it from State Farm, Allstate, Nationwide, or whoever sold their general policy—that is, until major catastrophes and sky-high claims put the NFIP and FEMA in the news cycle. Participating companies sell flood insurance with their names on the letterhead, from their offices and agents, often sold alongside their other insurance products. A policyholder will write their checks to the WYO company. The WYO company settles claims, issuing a company check, from the company's bank. However, unlike the initial arrangement with the industry pool, the private companies do not in fact take on any of the financial risk; the federal government is the real insurer, bearing full risk and responsibility for paying claims. Within a few years, over 90 percent of NFIP policies were issued by WYO companies.[131]

In the early 1990s, Gilbert White was again invited to weigh in on the status of the federal government's approach to flood losses and floodplain management. He led a 1992 National Review Committee report, which concluded: "The record is mixed." More communities had adopted floodplain regulations. But at the same time, annual flood losses had not been stemmed or reversed. "On balance, progress has been far short of what is desirable or possible, or what was envisaged at times when the current policies and activities were initiated," White and his coauthors wrote.[132] The best efforts of geographers, economists, engineers, and policymakers to rationalize the administration of flood-prone areas via insurance had not apparently prevented the explosion of development in hazardous areas. Neither had it assumed the central place in recovery funding that its designers had anticipated. Take-up rates remained low—it turned out the mandatory purchase requirement had been inconsistently and poorly enforced—meaning that uninsured losses remained high. Following the devastating 1993 Midwestern floods, for instance, the NFIP covered just 2 percent of the total damage estimate of $12 billion and comprised about 14 percent of total federal disaster relief spending.[133] That year, White gave the opening keynote at a conference to mark the NFIP's Silver Anniversary. He did not pull his punches: "The record of losses for the United States as a whole does not encourage the belief that great reductions in the net cost of flooding to the nation have been achieved since the mid 1960s."[134] The possibility had to be examined that the NFIP, like structural flood protection before it, had become as much the problem as the solution.

CONCLUSION

Hurricane Katrina in 2005 damaged more than a million housing units in the Gulf Coast region, about half of them in Louisiana. In New Orleans alone, 70 percent of all occupied housing units suffered damage.[135] The NFIP was not equipped to respond to the scale of the destruction. Its fund had only just managed to pay off debts incurred following the 2004 hurricane season. Coverage had increased in the region, due in large measure to Congress strengthening the mandatory purchase requirement in 1994. But the NFIP still had no real reserves, no financial capacity to weather the truly catastrophic storm. This is in part due to the unexpected political resilience of premium subsidies. Today, an estimated 20 percent of the entire program is still comprised of subsidized policies. According to a 2017 analysis by the Congressional Budget Office, an estimated 85 percent of policyholders in the highest-risk zones pay heavily discounted premiums.[136] FEMA does not actually know how many policyholders have grandfathered rates. The claims on the NFIP, as it faced the particularly catastrophic Katrina, surpassed the premiums it had collected, making it effectively insolvent and creating a huge new debt to the Treasury that the program seemed unlikely ever to be able to repay. By that point in the life of the program, policyholders were faring no better. The fixes of the 1980s—those policy exclusions and limitations on basements and garages, enacted to make the program financially self-sustaining on an average-year basis—had chipped away at the protections provided by the flood insurance product. Further exclusions are also not well understood by policyholders, such as lack of coverage for alternative living expenses (e.g., rent on other housing while property is repaired) and damage caused by earth movement (e.g., landslides), even when the earth movement results from the flooding.[137] Many policyholders who had dutifully paid their premiums found, upon making a claim, that some of their losses were not in fact covered.[138] Congress ultimately approved over $60 billion in outright disaster relief.

We can understand this outcome in New Orleans in part by situating the NFIP in its larger political economy. There, as elsewhere in the United States, safe land use was subordinated to the desire for local development. The regulations that would have militated in the opposite direction, a supposed condition of accessing the NFIP, were hard for the federal government to enforce and were watered down over time. Like many other American cities, New Orleans was caught up in a growth machine dynamic that pursues profit and relentless economic growth linked to local real estate development, without sufficient contemplation of what the limitations might be or who might pay the price.[139] Louisiana has energetically reengineered its relationship to water, draining wetlands and building levees to develop floodplains, and the NFIP has been an important part of that story.[140]

Insurance did not outright prohibit building in hazardous areas, after all; rather, its purpose was to insert the cost of the risk into the calculations made by residents, developers, and local officials. With respect to this political economy, it is therefore not surprising that the NFIP was hard to implement as planned and later to reform, given the ways it could transgress the interests of local actors and powerful industries. The program did not live up to the expectations of rationalized governance, on the basis of science and economics, held by technocrats and the politicians who relied on their expertise. Floodplains might be statistically discernable, but they were socially and politically unruly.

However, we can also understand the outcome in New Orleans, and the problem of the NFIP's historical failures more generally, as a product of the program's many tensions and contradictions—tensions and contradictions arising out of dilemmas of moral economy that, when they explode into controversy in crises like Katrina, have no technical fix. In taking a closer look at the NFIP's history, we can appreciate that the establishment of an insurance program, even one for natural hazards, is inevitably a moral project. It is a project that depends on the persuasiveness of claims about protection, blame, accountability, and fairness. The challenges that face the program have always been—and continue to be—problems of adjudicating which economic arrangements are fair, prudent, and right when it comes to managing flood losses. Different and powerful interests fight these things out, but the substance of the dilemmas themselves reveals complex and shifting understandings of who is to blame for flood loss—God, nature, individuals themselves—and who is or can be made responsible for them, and how, as a result. As Collier notes, if before the NFIP it had been assumed that "individuals could *not* be held responsible for their losses then insurance was a political technology for *making* individuals responsible" by shifting the risks of flood loss to occupants of floodplains themselves.[141] The NFIP, as conceived and described in the pages of HUD and task force reports, was premised on a moral vision that emphasized personal responsibility and the virtues of rational calculation over outright compensation and redistribution from collective resources. Yet in the congressional floor debates, policymakers discussed, debated, and ultimately authorized the NFIP on the basis of a distinct moral vision, one that emphasized instead collective solidarity with blameless victims of acts of God, people who had made investments in livelihoods and homes that the government ought to intervene to protect. Actuarial insurance might serve one public purpose, as a tool of land-use administration, but affordable insurance served another: it helped people attain and secure ownership of homes, an important imperative of American social policy more generally. Indeed, the National Flood Insurance Act ultimately became Title XIII of the Housing and Urban Development Act of 1968, a "watershed event in American housing policy" that pursued the further expansion of homeownership through homebuilding, programs to help low-income and poor people become homeowners, mortgage insurance guarantees, and other mechanisms.[142] Across the various actors involved in establishing the NFIP, what seemed to unite them was, first, a belief that if the government could scientifically and economically appraise the floodplains, then it should govern them on that basis and, second, an emergent preference for using individually targeted incentives and subsidies to pursue the public good. The outcome of all this deliberation was the reapportionment of responsibilities for loss, and the creation of some new ones, across governments, local communities, and households. It enacted a set of arrangements for shaping behavior and for establishing what floodplain residents and taxpayers owed and were owed.

The NFIP became a program that creates a community of fate for unwitting victims of catastrophe but also demands accountability for foreseeable events. It protects some investments but makes others less economically viable. It is meant to be actuarial but affordable; risk-based but reasonable; regulatory of development but not prohibitive; market-like but not private. Flood insurance was meant to solve many public policy challenges in the long run. But the short-term, day-to-day business of managing the nation's floodplains through insurance required policymakers to make a series of political accommodations related to how the NFIP classifies, prices, and distributes risk. Some of these were designed-in at the start; others were institutionalized as the NFIP sought to respond to its own emergent challenges of implementation. These tensions and contradictions have compromised the ability of the NFIP to achieve in practice *some* of what it promised on paper: significantly, to reduce flood losses through changing human behavior. But against some of its own competing objectives, the NFIP can also be viewed as a success: it has buoyed American homeownership, transformed some measure of relief into a contractual obligation to compensate loss, and enshrined a privileged role for science and economics in knowing and managing the problem of flood losses, now treated in terms of risk. The program's tensions and contradictions have also, perhaps, been essential to its longevity. They provide different people and political groups with multiple registers in which to make moral claims about the necessity and benefits of public flood insurance, even with all of its challenges. Claims of who or what is failing in the operations of the NFIP reflect ideas about what individuals, governments, and private industry can or should do when it comes to dealing with the problem of loss.

Just as Hurricane Betsy had, Katrina created a political opportunity to revisit the arrangements that were put in place for managing flood loss. The result, after years of lobbying and debate following Katrina, was the most substantial overhaul of the NFIP since its founding: the Biggert-Waters Flood Insurance Reform Act, passed in July 2012. Reformers won a transition toward a program with actuarial rates, meaning the long-delayed elimination of subsidized pre-FIRM and grandfathered rates. They won a mandate to update the nation's flood maps and to incorporate advancements in climate science. In other words, they sought to make the program actually do what it was expected to do in the late 1960s, to resurrect the original vision for flood insurance and do it better this time—and with an eye toward climate change. Only now, many more people occupy the nation's flood zones, which are themselves appearing to expand as hazards intensify. Taken together, the provisions of Biggert-Waters meant that the price of insurance would be increasing for NFIP policyholders—a change that would be felt first in the greater New York City area as it recovered from Hurricane Sandy.

Chapter Two

LOSING GROUND

Values at Risk in an American Floodplain

In the days when his Queens neighborhood was still flooded from Hurricane Sandy, Palmer swam through the polluted water to check on his neighbors. Before retirement, Palmer was a 9/11 first-responder with the New York Fire Department and he has a rod in his neck from injuries he sustained during that other dark chapter in New York City's history. Even still, he tells me, he took to the water because that's simply what you do in Rockaway—a sentiment I would hear expressed in different ways again and again. Storms could wreck their homes, but this community cohesion would be what made it possible for them to survive. It was a strength that would help them hold on and a virtue that warranted protecting.[1]

Over a year after I met Palmer, and on the two-year anniversary of Sandy, an official with the New York City Department of City Planning explained the implications of the City's proposed new flood insurance rate maps to a meeting of architects, planners, construction managers, and designers in Greenwich Village, Manhattan. She told them that the maps, combined with the insurance rating changes authorized under the recent Biggert-Waters reform, created "a substantial amount of economic and financial pressure to become resilient."[2] That same month, the Office of the New York City Comptroller calculated that the city had over U.S. $129 billion of property value at risk of flooding. The city's new flood insurance rate maps showed that the official flood zones had expanded; the property value at risk had increased as a result, 120 percent over the previous maps. In his report, the comptroller concluded that this new picture of "value at risk" should motivate spending today that would help the city's residents to adapt to a frightfully watery future: "With such immense value arrayed along the City's coast, we must act now to make the necessary investments to protect our homes, our businesses and our neighborhoods from the future effects of climate change . . . While the costs of resiliency projects are high, investing in the City's future will pay enormous dividends, both to our waterfront communities and our broader economy."[3]

For New York City in the aftermath of Sandy, information about value and risk, captured and conveyed in flood maps and insurance premiums, was meant to guide action—of individuals and of government—oriented toward a more resilient future. This is very much in keeping with the way the National Flood Insurance Program (NFIP) has long been imagined as a tool for rationalizing our relationship to natural hazards, as described in the previous chapter. This chapter pulls the NFIP out of the realm of national policymaking and program administration and situates it in the fabric of social life. It follows what happens as a flood insurance rate map grafts a new landscape of "value at risk" onto the physical and social world, which happens in communities around the country every time a map is updated. Through its technologies of maps and insurance prices, the NFIP is meant to tame uncertainty, empowering individual and collective actors to act with greater confidence, to take informed steps that will avoid or minimize future losses of property and economic value. Yet as New Yorkers like Palmer confronted new maps and learned about the changes to the NFIP under Biggert-Waters, they responded with alarm. The new maps were "scarier than another storm," in the words of another Rockaway homeowner.

What could make a flood map scarier than a storm? This sentiment makes sense, I found out, when we understand that the losses New Yorkers were worried about were not just flood losses, not just having their properties submerged again in the future. The map framed calculative decision-making about loss as a matter of protecting property value at risk of flooding, in the straightforward way suggested by the comptroller. But a broader set of losses concerned people and shaped what they decided to do. This comes into view when we are attuned not simply to (financial) value at risk (of flooding) as a motivator of action, but rather to plural and interacting *values at risk*. In other words, local experiences and understandings of loss reflected other kinds of values, as well as multiple perceived risks; property values and floods were only part of the problem. The map was "scarier than another storm" because dealing with flood *insurance* seemed to threaten other things people held dear: obligations to family, connections to places, moral commitments, and that sense of collective cohesion, belonging, and security that Palmer celebrated. The map also created and provoked worry about risks and uncertainties beyond flooding—risks that would unfold along multiple timelines. The map, rather than the flood risk it depicted, became a source of economic strain, seeming to pit near-term needs against long-term goals and plans. The uncertainty that preoccupied people was not chiefly about future floods and storms, but about if or when political and institutional changes would take place. And though New York City connected the map to climate change (an effort discussed in more detail in the next chapter), for users on the ground, it provided an ambiguous signal of when they would be exposed to certain risks or how those risks would be taken into account. As a result of these *values at risk*, New Yorkers were dealing with a much more complex picture of loss than the one visualizable in a flood insurance rate map.

This chapter reveals these larger stakes for floodplain communities as they confront new visualizations and economizations of a natural hazard risk. It is as much about flood *zones* as about flood waters, about the way changing hazards are reassessed as risk, depicted on maps, transformed into insurance premiums, and governed on that basis, after the storm has passed. Far from producing clear strategies of action, the flood map produced ambivalent actors and outcomes—in part, because people recognized that compensation for some of these losses wouldn't be fair or even possible. In addition, even when people took steps to reduce their flood risk, they often did not feel that they were better off or more secure for having done so. However prudent or rational such actions might be, in terms of dealing with flood risk, their exposure to other kinds of losses as a result did not seem wholly justifiable.

In encounters with flood insurance in New York City, we see that moral economic questions of compensation for and justification of loss are unsettled and unsettling as communities confront further climate change. Ultimately, even when flood insurance works the way it is supposed to, these multiple and interacting values and risks complicate determinations of what is in the best interests of communities, as well as understandings of what constitutes rational or prudent responses to changing hazards, in anticipation of future losses. This was true not only for the affected residents themselves, but also for other users of the NFIP's maps on the ground: insurance professionals, New York City and federal government officials, housing and consumer advocates, lawyers, urban planners, floodplain managers and engineers, and New York state legislators. The meaning and significance of the new map for residents was produced in interactions with these experts and professionals, who, in a variety of contexts, helped people to situate themselves in relation to the redrawn flood zones and changes to insurance, as well as relayed their concerns to local and federal authorities. As these experts and professionals encountered the dilemmas facing flood zone communities, they too became entangled in complicated and conflicted calculations of what to advise and when.

ECONOMIC AND FINANCIAL PRESSURE TO BECOME RESILIENT

As described in the last chapter, the NFIP shifted the financial calculation of how to manage local flood hazards from the federal government to local communities and individual property owners. This was important to Gilbert White and other architects of the program primarily because of the preventative function of insurance. Put more plainly, if the people who benefit from inhabiting the floodplain are made to calculate and bear the costs of doing so, they will—assuming economically rational decision-making— take steps to minimize or avoid those costs. The idea here is that by providing both information and incentives, flood insurance could introduce or reinforce risk reduction mechanisms for decision-makers, reducing individual and aggregate losses and exposure to risk in the first place (an analogous logic to the idea that a higher health insurance premium might encourage someone to quit smoking). This is, in a very general sense, what the city official meant when she said the maps created "economic and financial pressure to become resilient." For this to work, insurance experts often stress, actuarial insurance rating—that is, setting premiums according to an accurate view of the underlying risk—would be essential. Only a risk-based insurance premium can signal something about the world, helping individuals to make informed decisions about how and where they conduct their lives. By this logic, subsidized (i.e., below-risk) premiums are problematic in part because they encourage moral hazard: if individuals do not know or bear the full cost of risk, they will take less care to avoid loss. Again, this is believed to be a rational response to a subsidized price. In addition, for the preventative function of insurance to work, the terms of the contract between insurer and insured have to be such that the price signal is clearly communicated and connected to a set of risk-reducing actions.

Before turning to how these pressures to become resilient were experienced in New York City, we need to establish how the technologies of flood insurance—the maps and insurance premiums—are meant to shape the decisions facing property owners by creating a specific set of regulatory requirements and incentives. For individual homeowner policyholders in the NFIP, the risk-reducing actions that can lower the cost of an individual's insurance are principally (1) elevating the structure above the base flood elevation (BFE, the height of expected floodwaters during a typical flood event) in the flood zone; or (2) relocating to areas that are officially designated as lower risk.[4] Commercial property owners have a few other flood-proofing options. As the FEMA illustration (see figure 2.1) shows, elevating the home so that its lowest livable floor is at or above the BFE reduces the annual premium.

Individuals who take this decision reduce the likelihood and costs of flood loss for both them and the NFIP over the long term. Floodwaters can rise, but the lowest floor of the house stays dry. Though this may be an expensive undertaking in the short term, the mitigation will pay for itself after a certain number of years of reduced flood insurance premiums, as figure 2.1 is meant to convey.

A homeowner may determine that the price of insurance is too high and they cannot or do not want to elevate the home, perhaps because they live in a conjoined row home or, for instance, because they are elderly and elevating would mean the introduction of stairs. In these types of cases, the price signal can motivate relocation to safer ground. Moving out of the official flood zones eliminates the need for flood insurance altogether. Recall that Congress established the mandatory purchase requirement in the 1970s. Though this requirement has been inconsistently enforced, the rule is that homeowners with federally backed mortgages in official high-risk flood zones must purchase and carry flood insurance on their property. In New York City, compliance with the requirement increased from 61 percent in

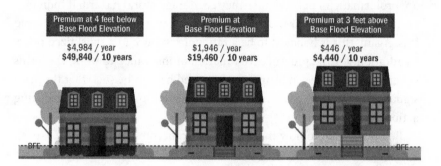

FIGURE 2.1 Building above the base flood elevation can save you money over time. Graphic from *FEMA Build Back Safer and Stronger Brochure*.

2012, when Sandy hit, to 73 percent in 2016.[5] Homeowners can avoid this requirement by avoiding the flood zone or by moving even just outside of it—though we know of course that actual floods do not helpfully stop at the boundaries of the flood zones on a map.

Flood insurance is in this way designed to govern the nation's flood risk in part through setting in motion these individual decision-making processes. Over time, through governing individual behavior, the aggregate effect would be, in theory, to transform the built and social environment, as people were nudged away from uneconomical uses of the floodplains. As Brett Christophers notes, such techniques do not have to presume the existence of already-rational actors. Arguments for their use instead suggest that incentives can *engineer* rational behavior: "Actors could be encouraged or educated, if you like, to behave rationally—if the incentives were gotten right."[6] This was, as we learned in the previous chapter, meant to be coupled with land-use provisions that would prevent (re)building and real estate development in the nation's riskiest floodplains—provisions the federal government has largely failed to enforce. The NFIP has also continued to subsidize a significant portion—now around 20 percent—of insurance policies nationwide. Grandfathering has allowed many homeowners to retain affordable flood policies even as the underlying hazards have changed and flood insurance rate maps have been updated, meaning that over time, many premiums have moved further and further from risk-based rates. When Biggert-Waters, passed a few months before Sandy, mandated the phase-out of premium subsidies and the elimination of grandfathering, new maps suddenly had dramatic financial implications over the near- and long-term for many residents in flood zones.

NEW MAPS FOR NEW YORK CITY

New York City is a center of global power and affluence, a place of gleaming skyscrapers, luxury apartments, splashy celebrity glamor, and frenetic commercial activity. It is also known for its high levels of inequality and poverty, with concentrated pockets of deprivation. Like many major global cities, New York City is a place of extremes. But somewhere in the middle are low- and middle-income homeowners, many of whom live in the furthest reaches of the city, at the watery edges of Brooklyn, Queens, and Staten Island, in neighborhoods on or not far from some portion of the city's 520 miles of shoreline. Many of these outer borough communities are populated by single-family homes, with a more suburban than urban look and feel. Many are majority white neighborhoods in this minority-white city.[7] Breezy Point, Queens, for instance, among the areas most damaged by Sandy, has long been known as the Irish Riviera. The racial homeownership gap is profound across New York City, as it is nationwide ("bigger today than it was when it was legal to refuse to sell someone a home because of the color of their skin," according to the Urban Institute). Black homeownership has declined, but some parts of Brooklyn most affected by Sandy and the new maps, like Canarsie, have been strongholds of black homeownership.[8] Though many are facing the increasing pressures of gentrification, these parts of the city are where it has remained possible for firefighters like Palmer, cops, sanitation workers, teachers, nurses, and other public-sector workers to capture a piece of the conventional American dream of a house, with a small yard, and a car or two. "I moved to Rockaway for the parking," one man joked to me. There is more elbow room, more space to breathe. Some moved because they wanted to be on the water. Many are there today, they told me, simply because their families always had been; it was the only home they had ever known.

Much of the destruction from Hurricane Sandy was concentrated in outer borough neighborhoods. Most of the forty-three deaths during the storm were on Staten Island. Homes were partially or completely destroyed.

And the flood insurance rate maps on the books at the time had done a poor job of setting expectations for the extent of the devastation. Those maps captured only 54 percent of the Sandy-flooded area in Queens and 67 percent of the Sandy-flooded area in Staten Island.[9] An estimated 304,000 people, including 45,000 adults age sixty-five or older and 17,000 children, lived in areas that flooded during Sandy but were not accounted for in New York City's maps.[10] About 80 percent of people who suffered flood damage from Sandy did not have flood insurance, many because they lived outside of the official high-risk zones.[11] These failures of prediction have been attributed to the age of the maps. They were based on topographical and hydrological data and coastal modeling from 1983, produced as part of the city's very first flood insurance rate map. City and state officials had in fact long been requesting updated maps. In January 2005, New York State's chief of floodplain management wrote a letter to FEMA protesting a national shift in strategy and funding from updating the flood maps in high-priority areas to one of producing digital flood maps nationwide.[12] He warned:

This means that in much of New York, and I imagine in most of the rest of the nation, there will be sufficient funding to do little more than digitize existing maps with perhaps better quality approximate studies. This is insufficient and will result in poor quality, but really good looking maps that fail to provide the data needed to adequately manage development in floodplains.[13]

Indeed, in 2007, New York City received digitized maps, but based on much of the same underlying 1983 data and modeling.[14] That year, Mayor Michael Bloomberg launched his PlaNYC effort to make New York City "greener" and "greater," specifically launching initiatives to deal with climate change that ultimately included, again, formally calling upon FEMA to update the city's flood insurance rate map to account for sea level rise.[15]

In 2009, FEMA's Region II office received funding to begin a more substantive update to New York and New Jersey's flood insurance studies and rate maps, and the mapping work began in earnest in 2011.[16] Thus, new maps were underway when Biggert-Waters passed in July 2012 and when Sandy hit three months later. These major events did not change the mapping process in progress; rather, it changed what those maps would mean. With Biggert-Waters in place, when this new map was adopted (a process described in more detail in the next chapter), it would enact the NFIP's shift toward full actuarial rating. New York City was the first major metropolitan area to undergo such changes, but this would eventually take place in communities all over the country as their own maps were updated.

In the wake of Hurricane Sandy, local and federal officials wanted residents to have the best available information about flood risk and insurance—especially because property owners who received federal assistance after Sandy would be required to purchase flood insurance.[17] In addition, of the policies in force, 75 percent were eligible for pre-FIRM subsidies, which would be disappearing under Biggert-Waters.[18] In the days and weeks following the storm, residents were already working to get back to normal, rebuilding back to the way they were before the disaster, to building codes that had not yet been revised to incorporate changing risks. They might spend time and money reconstructing a house only to find out, when FEMA finished its flood insurance study and released its preliminary flood insurance rate maps, that they were in a flood zone for the first time, or in a riskier one than before, or that the base flood elevation had gone up. They might, in other words, rebuild their homes only to find out they could no longer afford to insure them.

FEMA and the city therefore wanted to get as much of the available risk information out to the public as quickly as possible, "not only for safety, but particularly in the face of Biggert-Waters, where they're going to get slammed by insurance premiums down the road," as one city official put it.[19] Shortly after the storm, FEMA announced it would be releasing advisory BFEs (ABFEs), an unconventional product that would summarize what FEMA knew at that moment about the current flood risk.[20] After some consultation with city staff, FEMA released a series of draft maps over the course of the year—first the ABFEs, then preliminary work maps, and finally the preliminary flood insurance rate maps or pFIRMs that would undergo a formal review and adoption process. Each draft revised the boundaries of the flood zones and the BFEs, but the general tendency was apparent from the first: the official flood zones had grown and the BFEs were going higher (see figure 2.2). Ultimately, the maps put almost 400,000 New Yorkers in the city's new high-risk flood zones, making it the nation's largest floodplain by population, and more than doubled the number of structures inside the zones from around 35,000 to 71,500. The New York City

Building Code required that new and certain categories of rebuilt build-ings have an elevation of two feet above the BFE.[21]

Not surprisingly, the areas that saw the most change were the outer-borough areas that had flooded during Sandy. Across the newly mapped high-risk flood zones, 90 percent of one-to-four family properties were owner-occupied; just under 40 percent of households were low-income. According to a RAND study commissioned by New York City, with the loss of subsidies and grandfathering, the median premium for one-to-four fam-ily properties in high-risk zones would increase from $3,100 to $5,600 per year, and at least 25 percent of policyholders would pay premiums in excess of $12,300. For properties mapped into the flood zones for the first time, the median premium would increase from $2,700 to $4,200, and at least 25 per-cent of property owners would pay in excess of $4,700. In the borough of Queens alone, 23,500 families were facing higher rates.[22] Thirty-three per-cent of households would be housing-burdened (i.e., a ratio of homeowner-ship costs to household income greater than 0.4) by the increases to flood insurance under the new maps and with grandfathering eliminated. This could increase the likelihood of loan defaults.[23] Some of the most affected areas, like Canarsie, were also predatory lending hotspots with high fore-closure rates before Sandy and Biggert-Waters, meaning that the cost pres-sures of flood insurance would compound existing mortgage distress, related to the 2007–2008 housing crisis and longer histories of racialized practices of subprime lending.[24] Eighteen-hundred owners of one-to-four family homes in the storm surge area had foreclosure proceedings started against them in the two years prior to the storm.[25] RAND concluded:

Taken together, these changes in the flood insurance market could put many resi-dents along New York City's vulnerable coastline at risk of losing their homes if they cannot afford the mandated insurance policies. Hardest hit will be low- to moderate-income residents, including communities of working-class families who have lived on or near the coast for generations.[26]

VALUES AT RISK

The flood insurance rate map frames value at risk as the relationship between objective measures of specific properties of things, that is, the spe-cifically *financial* value of the built environment in a given location and its

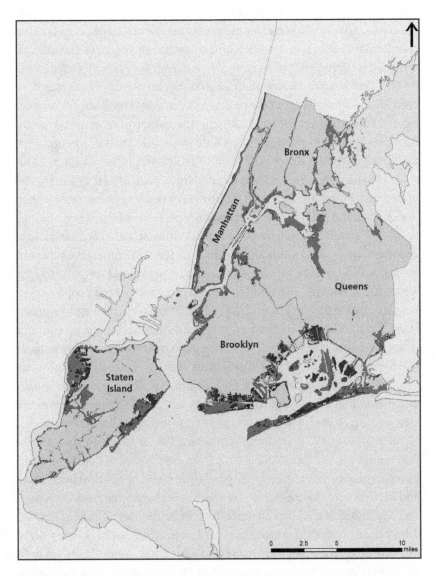

FIGURE 2.2 Citywide comparison of the 2007 FIRM and 2015 pFIRM 1-percent-annual-chance floodplains. *Note:* **Light gray** areas denote high-risk zones according to the 2007 Flood Insurance Rate Map (FIRM) and **dark gray** areas denote high-risk zones added by the pFIRM. *Source:* Lloyd Dixon, Noreen Clancy, Benjamin M. Miller, et al., *The Cost and Affordability of Flood Insurance in New York City Economic Impacts of Rising Premiums and Policy Options for One- to Four-Family Homes* (Santa Monica, CA: RAND Corporation, 2017). Courtesy of RAND Corporation.

risk *of flooding*. When authorities deploy the map, they assert and privilege the characteristics of a place that are presumed relevant to decision-making, standardizing this across users who may be facing very different circumstances, resources, and constraints.[27] Flood insurance specifies a temporality of action based on a singular risk, wherein knowledge of current flood risk, based on knowledge of the past, is meant to motivate behavior oriented toward future expectations.[28] As such, the comptroller emphasized the financial returns to mitigation not only in the form of savings on yearly insurance costs, but also in the form of protected property values. In the wake of Sandy, New Yorkers also by and large understood they were at risk of floods; a poststorm survey of homeowners in flood prone areas of New York City found that 86 percent of respondents believed they lived in a high flood risk area.[29] Yet despite the financial value at stake, and despite the apparent flood risk, communicated through the flood insurance rate map, for many in New York City the matter of how to respond was not straightforward. Encounters with flood maps and insurance forced people to contemplate multiple meanings and experiences of loss. We can begin to understand this by taking a broader view of risk, an analytical approach common in sociocultural risk research. This research tradition has shown, across a variety of sites, that people situate risks relative to the "time and place coordinates" of their lives. At the experiential level, people formulate understandings of risk and responses to it in light of a range of contextual factors, only some of which might have to do with natural hazard or technological risk. The risks residents perceive, or to which they ascribe paramount importance in their daily lives, may not be of floods, or hurricanes, or nuclear meltdown, but instead issue from the political institutions and experts who describe their communities as risky, or from more general conditions of anxiety and precarity.[30] When people talk about or make decisions in light of these other relevant factors, they do not do so by deriving and comparing statistical probabilities. These other "risks" may be hard to articulate, let alone quantify. But they are nevertheless risks in the sense that they involve people's best efforts to manage the uncertainties of the future, to try to work out what will happen next and what they can do now in light of those expectations.[31] So when New Yorkers—not only residents but also the officials, experts, and professionals who interacted with them—confronted the changes to flood insurance maps and rates, what did it mean to be "at risk," and what were they at risk *of* or *from*?

Risks and Relationships to the Past, Present, and Future

For Grace, a construction manager in Broad Channel, Queens, the risk she faced was not just flooding, but economic strain she attributed to the flood map itself. She raised her home once before in order to mitigate her flood risk and lower her insurance premiums. The new map showed she was at higher flood risk and she was considering elevating again, but this was an expensive proposition:

We bit the bullet; we brought the house up . . . Now we've invested all this money in the house. Ten years later, here we are: we've raised the house. We've done our due diligence because we wanted it done right. And then they tell us, "You have to raise your house again." Now you're going to turn around and tell me, "You raised it in 2004, now there are new maps. You're going to have to come up with another 100,000 dollars"—where am I going to get another 100 grand? Do you know how much it took for me to save 100 grand? OK, maybe I'll save it—but my kids won't go to college![32]

Grace knows that raising her home again will save her money on flood insurance in the future, avoid future flood loss, as well as protect the resale value of her home; she understands the financial incentives. But she also knows what it took for her to raise the money before, and she knows that spending the money on this now will require trade-offs over time that she feels are inhuman. Protecting the home from flooding today may mean no money in the future to support her children's education—the creation of another kind of economic risk, in the broader context of her life and in her "projections of family biographies" via her children.[33] For Grace, making the decision to mitigate again is not a simple calculation based on current flood risk. Rather, it needs to be reconciled with her previous financial efforts to do so and her felt financial obligations going forward.

A few streets over, Trish also sought to mitigate her personal flood risk through home elevation, but she ran out of money for the job and could not get a second mortgage to finance its completion, leaving her family indefinitely physically and economically insecure: "I do things to protect myself," she told me, but "we're struggling now. Going into debt, at 52 [years old], is not where I wanted to be."[34] The decision to address flood risk might be framed by the NFIP as prudent and cost-effective in the long term, but residents had to manage immediate economic problems. Following through on mitigation and realizing its rewards is a protracted process, which can introduce economic uncertainties that families will have to manage for unknown stretches of time. Grace and Trish had survived the flood; they had repaired their homes, at least to a livable standard. For them, it was the map that presented an economic threat now that the waters had receded. The map, and the risk-based insurance premiums it made possible, might work to reduce flood risk across the city, but like other risk-reduction strategies, it could increase exposure to other perils for the residents therein.[35] And as Grace's and Trish's experiences suggest, these economic risks can lead to experiences of moral struggle, as they challenge the stories people have about their own honor and self-worth. When people face conditions of economic strain and environmental precarity, the desire to maintain one's sense of honor and self-worth can powerfully shape attitudes and actions, even in ways that seem to transgress one's own interests—in this case, providing emotionally compelling reasons not to follow through on flood risk mitigation.[36]

Exposure to new kinds of economic risk was familiar to Meg, a legal aid attorney working with families on Staten Island, who showed me a list of reasons that her clients were refusing home elevations. City officials also told me about these refusals, with discernable confusion. But according to Meg, for many, there simply was no money for it. The city's Sandy recovery program, called Build It Back (the name implies a kind of heroic confrontation with a watery future, a refusal to relocate from the water's edge) offered additional financing for some home elevations. Yet even when eligible, many clients could not afford temporary rent (often in addition to a mortgage payment) to bridge the unknown length of time that they would be displaced from their homes during construction. Like Grace and Trish, many of Meg's clients felt overwhelmed by the prospect of undertaking a lengthy mitigation project: "One [thing] we hear a lot is: I'm just exhausted. I'm too tired; don't talk to me about this. I'm done. It's over."[37] Scott, an insurance broker who sells NFIP policies, had experienced the same thing: "The biggest reason people aren't doing [elevation], believe it or not, is they're beaten down. They're beaten. They've had enough . . . I get it."[38] Taking on such tasks to prepare for the future was too disruptive to their already disrupted normal routines and economic circumstances.

These were among what city officials, lawyers, insurance professionals, and housing and consumer advocates often described in interviews as "sad cases." Homeowners with mortgaged properties below the BFE who could not afford the high yearly premiums were at risk of foreclosure, as the banks could purchase insurance on their behalf and include the premiums in their monthly mortgage payments (called "forced place insurance"). Homeowners could avoid this with elevation, but in New York City, elevating a free-standing home costs about $100,000, the figure Grace mentioned, which even FEMA acknowledges may be "cost prohibitive."[39] Many New Yorkers did not even have this option, because they lived in conjoined row homes, often made of heavy masonry rather than light woodframe construction. In these circumstances, typical of many urban floodplains around the country, entire city blocks would have to be raised.[40] For some people then, the rational course of action would be not to "build it back," but to relocate out of the floodplain entirely—but who would want to buy a house with a hefty annual flood insurance premium attached to it? In tears, one woman from Gerritsen Beach, Brooklyn, explained to a housing counselor at a community flood insurance help desk, convened by the Center for New York City Neighborhoods and other local organizations, that her mortgage was underwater. "A lot of my neighbors, they're going," she said. "What if we want to walk away? No one wants to come down the block to see our house."[41] In New York, the increasing flood insurance premiums formed part of a broader context of financial hardship due to expensive—and most typically debt-based—recovery from Sandy, which some called a "second Sandy."[42]

When faced with a particularly sad case, a lawyer with a city housing organization confessed to feelings of impotence:

I was talking to [the homeowner], and I was like, "I'm so sorry. I guess there's nothing I can tell you. We wrote a report about this issue. We're trying to get—" you just sound so stupid when you say shit like this—"We're really trying to make FEMA aware of the problem." . . . He's four feet below on the new maps, so it's rough.[43]

She had helped this homeowner understand the implications of being four feet below the base flood elevation on the map. Even though her job involved urging him down a rational path aligned with NFIP requirements, she, and others like her, described the situation as offering no good options. In the wake of the storm, as many were calling for smarter rebuilding and land use, these professionals, who interacted with homeowners facing tough choices, said that people were not in denial of the flood risk. Rather, it was that though the end result of risk mitigation might be financially desirable, the time it would take to get there was indeterminate but anticipated to be long, generating or intensifying economic risks that were difficult or impossible to bear.

New Yorkers also understood themselves to be at risk of further political developments related to flood insurance, which had in the past, and could again at an unknown point in the future, lead to unpredictable changes to the map or to the program more generally. This could change the situation on the ground, even in the absence of further flooding. All insurance systems are politically determined but the NFIP, as a public, federal program, has been conspicuously shaped by shifting political priorities, funding commitments, and reform agendas. Whenever the NFIP is reauthorized, changes to regulatory arrangements for managing flood loss, like those under Biggert-Waters, can set off further local changes to land use, building codes, and zoning regulations. For instance, local authorities may require new elevation certificates (which establish the height of a property relative to the base flood elevation). In addition, the lines that now delimited the high-risk flood zones could, and likely would, change again in the next map update. The base flood elevation could also go up or down. NFIP policyholders have to adapt not only to changing flood hazards, but also to a new political reality with ambiguous staying power. As then-FEMA administrator Craig Fugate put it at a March 2014 congressional budget hearing: "The question's always been, when you update the maps, what happens when if you built to the previous codes, and now new data says that's not high enough, and now you get slapped with these increases, but you did what you thought you were supposed to do at the time." Trust (or lack thereof) in the stability and authority of scientific and political institutions is also relevant to the frame of reference through which people interpret and act on the problem of flood loss and understand its representation as risk on maps and in insurance premiums.[44]

In New York City, these political risks associated with the NFIP, familiar from past experience with the program and an anticipated feature of its future existence, introduced an additional factor complicating the decision of not just when, but also whether or how to mitigate flood risk. Sophia's house in Broad Channel was completely destroyed in Hurricane Sandy. She planned to rebuild at higher elevation. However, "if the federal government can come in and say, OK, you built to code in 2014, but now it's 2025, and you're no longer up to code—then what? They're going to keep changing the rules of the game mid-way?"[45] Sophia knew those rules could change further, or change back, at the next NFIP reauthorization, map update, or sooner. At a flood insurance help desk on Staten Island, a housing counselor described the situation to me:

We know flood insurance is going to go up . . . the question is, is it 15 percent, is it 18 percent, is it 25 percent? . . . What are people to do? . . . They're facing flood insurance rate increases very, very quickly, and most people in this community are on the margins of being able to pay their mortgage . . . Homeowners have an enormous amount of distrust in government, and the government hasn't helped their case any, with all the promises, and broken promises, and when things are going to happen.[46]

Based on the consultations he had done, he said: "I wouldn't say people flat-out don't want to elevate." Instead, they seemed to want to "wait and see" if the changes to the map and insurance rates would stick. Researchers have reported similar findings from focus groups in New Jersey, which received new maps at around the same time; participants evinced "skepticism about [the maps'] precision and permanence . . . The existing maps and elevation requirements were complex enough, but the idea that people would be rebuilding under interim maps that were subject to further revision added immense confusion."[47] The maps were political artifacts that would take years to be formally adopted and go into regulatory effect. Dave, a Rockaway resident, summarized, with some exasperation, the questions about the changing map that local residents put to FEMA officials at a civic association meeting in the winter of 2013:

You're telling me my house, where it's sitting, the way our area is configurating, that I'm in the most vulnerable flood zone, therefore my insurance is X, Y, Z. But if these resiliency measures are taken, does that, is that taken into account, and does that move me out of the floodplain, or does it affect my insurance? At that time, the answer was, "I don't know," I believe, at that meeting, because nobody was thinking that far ahead.[48]

Residents wanted to know if, in the near future, the city invested in structural flood protection or other community-wide flood risk mitigation, they would each see reductions to their flood insurance that would protect their property values and prevent them from having to take on expensive personal mitigation projects or consider relocating now. This was a possibility if the city decided to take advantage of FEMA's Community Rating System (CRS), a voluntary and underutilized NFIP program that provides community-wide discounts if the community institutes one or more of a set of floodplain management policies.

The terms of assessing, pricing, and distributing flood risk would always be in some respects politically tentative, subject to tweaking or wholesale reimagination at unpredictable junctures over the near and long term. Preparedness for the future implied not simply a response to intensifying flood risk, but also some ability to absorb the vagaries of political processes that might repeatedly change the rules over time. Local actors understood the situation on the ground as dependent not just on changing flood risk, but also on larger political and regulatory forces, which can, sociocultural risk researchers have noted, breed "complex resentments and frustrations."[49]

Adding to such resentments and frustrations were the lengthy and labyrinthine processes of navigating the NFIP's claims processes, which left Sandy-affected policyholders feeling misled, mistreated, and "low-balled" when it came time to seek compensation for their flood losses.[50] "When it's their time to pay, they don't," one man complained at a flood insurance help desk in Coney Island. "We've been paying all these years, doesn't that count?" his wife added. Getting claims money paid and spent required coordinating with multiple insurance adjusters, banks, lawyers, and contractors, and often many government offices: FEMA, the New York City Build It Back program, the Small Business Administration. When money was allocated, even local experts and officials had a hard time assessing things like how to interpret BFEs and building elevations. The couple in Coney Island had elevated their home six feet only to find out later that they needed to be two feet higher.[51] At a help desk on Staten Island, architects and city planners argued back and forth about how to understand the technical details of the various insurance and building code requirements.[52] Often, residents and the experts they consulted would claim that they "can't get a straight answer from FEMA" on these questions, in the words of a lawyer from Neighborhood Housing Services.[53] The prolonged and confusing recovery generated a great deal of ill-will toward FEMA and the NFIP, undermining the notion that flood insurance was part of keeping floodplain residents safe and secure or that the NFIP would even be capable of helping homeowners be "made whole" if and when flood hazards worsened in the future.

As we saw at the start of the chapter, the comptroller's report also confidently connected the new depiction of flood risk to climate change adaptation that would protect the financial value at risk in the city. But for people on the ground, the new map and insurance prices were an ambiguous and politically contentious signal of how near or far climate change might in fact be.[54] From a technical standpoint, the map did not formally account for already occurring or future climate change, or even for the flooding from Hurricane Sandy (this is examined in further detail in the next chapter). FEMA's remapping work—the data collection and modeling—had begun before Sandy. The map was based on data as up-to-date as flood events previous to Sandy. This was historical data, not a projection of future sea level rise or of storms to come. Yet sea levels had already risen in the region and, with the recent experience of Sandy, New Yorkers debated whether the map was indeed reflecting local effects of climate change. Dave from Rockaway described the new map as a "fantastic Exhibit A for climate change":

I think that, just from the changing, the amount of homes in flood zones has at least doubled. And that tells you something—and that's not out of preparedness— it's a reaction to what happened . . . I think that it's a very real thing now, and I think that people here are very keenly aware of that. Everybody—all the people that are educated—are saying that. So I think that's very real, and I think that, the hotter summers and all of that sort of thing, I think that that's very real.[55]

He had attended a meeting of the Rockaway Waterfront Alliance in Arverne, Queens, where a professor from Columbia University had shown the crowd charts and graphs of storms and floods and explained how 100-year storms were becoming much more frequent. "Of course, there's a big pushback about this is all a hoax, it's fear," Dave said. "But when the ocean's at your front door, you have to say, things are different. You know?"

But Meg, the legal aid attorney, was uncertain about whether to make flood insurance "a climate change issue" in her work with clients:

That has been such a volatile issue, that I don't want to associate anything I'm saying about flood insurance increases and what you need to do with something that some people may consider still fiction. Because this is not fiction—whether you believe that or not, [flood insurance] is reality. I know the city is trying to talk about it a lot that way, and [New York] Governor Cuomo came out strongly about that, and that's great. But for me, we've got all these hurdles of credibility to overcome. So I don't mention climate change. But we do hear people in the community on either side of that. Some who are saying, look, this is climate change, and we've got to deal with what we've got to deal with, and others who say, hell with it.[56]

Amy, an insurance consumer advocate whose organization advises policyholders in the wake of disasters, said she knew "rising water is going to wipe things out." Yet she said she had trouble figuring out, "where should my organization be?":

I figured out early on, there was a bit of a schizophrenic problem here. Like I could be lockstep with my environmental colleagues in saying, don't allow new construction, don't allow new construction. But how do you say to someone who's been living—the firefighter—how do you say to them, "I'm sorry" . . . But see, you can hear how my focus keeps coming back to wanting people to be able to have insurance, which is not a radical—the radical thing is, "Don't let them live there." And I can't be there, because my constituency is the people who are trying to live their lives, and they don't know from rising sea levels, they just know I've got to drive my kid to school, I've got to get to work, you know?[57]

Amy feels conflicted as to whether she should interpret the new map as grounds for urging homeowners, even if they can make it work financially today, to move out of harm's way given a potentially riskier (and more expensive) future. Though the city and state governments connected the new map and insurance premiums to rising sea levels and climate change, map users on the ground grappled with how or whether to factor climate change into planning for next month's mortgage payments, next year's insurance renewal, or the next property sale. As John Tulloch and Deborah Lupton found in their study of "risk biographies," people grapple with a not yet/no longer temporality in the context of their own lives—in this case, an ambiguous temporality connected to the flood map.[58] The city was *not yet* facing sea level rise that made its waterfront entirely physically or financially uninhabitable, at least for those who could afford to rebuild and insure. But at the same time, the changing picture of risk on the map suggested that some of the city's waterfront communities were *no longer* as safe or economically viable as they once were for many of the residents who had long occupied them. As Liz Koslov observes in her ethnography of managed retreat (coordinated relocation of entire communities) on Staten Island, the official "flood-zone temporality" may be "out of sync with other ways of knowing and navigating the past, present, and future" that shape how people think about threats like climate change.[59]

In sum, in delivering new information about current flood risk, the flood map generated and exposed other kinds of risks relevant to local understandings of loss: what New Yorkers were poised to lose, what was causing that loss, and how best to respond. For many, the map, rather than the flood, seemed to become the key trigger of loss. It did this by generating economic risks attendant on mitigating flood exposure over the short and long term that, in turn, forced people to confront emotionally and morally significant losses: a loss of honor, related to providing for one's children; a loss of self-worth, from being a person who has to take on debt in middle age; or a loss of stability or routine from uprooting one's household to begin a lengthy mitigation project. The map, with the attached changes to flood insurance under Biggert-Waters, also made the NFIP a conspicuous source of loss, as the rules and zones and BFEs, ever at risk of changing time and again, seemed to penalize even people who had played by the rules. The map also raised questions about the present and future role of climate change in driving loss, and when the costs of insurance would be too high to bear. Feeling at risk in all of these ways, residents wanted to or felt compelled to make a decision, but also found reasons to wait and see. Some residents, like Grace, Trish, and Sophia, did respond ostensibly rationally and relatively promptly to the changing economization of flood hazards. However, even for them, the relevance of these multiple risks to their personal situations made them feel less rather than more secure, that in responding to avoid future flood loss they had been forced to sacrifice something else. Through their interactions with residents, engineering, insurance, legal, and housing experts also understood these multiple risks as relevant to what they would advise and when. They appreciated that the decision was a complicated one. People who might appear ignorant or irrational, in terms of dealing with their flood risk, were perhaps really just focused on protecting other things that mattered.

Values Imperiled

Through economizing flood hazards, flood insurance makes an assessment of physical risk financially consequential, in New York City generating economic hardships and dilemmas. However, the stakes on the ground were more than financial. Just as we need an openness to multiple meanings of risk at the experiential level, so too do we need a more plural understanding of value and the forms it can take. The flood insurance rate map makes it possible to make an assessment of the financial value that could be lost to a flood by indicating the boundaries within which we might tally up property values. But using that map to make individual calculations brought to the surface other concerns and considerations about values that might be transgressed, endangered, or lost. This can be especially poignant in the case of housing, which has both an exchange value, as real estate, and a use value, as a home.[60] We talk about properties as financial investments all the time, particularly in the context of policymaking and governance, but, as Debbie Becher explores at length, homes are also investments where value can take many forms: money, but also social networks, material goods, wisdom, love, and skill. People invest their time, effort, and emotional energy into homes, their individual properties, but in doing so also participate in hopes about a collective future, in which the value of a place, in this broader sense, grows and deepens over time.[61] Economic sociologists know that financial or monetary value is embedded in and interacts with other aspects of social organization, which can impact how those values then shape social action. Nonmarket orders of worth shape our understandings of what counts and what is valuable. As a result, when processes of quantification and economization produce prices or property values, which are then expected to motivate action, these can feel like inadequate, inappropriate, or incomplete representations of worth.[62]

The new map depicted parts of the city as risky, perhaps too risky—and too expensive—for some communities to remain intact. Some residents might be able to elevate their homes in place, but some would have to move on. Individual fates and the character of the community would change in ways people imagined as worse; the flood map seemed to pose an existential threat. A New York state assembly representative for Rockaway described it as "a brick to the head."[63] These were risky places, perhaps even economically less valuable places, but they were places imbued with social and emotional value, understood as sources of treasured relationships, collective experiences, and ways of life, which provided a sense of belonging, well-being, identity, and security to residents. When I asked Dan in Broad Channel if the new map might lead him and his neighbors to move, he replied: "You're wasting your breath . . . we're never going to move away." He described Broad Channel:

This is working-class families . . . The people who live here are the people who pick up your garbage; they teach your kids; they keep you safe from criminals; and they run into burning buildings. That's who lives here . . . There's a sense of community down here that's existed since the '20s, and after the storm, this town had the first resource center up, two nights after the storm . . . We have a sense of community that I think is very strong, and something that is admirable, and something that the country's always sought to support.[64]

Dan described a place character that was threatened by the rising price of flood risk and that he vowed to defend.[65] While they may not be sufficiently flood-resilient, they were socially resilient, able to get organized in the face of the storm's devastation, a point of pride. What's more, they were used to neglect and hardship; they could get by. Of Rockaway, Dave said: "We're in the middle of nowhere, transportation is at a minimum, jobs on the peninsula don't exist," but it's "wonderful people there" and he doesn't want "to see circumstances drive you from your home if you want to stay there. Because that's wrong."[66] The riskiness of a place can be experienced as a kind of stigmatization, which local residents resent and resist when it threatens their emotional and social attachments to place.[67] Trish, choking up as she spoke, said, "Living on the water, we saw the change." She was not in denial; she believed what the map was showing her about her community. "Sure, you can walk away," she said. "But I, I don't want to. I'm not ready." Her favorite old joke about Broad Channel was that they all swim breaststroke because Jamaica Bay was so filthy with sewage that they always had to keep their heads above water. Even still, she was emphatic: "I'm not moving."[68] Neighborhoods change all the time, but flood zone residents understood themselves as kinds of incumbents who had made these places valuable, against the odds, through their investments of money, time, and care.[69] For New Yorkers, this complicated any rational calculation of the costs—explicit or otherwise—of staying as is, mitigating the risk, or relocating elsewhere. And this meant a loss of value was felt more profoundly than a percent-reduction in property values could capture.

The emotional and social value of threatened places also resonated with experts and local officials. For those whose jobs required explaining the changes to flood insurance to homeowners in the flood zones, assisting with these calculations on a case-by-case basis was an emotionally taxing undertaking. In helping to communicate the risk and its price, these professionals were often delivering bad news about the future of homes. Clients yelled, wept, begged; the most anyone could do was try to calm and reassure them. Dealing with flood insurance even became a pastoral matter; reverends attended flood insurance workshops held by housing and legal aid organizations in Coney Island, Brooklyn, so as to better support their parishioners facing tough circumstances.[70] At an event to mark the second anniversary of Sandy in Bowling Green park in Manhattan, a reverend from Brooklyn called for an "aggressive education campaign so that our neighbors understand the increasing flood insurance premiums" before leading the crowd in a prayer.[71] A city official who works on flood insurance issues said, after explaining all the reasons someone might move, "It's about their home, the place they love to live."[72] At a Staten Island flood insurance help desk, in between consultations with homeowners, a city planner mused to colleagues:

There's something kind of beautiful about the neighborhoods in these areas that are not going to exist in 50 years, who feel such a strong connection to place, that they don't want to go anywhere. You can look them in the eye and tell them it won't be there in 50 years, and they'll say, "OK, but until then . . ." There's something kind of beautiful about that.[73]

He could understand delaying or rejecting the push toward risk reduction as deriving from an intelligible affection for and desire to, in a counterintuitive way, defend cherished places from changes that felt destructive of certain forms of value, even as they protected others.

Values can also pertain to shared, affectively charged beliefs and moral commitments: a sense of what is good, right, or virtuous. As David Stark puts it, "*value* is almost always bound up with *values*" (emphasis in original).[74] The notion of economically rational action on the basis of financial value and flood risk is irreducibly a value judgment; it adjudicates between a kind of right and wrong behavior on the basis of economic costs. But in New York City, right and wrong were also bound up with shared values of fairness and equity, as they related to ideas about what flood zone communities were owed or entitled to, when people contemplated how insurance-driven flood risk reduction would transform the areas subjected to it.

The zones on the flood map set down lines that demarcated "communities of fate": entire neighborhoods that shared a designation as newly or more intensely risky and whose residents would bear more intense individual financial burdens as a result. For some, this raised concerns about the fairness of these shared fates, particularly in relation to questions of collective responsibility for *causing* flood loss. A flood map engineer who worked on the region's maps suggested that individual mitigation should be "one piece" of a broader effort to make entire communities more resilient, justified in part by the collective failures that had put people in the floodplain to begin with:

Those people are at huge risk . . . And obviously I can't tell people to get out of their house. And that will be unfair because as I say, for them it's catch-22, and we as a society put them there, partially. So we have to find a way out, but it's not only the insurance rates. That's one piece of the whole puzzle, of mitigation options, approaches, and basically being able to help those communities, the whole society, not to be constantly on the hook for billions of losses after every single flood event.[75]

Though the map made the problem of property at risk one for the local community and its residents, he acknowledged that "we as a society put them there," making the losses they faced as a result seem less justifiable. For him, weak land-use enforcement in the past implied a broader sharing of financial responsibility today as a matter of fairness to those places now facing such high risk. Others also pointed to the ways that we as a society put them there; in New York City, that had to do with earlier city decisions to fill in and build on top of wetlands. "People didn't realize they were building themselves into a problem," in the words of a Staten Island resident.[76] During a flood insurance help desk, two planners with the Department of City Planning discussed the situation on Staten Island with a housing counselor, during a break between consultations with homeowners:

PLANNER 1: We have some maps of the elevations, the ground elevations towards the wetlands, the creek, and it is *frightening*—how large the area outside the wetland is, that is the same elevation as the wetland. The only thing that separates them from being the same elevation in most cases is that the streets are a little bit higher, but the properties aren't necessarily any higher, so it ends up being just—once water gets in, it doesn't go anywhere.

PLANNER 2: You can actually see, in the ground elevation maps, where the wetland probably used to be. If you somehow had an aerial photo from 150 years ago, the wetland would probably be the exact same line of what the ground elevation is. The really low, low, low elevation. Yeah, it's a problem.

HOUSING COUNSELOR: Welcome to development in New York City.

PLANNER 2: It's tough. There's a way to build correctly in those areas that a lot of people haven't.[77]

Scott, the insurance broker, also thought that responsibility ought to be distributed differently: "It's maybe time to look at [flooding] and look at the causes. Now, where do I think the funding should come from? Everybody who's contributing to global warming—forget the cap and trade—tax the bastards and have them pay for all this."[78] If loss is a function of climate change then, in Scott's view, homeowners shouldn't be left holding the bag. For these professionals, who worked with flood insurance in interaction with homeowners, the map highlighted the contradiction between a collectively produced but locally emplaced financial burden. The flood risk was what it was, but the value of fairness shaped their understandings of how its economic consequences, enacted through flood insurance, ought to be managed.

The flood zones on the map also overlaid existing spatialized socioeconomic differences reflected in the geography of the city, generating tensions around equity. In some sense, flood insurance does treat each floodplain community equally, subjecting them all to the same processes of risk assessment and economization (processes that are described in greater detail in the next chapter). The same broad flood zone designations apply whether the floodplain in question contains luxurious beach houses or humble bungalows; like all maps, the FIRMs take a complex reality and simplify it, making it legible and amenable to administration.[79] However, procedurally equal treatment would result in highly unequal effects. More affluent communities, in New York City and nationwide, can better absorb higher household costs and protect their own property values as intensifying flood risk is reflected on new flood maps. If New York City maintains development on its waterfront, who will ultimately live in redeveloped, more flood-resilient places is an open question. After Sandy, some homeowners whose houses were or would soon be financially underwater had the option of letting New York City acquire their land through Build It Back—which it could then redevelop. Meg, the legal aid attorney, said professionals in her world "have a real concern that what's going to happen is they're going to be redeveloped for wealthy people." She pointed out that using financial value as a lever to incentivize redevelopment did not come with a "right of return for all those people who have already been pushed out."[80] With lower property values, residents who sold homes they could no longer afford to insure, or that would not sell for a return, might not be able to find affordable housing elsewhere in this very expensive city. Residents voiced these concerns, as well. One man on Staten Island, talking to a FEMA volunteer liaison, said he understood the flood insurance "ain't going down; nothing's going down," but when he thought about trying to sell his house: "It's tough, because we're left with nothing. That's the kicker. Then it doesn't pay . . . Where you going to go?"[81] In the words of Grace in Broad Channel:

They would take this entire community, level it, and sell it to the one percent, the two percent of the population that make a hell of a lot more money than I could ever dream of. They'd put up houses here, or condos, sell them at two or three million dollars apiece, but meanwhile, the regular Joe Shmoes out there, they're making 50,000 dollars a year . . . Are they going to turn around and say that the Hamptons—we're not talking million-dollar homes, we're talking multimillion-dollar homes—they're phenomenal out there, swimming pools and everything else—are they going to tell them that *they* can't rebuild their neighborhood? I sincerely, with my heart of hearts, do not believe that.[82]

Her neighborhood might be a risky place to live, but so are the Hamptons on the coast of nearby Long Island, where the rich and famous keep their summer homes. Though from a technical standpoint the map treated every place equally, poorer places would experience these options as a threat to their continued existence and the pressures of insurance would heighten spatially uneven economic well-being in the city and region. Why was it acceptable, even desirable, for Grace to face the loss of her home for the sake of adaptation when more privileged people would not? Class inequalities mean that the burdens of risk exposure, visualized on the map, and adaptation, incentivized through assessing the value at risk, will be unequally felt.[83] These distributional effects on more versus less affluent places undermined the legitimacy of the map's ostensible purpose of helping to *protect* at-risk places from facing future loss. In the words of Kevin Boyle, then-editor of the local Rockaway newspaper *The Wave*, "I'm not a denier about rising sea levels, but I'm looking for remedies here. I don't want our town being killed, or anybody else's town being killed by this."[84]

CONCLUSION

In the service of managing loss, the remapping and repricing of flood risk is always meant to change understandings of the landscape. The expectation or hope is that new information about the dangers people face, particularly when those dangers become immediate economic realities in the form of new or higher household costs and threatened property values, will motivate economically rational risk-reducing action. This is why, in New York City, the city and FEMA pushed new information about value at risk: they wanted to reorient people's decisions about whether or how to rebuild after the storm. And this happened, for many New Yorkers. While some residents rebuilt back to normal, others did mitigate their property-level risk. Some relocated out of harm's way, notably on Staten Island, where entire neighborhoods opted to take a state buyout of their homes so the land could be "returned to nature."[85] Officials and experts may have emotionally connected to residents and expressed concern, but they did their jobs, helping—or forcing—residents to make the kinds of financial calculations that would have bearing on their short- and long-term futures.[86] While many studies in economic sociology ultimately produce evidence that humans are not rationally calculative in the way economists imagine, the story here does not show that the technology of flood insurance fails to produce the kinds of effects it is designed to produce. The rational calculation engineered by flood insurance did produce the expected and desired changes in behavior, albeit unevenly.

Yet however rational the ultimate outcome, the relationship to loss in a sense "overflows" the narrow bounds of calculation framed by flood insurance and its technologies of maps and insurance premiums. Michel Callon coined the term "overflowing" to capture the inevitable failure of economic activities to stabilize the objects and actions that need to be taken into account in a calculation or transaction.[87] For New Yorkers orienting themselves to the threat of future flood loss, the things that overflowed involved multiple and interacting risks and values. The calculation was meant to take place now, but users of flood insurance on the ground had to situate themselves along multiple timelines, over which a variety of perceived risks—economic, political, and ecological—might unfold and recast the decision. Dealing with the problem of flood risk and its cost also involved contemplation of commitments to values of fairness and equity vis-à-vis threatened places, which shaped judgments of what was the right or best course of action. We saw New Yorkers grapple with the conditions that justify a loss, of any kind—conditions that have to do not only with blame for causing the loss, but also with matters of who suffers most or suffers at all from collective efforts to manage loss. Elements of the political economy of flood insurance, that is, the particular ways in which it distributes risks and interacts with existing inequalities, became salient matters of moral economy. People questioned whether the existing arrangements of insurance, and the technologies that enacted them, were in fact protecting people and places, or if instead they were actually threatening people—and some people more than others—with losses of various kinds. They voiced concerns about inequitable outcomes and mistreatment after playing by the rules, which seemed to discredit the operations of flood insurance and raised larger suspicions about the prospect of having to relocate, however sensible doing so might be in a world in which climate change worsens floods. Emotional and social values "rooted in the connections . . . built up over time between person and place"[88] also constitute the worth attributed to places and, when those kinds of values are imperiled, they inform the individual and collective outcomes that seem acceptable. The economic and noneconomic cannot be easily parsed in practice. Though meant to motivate confident, informed action, using insurance technology to depict and communicate value at risk exposes the presence of interacting, plural values and risks relevant to the steps taken today, only some of which might have to do with mitigating the natural hazard risk itself in preparation for a potentially watery future.[89]

But it is not simply that flood insurance cannot bracket-out these considerations, or contain these overflows; it *provokes* them. The effort to impose some order on the floodplain, to carve it up into zones of high and low risk, is meant to simplify decision-making by reducing the amount of information people have to process. But this simplification itself spawns new uncertainties and ambivalence, multiplying the potential sources of loss. The map becomes the problem for people, in some ways more of a problem than the threat of flooding—"scarier than another storm." Higher insurance prices indeed act as a signal, but not simply or primarily of higher flood risk; they also activate interest in and awareness of political events and institutional changes. Even when people take steps to mitigate their flood risk, they may not feel that they are in fact better off. Even when experts and officials do their jobs, they may feel the policy and the situations facing residents are in themselves unfair. The rationality people experience is not empowering and confidence-building, but instead coercive, objectified in technologies and practices that they do not control.[90]

This illustrates that risk-reduction is often "conflictual and contradictory"—and, we can add, conflicted.[91] Diagnosing these conflicts and contradictions in flood insurance can clarify whether, how, when, and with what results risk-reducing action is taken. Given a particular constellation of risks and values, it may indeed seem better not to protect yourself against flooding,[92] at least for a time, as New York City's lawyers and housing counselors discovered in their work with residents who were refusing home elevations, even partially financed ones. The conflictedness, this sense of having no good options, even when the rational options are there, may be paralyzing for some. This helps us to see that even those residents who make ostensibly "irrational" decisions do not necessarily do so out of "naïve expectations of zero risk"[93] (recall that 86 percent of New York survey respondents believed they lived in a high flood risk area). For the experts, officials, and professionals that interacted with residents about these issues, this conflictedness enlarged the relevant problem they were part of solving. It brought into view the ways in which individuals and communities evaluate their economic and physical conditions in relation to other things they don't want to lose. Values and risks can combine in ways that make people feel the losses they face are losses of honor, self-worth, connections to past generations, stable routines, cherished relationships with neighbors, and emotional attachments to homes and places. These are losses that cannot be compensated; one may never be made to feel whole again. Flood insurance involves its users in more complicated questions than simply whether or how individuals should address their personal, calculated share of exposure to flood risk.

At the point in New York City's history examined here, climate change occupied an ambiguous position in present conditions and imagined futures. For some, flood insurance was absolutely about climate change. The changes to the city's risk, depicted on the map, reflected already occurring sea level rise, and flood insurance was one part of the adaptation picture going forward. For others, flood insurance was not about climate change. They didn't make the connection, sometimes strategically, because it seemed to activate a more complex and contentious set of issues.[94] For still others, the relationship was a murky one; it wasn't clear whether flood insurance revealed climate change to be a problem of today or tomorrow. In any case, flood insurance—along with other insurance institutions—is already working to format local experiences of climate change's effects. It channels changing ecological conditions into the lives of individuals and shapes the fates of communities in ways that affect homeowners and nonhomeowners alike (though not in the same ways). Detailing experiences with insurance—how it actually works on the ground, as opposed to in theory—reveals how people, when they engage with insurance technologies like flood insurance rate maps focused on one kind of loss, are made to contemplate others. However well insurance performs at visualizing and pricing future climate risks, people operate with a larger sense of what needs protecting and of the losses they want to avoid, and this may shape the demands they make on the authorities and experts who run insurance institutions. In the chapters that follow, we will see how such concerns shaped debates about how flood risk could and should be defined, priced, and distributed going forward.

*   *   *

Palmer had protected his neighbors from the flood when he swam door-to-door, checking on them, making sure they had what they needed to get through the disaster. Now he would protect them from flood insurance. Palmer ultimately decided to fight the new maps and the insurance prices. He joined an effort of New York City homeowners pressuring local officials to contest the official depiction of the city's flood risk, arguing that FEMA had used faulty data and models that led it to exaggerate the real risk. Palmer had survived a flood, but the map threatened to regulate his community out of existence. It would become the target of intense scrutiny.

Chapter Three

VISIONS OF LOSS

Knowing and Pricing Flood Risk

On a Monday evening in late October 2014, two days before the two-year anniversary of Hurricane Sandy, hundreds of New Yorkers turned up for a town hall at Beach Channel High School, located at about the halfway point of the Rockaway peninsula. Two city councilmen, who represented opposite ends of Rockaway, were cohosting the event, and the choice of location was meaningful; in the words of one of them: "We wanted to have one meeting, in the middle of the peninsula." He was alluding to the way racial and socioeconomic difference was arrayed across the topography of this 11-mile-long stretch of land, with the whitest and more affluent neighborhoods clustered toward the western end and more deprived areas concentrated in the east, where the peninsula's public housing developments were located. Bright yellow and green homemade posters reading, "PROTECT OUR HOMES," "STOP FLOODING NOW," and "OUR COMMUNITY IS DROWNING. STOP NEGLECTING US," were scattered throughout the crowd. Representatives from city agencies were there to take questions and hear grievances, on everything from how to get boilers replaced, to when the boardwalk would be rebuilt, to sewer overflow, to unresolved repairs in public housing apartments, to home acquisitions. A diverse group of New Yorkers wanted answers as to when Sandy's losses would be addressed, when they would be made whole again.

Flood insurance was on the agenda that night. Dan Zarrilli, the city's Chief Resilience Officer, told the assembled residents that one of the major areas of work for his office had to do with FEMA's new flood insurance rate maps for the city and the shift of premiums to actuarial rates. "The rates are starting to skyrocket," Zarrilli said. "The city has been advocating forcefully with FEMA to continue to make sure that flood insurance can remain affordable and available." At the same time, he noted, Sandy had shown everyone that the city was at "increasing risk from extreme weather events and climate change." The new maps, with their larger flood zones and higher base flood elevations, reflected that. The city would have to adapt. But later that evening, Zarrilli told the audience that FEMA would actually be opening its own analysis to scrutiny. During a ninety-day appeals period, a required phase of every map update, local communities can produce their own rival technical assessments of the local flood risk based on different models, data, or both. The result might paint a different picture of where the boundaries of the flood zones ought to lie, or how high the base flood elevations should be. "It's a rigorous process to challenge the maps," Zarrilli said. "FEMA will have to respond to those appeals, and have to resolve those issues" before the maps could be used to set insurance requirements.[1]

Even if most everyone agreed that flood risk in New York City had generally worsened—something Sandy made it hard to deny—*how much* worse was it really? Where was it worse? With the very existence of an appeals process, FEMA seemed to be acknowledging that it might not have the most accurate view of the risk possible. So how does FEMA, in fact, come to know an area's "real" flood risk? And how does it arrive at the "true cost" of that risk? This chapter investigates these questions by focusing on the production of the central instruments of flood insurance: rate maps and insurance premiums. These two technologies classify and calculate; they assess risk and assign costs. They are used together to objectify hazards into degrees of chance of harm and to establish the price at which an insured entity can secure financial protection in the event that such harm comes to pass.[2] They are policy devices that help policymakers see and make decisions about the world, essential to efforts to govern floodplains on the basis of scientific risk assessment and economic calculation.[3] They have also been the objects of intense contestation in the life of the NFIP.

In much of the commentary on the NFIP, and in discourse about natural hazards more generally, flood risk is treated as objectively discoverable.

In other words, "the actual risk"—a probabilistic assessment of the likeli-hood of real, underlying hazards—can be determined, measured, and quan-tified using the best available data, models, and scientific and technical techniques. It is the job of risk experts to refine and update such informa-tion and techniques in the pursuit of ever-more accurate depictions of this "real" risk. In the context of insurance, at least under an actuarial system as the NFIP is meant to be, the cost of coverage is supposed to reflect this real risk; there is a true cost and objective assessments make such risk-based rating possible. For an insurance system to remain solvent—that is, for it to bring in enough in premiums revenue to cover its expected losses—the insurer needs a clear view of the real underlying risk. Such a view also helps the insured, as well as governance authorities, to take steps to plan for and ideally to mitigate their risk on the basis of objective facts about that risk.

The premise of objectively discoverable risk reflects a more general real-ist epistemology around risk and disaster, and it undergirds a common narrative about the NFIP: that the program is error-prone and has shown a long-standing failure to map and price risk "accurately."[4] The maps use old data. The maps use bad data. The maps are missing data. Too many years go by between map updates. The maps aren't precise enough. These are sto-ries about bureaucratic ineptitude and resource constraints. There is also a story about politicization. What would otherwise be a robustly scientific process is tampered with, driven off track by self-interested homeowners and real estate developers, with the assistance of short-sighted politicians. They manipulate the mapping process, particularly that appeals phase Zar-rilli described to New Yorkers at the town hall, in order to avoid higher flood insurance costs by unduly lowering base flood elevations and shrink-ing flood zones. This leads to underinsurance, further floodplain develop-ment encouraged by underpriced insurance and, ultimately, to financial strain on the program as a whole—which becomes a problem for taxpayers nationwide when the NFIP needs to be bailed out. This is a story about science and politics on opposing sides; about experts, with their objec-tive, rational scientific risk knowledge on one side, versus laypeople, with their emotion, misguided outrage, irrationality, systematic biases against understanding objective risks, and irresponsibility on the other. We see both of these stories in much of the reporting about the NFIP, with head-lines like "Bureaucracy and Old Data Hobble FEMA Flood Maps" (Texas Public Radio), "Outdated and Unreliable: FEMA's Faulty Flood Maps Put

Homeowners at Risk" (*Bloomberg*), and "National Flood Insurance Is Underwater Because of Outdated Science" (*Scientific American*). The *New York Times* has written stories about "gerrymandered maps of risk" and the *Houston Chronicle* faults "greedy developers eager to make a quick profit and government officials desperate to promote economic development."[5]

There are facts to support these narratives. FEMA has indeed always had a difficult time updating maps, due in no small part to the fact that its mapping work has been inconsistently funded by Congress.[6] The agency more generally has been plagued by volatile bureaucratic changes, staff turnover, shifting responsibilities, and unpredictable resource allocations, particularly since 9/11, when FEMA became part of the new Department of Homeland Security.[7] According to a 2017 investigation by Bloomberg News, almost two-thirds of the flood insurance rate maps for the NFIP's 22,000 participating communities were at the time of writing more than five years old. Some maps have been in place for more than forty years.[8] Recall that the maps in New York City, before Sandy, were based largely on data from 1983. The program's incredible and persistent liability to the U.S. Treasury indeed implies a significant problem of underinsurance. The official flood zones in many communities likely ought to be bigger; already, over 20 percent of flood insurance claims come from losses outside of currently mapped high-risk zones (where flood insurance is available but not mandatory).[9] In Harris County, Texas, for example, Hurricane Harvey in 2017 damaged more than 204,000 homes and apartment buildings, almost three-quarters of which were outside the federally regulated flood zones—resulting in high uninsured losses.[10] With a different, better view of the flood risk, perhaps those homes would not have been built at all, or would have been built at higher elevations. The previous chapter described the high stakes for residents "mapped in" to the official flood zones on new maps, but these are some of the serious consequences of leaving people out.

There is also evidence that powerful individuals and interests can indeed bend the flood mapping process to their will. Former NFIP administrator J. Robert Hunter was dealing with this as early as the 1970s, as described in chapter 1. More recently, in February 2014, NBC News released the results of an investigation into FEMA's flood mapping, focusing on instances of successful appeals for map revisions. Their team found that the appeals process seemed overwhelmingly to benefit the commercial real estate owners of luxury beachfront condo developments, who can afford to hire the engineers and other experts necessary to craft a successful appeal. Companies devoted entirely to helping commercial real estate developers navigate these appeals have thrived. In some cases, FEMA has agreed to amend maps even for properties that have filed repeated claims for flood losses.[11]

This chapter acknowledges these facts but emphasizes the unexamined moral economic dimensions and significance of flood risk mapping and pricing. It does so for two reasons. First, it allows us to see more clearly the moral visions implicit in those techniques and technologies themselves. This means, unlike the conventional narratives, not positioning science and politics or experts and laypeople on opposite sides. Instead, applying insights from a long tradition of sociologies of science and expertise, we understand scientific and economic enterprises of risk assessment to have their own political character. As Andy Lakoff and Eric Klinenberg have argued, there is in fact no position outside politics when it comes to creating a tool for making decisions in the face of uncertainty.[12] While threats like floods are real, acting on those threats specifically on the basis of risk assessment and economization asserts a particular framing of the problem and its solution. The arcane technologies and procedures used in governing on the basis of risk appear to operate technically, but also always operate morally.[13] The often-contentious negotiations between multiple stakeholders over flood insurance rate maps reveal not only the interests at play, but also the underlying norms and values that are constitutive of technical, scientific, and economic processes as they construct and manage risk.[14]

The second reason to examine the relationship between moral economies and scientific risk assessment and economization is that what these contentious processes ultimately produce is a particular vision of the problem of flood loss that is not so much definitively accurate, but rather one that can be accepted as *reasonable* for the actors involved. The reasonableness of this vision, in turn, depends on how new or updated technical parameters of risk assessment interact with moral economic concerns related to the legitimate distribution of responsibilities for bearing or sharing flood risk, as well as for preparing for the possibility of future losses. The technical arrangements in flood maps and insurance prices establish who bears how much of the cost and when. The outcome of conflicts over those arrangements determines whose vision of the future is used to govern the present. As we will see, actors involved in assessing and pricing risk operate in a context in which they are made mindful of the distributional effects of those assessments and prices. They respond to objections about fairness and equity when they contemplate how risk assessment and insurance pricing will alter the affordability and accessibility of insurance, today and in the future. These objections are made possible in large part by the insurance technologies themselves, which outline collective actors through their classifying activities; the lines drawn around flood zones on a flood insurance rate map are lines that group together people who then have in common their exposure to flood risk and insurance. Those actors problematize the technologies and their effects, which then shapes how the problem of loss can subsequently be framed and distributed through the assessment, visualization, and pricing of risk.

THE PRODUCTION OF A FLOOD INSURANCE RATE MAP

As chapter 1 described, the production of a flood insurance rate map is a lengthy and expensive process, which the NFIP's architects did not seem to fully appreciate when they placed this task at the center of the new program's objectives. The ultimate outcome is a document that carves up a *floodplain*—a complex ecosystem involving human and nonhuman elements—into simplified *flood zones*: geographic areas officially deemed to be high or low flood risk. The word "risk" has different colloquial, technical, and academic meanings. These meanings are also, as Mary Douglas's anthropological work has shown, historically, geographically and culturally specific.[15] In everyday usage today, "risk" is often used interchangeably with "harm," "disaster," and "peril," and, as we saw in the previous chapter, it can characterize a broad experience of threat and expectations for the future. With the NFIP, however, we're dealing with risk in a narrower, technical sense. The NFIP's high-risk zones, called Special Flood Hazard Areas (SFHAs), are the geographic areas determined to be subject to flooding by the "1-percent-annual-chance" flood event, sometimes called the 100-year flood. This nomenclature is often a source of confusion. FEMA is referring here to a statistical probability of a flood occurring every year, not the time between events. On average, this type of flood event will occur once every 100 years, but the number of such events that actually occur every 10, 20, or 50 years is highly variable. Also, while "100-year flood" sounds dramatic, this does not necessarily denote devastating flooding but, in fact, can apply to a wide range of flooding events. The maps also depict the "500-year-flood," or the areas that have a 0.2 percent chance of flooding in a given year. When producing a map, FEMA also establishes the base flood elevations (BFEs): the height the floodwater is expected to rise during a typical flood event. High-risk zones are called "A zones"; high-risk zones also subject to storm surge are called "V zones"; low-risk zones are "X zones" (see figure 3.1).[16]

Flood risk is dynamic, changing not only when the climate changes but also when humans change the landscape: when new buildings are erected in the floodplain, when the population inhabiting a floodplain grows, and when once-permeable surfaces are paved over. Such actions alter the way water moves through an area and determine what is in its path. As such, a map of flood risk is necessarily a static snapshot of changing conditions, an attempt to stabilize what is in constant flux.[17] FEMA is meant to update flood insurance rate maps regularly, to try to keep up, in some sense, with changing conditions on the ground. The process of making or updating a flood insurance rate map can be initiated by either FEMA, under the purview of one of its 10 regional offices, or a local community.[18] FEMA also

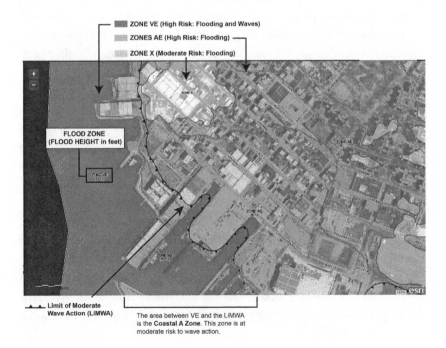

FIGURE 3.1 FEMA flood insurance rate map.

relies on local governments to provide notifications of changing flood hazards and to help with data collection required to update the flood risk
maps.[19] The mapping work is accomplished through the collaborative efforts
of a study team comprised of different kinds of experts: engineers, coastal
scientists, surveyors, and mapping specialists. Often, they are the employ-
ees of large, private engineering and consulting firms contracted by FEMA;
in flood risk assessment and mapping, as in many other areas of its mission, FEMA relies on purchasing and arranging services rather than providing them directly.[20] A flood insurance study for the area precedes each
map. When available, the study team will analyze topographical data, lately
produced using a laser technology called LiDAR,[21] as well as engage in on-
the-ground field reconnaissance that involves physically visiting locations
to verify shoreline, vegetation, marsh, and structure information. The team
also analyzes the hydrological (the movement of water) and hydraulic (how
water moves in confined spaces, under pressure) conditions of the area.

In addition to current conditions at the time of mapping, assessing the
likelihood of a future flood is based on an analysis of the historical record.
Current mapping practice relies on data about the past: historical climate
information that captures trends in streamflows and coastal water levels.[22]
In coastal areas, this includes data on historical storms. To assess the risk
of coastal storm surge, relevant to New York City and many other large
U.S. municipalities, the mapping team uses this data to create a representative set of storm events, which are then modeled in order to generate
probabilities of storm surge events of different magnitudes. Similar computer simulation models are used to evaluate the effect of waves on coastal
flooding probabilities. These models are added to the topographical data
for an area to produce the map, with the boundaries for the different zones
and the BFEs.

How does this process of risk assessment and mapping frame the problem of flooding? At the most fundamental level, these technical, scientific
activities of the NFIP define flood as a "risk object."[23] FEMA's engineers and
scientists assemble a range of data produced by different sources, modeling techniques, and expertise in order to identify objects and link them to
harm. They then communicate those harms in terms of quantitative, estimated probabilities. In this way, flood insurance participates in the *social
construction* of risk.

When sociologists say that risks are socially constructed, we are not claiming that harms and dangers do not exist. A social constructionist approach does not deny the physical (and patterned) reality of flooding, but rather underscores that conveying that reality in terms of *risk* represents only one, and a very particular, way of seeing the world and intervening in it. Risk is its own kind of discourse: a system of representation that influences and legitimizes certain perspectives and meanings over others. While devices of risk assessment and economization may seem to provide objective solutions to pregiven problems, they are in fact central to the definition of problems themselves. They define the terms of discussion, including and excluding elements of the physical and social world on the basis of their presumed relevance to the situation.[24] And what is deemed relevant to defining a problem may implicitly mobilize the particular social models, value judgments, and moral commitments held by scientists, policymakers, and the culture at large. Calculation and judgment do not stand in opposition in the world of risk assessment; as Theodore Porter shows in his own work on insurance, judgment is used to set up computations and to adjust and interpret the results.[25] Inclusions and exclusions of evidence or in model parameters can also reflect the ways that social relations, organizational decisions, and institutional constraints inevitably influence risk analyses, however objective they are made out to be.[26] When used to make decisions about public policy, techniques of risk assessment can have the result of "potentially obscuring or strategically deleting alternatives" where those alternatives do not fit the model.[27] And the model only holds under very specific circumstances; its truth is not absolute, but may "break down horribly in the unbounded wilds of society and Nature," in the words of Andy Stirling.[28] For all these reasons, risk is best understood not as "out there" and "objectively discoverable," but rather as a particular category of understanding, a state of knowledge that has to be practically accomplished through the combined work of many actors.[29]

What then is deemed relevant to FEMA's specification of flood risk and what is left out? And what does that specification look like when it is mapped? Harm from floods, as rendered in FEMA's risk assessments and on its maps, is a function of the elevation in the surface of the water. The maps leave aside harms associated with the duration that an area is underwater, the velocity of water discharge, or the damage that might arise from the movement of suspended material through floodwaters.[30] FEMA's approach to risk assessment also defines current risk, used to predict future floods, based on knowledge of the past. Risk experts characterize this as "the rule of stationarity": the assumption that data and processes do not change over time. For example, the predicted rate of shoreline change is assumed to be the same as the historical rate of shoreline change. Past predicts future. But if different factors are brought into the frame of how flood risk is calculated—notably, projections of *future* conditions—these rules of stationarity may not hold. We will see FEMA and New York City grapple with this in the next section, when climate change enters the calculative frame as a source of potential future losses.

However, even within a specification of risk based on historical data, there is necessarily a great deal of uncertainty involved in the estimation of local flood risks that cannot be depicted on the version of the map that is ultimately produced—a version that becomes regulatory, an authoritative representation.[31] A 2016 report of FEMA's Technical Mapping Advisory Council (TMAC), a panel of experts convened to provide recommendations for improving FEMA's mapping, observed: "While we are accustomed to relying on observations of past floods to estimate the extent and depth of future floods, there has always been uncertainty associated with our estimates, whether we have acknowledged it or not."[32] For instance, in the best-case scenario in many areas, risk experts will have 150 years of data, making a 100-year flood estimate necessarily quite uncertain.[33] The best available (which often really means the most affordable) existing topographic data for many communities has been the National Elevation Dataset maintained by the United States Geological Survey (USGS), which can be decades old for some locations.[34]

All measurements and models include some uncertainty. This is "epistemic uncertainty": uncertainty arising from imprecision in analytical methods and data. There is also "aleatory uncertainty" in flood maps: uncertainty arising from random, rather than systematic, variations inherent in the behavior of natural phenomena. There are no strict standards with respect to the acceptable amounts of uncertainty in flood hazard identification, nor are such uncertainties published with the maps. What this all means is that risk assessment, while a scientific enterprise, unavoidably involves judgment about what kinds and how much uncertainty is acceptable. And while demands are made on the maps to be precise and accurate, what this complex process of assessing and mapping risk can only ever really hope to achieve is, in the view of the TMAC, a "high-quality" and "reasonable" representation of historical flood conditions on the basis of model validation, expert judgment, and review.[35] The Government Accountability Office (GAO) notes that FEMA has to evaluate its risk studies and maps in terms of their "relative correctness" or "general reliability."[36]

As Liz Koslov has observed, "even as the FIRMs incorporate data from past events they promote an ahistorical understanding of flooding" because, on the maps, "flood risk looks like the natural attribute of a place rather than the result of human action and decisions made from afar."[37] Historical losses and current flood risk are a product of human activity unfolding over time: the reengineering of waterfront areas, land use and zoning, real estate development, and so forth.[38] This kind of historical data is not depicted on a flood risk map and it is not relevant to the governance of flood risk through insurance—though these histories are consequential for shaping the fates of different communities. The same kinds of risk zones apply whether the area being mapped is rural or urban or suburban, whether it developed largely in the 1950s or the 1990s, whether in California or Colorado or Connecticut. As we saw in the previous chapter, flood insurance flattens differences between people who live in flood zones in ways that they perceive as morally troublesome. But the map also provides a visualization of flood risk that flattens historically generated differences between places. The NFIP is a nationally standardized flood insurance system that administers not floodplains per se, but rather types of flood zones: broad risk classes that treat places as administratively comparable units.[39]

For example, large areas of Red Hook in Brooklyn, New York, and Tampa, Florida are both identified as high-risk A zones on their respective maps. While they might both be at-risk of the one-percent-annual-chance flood event for the purposes of FEMA and for insurance rating by the NFIP, the histories and patterns of development in these two places are quite distinct, leading to very different experiences of flood loss and to very different options when it comes to flood mitigation and land use. The building stock in Red Hook's A zone is, in general, much older than the building stock in

Tampa's A zone. New York City estimated in 2013 that 85 percent of the structures in the city's high-risk flood zones, according to the most recent version of the updated maps, were built before 1983, meaning they predate the first effective flood insurance rate map for the city and are therefore not necessarily built to a flood resilient standard.[40] Many of the homes in Red Hook are the conjoined row houses typical of urban areas, made of heavy masonry rather than light woodframe construction, while Tampa shows a more suburban pattern of detached, single-family homes. In Brooklyn, small businesses occupy the ground floors of many buildings; in Tampa, there are more discrete residential and commercial areas. The one-percent-annual-chance flood event will hit these two areas but will damage very different landscapes, in very different ways. In addition, for all of these reasons, it is much more difficult to pursue individual, property-level flood risk mitigation in a place with a built environment like Red Hook's relative to a place like Tampa. In a 2014 report, the New York City Department of City Planning found that only 37 percent of buildings within the city's flood zones were the kind of one- to four-family detached buildings on standard lots upon which the NFIP had premised its regulations. The remaining 63 percent of buildings "will encounter additional challenges when retro-fitting under the current federal regulations."[41]

Despite the considerable variation that characterizes actual flood events, which may or may not (and in fact often don't) helpfully obey the boundaries of FEMA's official flood zones, the maps have no shades of gray: you are either in or out of the high-risk flood zone. Inside you have to purchase flood insurance; outside you don't. Inside the zones you also often find tougher building codes and zoning ordinances. Within a given zone, structurally similar properties pay the same rate, even if, for example, an A zone house is located just outside of the V zone, where wave-damage is expected.[42] As Austin Zeiderman observes in his own case of risk mapping in Colombia, "the movable boundary of the risk zone is also the flexible geography of governmental responsibility." Different requirements—not only for governments, but also for residents—obtain inside and out.[43] The designation of high- and low-risk zones also assumes that existing structural flood protections, such as levees, will behave as they are designed to: they really will keep water away from the people behind them. This assumption inscribes a faith in our ability to design and maintain major infrastructure into the assessment of risk. Yet such faith can prove catastrophically misplaced, as Hurricane Katrina dramatically illustrated when the levees failed.[44]

All maps are simplifications.[45] But as critical cartographers have shown, decisions of what and how to simplify, and the effects of doing so, are never socially or politically neutral. Though maps are understood in public discourse and deployed in governance as a representation of an underlying physical reality, they are themselves social documents, which need to be understood in particular historical contexts. Beneath the abstract, instrumental space of coordinates lie design choices.[46] In the case of the NFIP's flood insurance rate maps, one particularly important choice relates to how broad or fine to make the designations of flood zones. This has always been a matter of reconciling technical capabilities with the desires of the maps' ultimate users. In fact, in earlier years of the program, risk mapping involved more granular assessments. When the NFIP started, it operated according to "community risk zones," with "much finer" rating distinctions: broader zones were each divided into separate subzones based on topographies and were refined further based on "community-specific rating factors."[47] In 1972, the rating scheme was simplified; the NFIP replaced the community risk zones with "nationwide risk zones."[48] The zones were further simplified in 1985, when FEMA undertook a Map Initiatives Project that involved more than two years of review and discussion by a task force of representatives from different groups of map users—local floodplain administrators, engineers, surveyors, lenders, real estate agents, and insurance agents—on how to make the flood risk maps more "user-friendly." Floodplain administrators, engineers, and surveyors "universally sought more detail, such as building footprints and topography." Insurance agents and real estate agents, on the other hand, "usually suggested less detail and maps that would, in their opinion, be easier to read."[49] Ultimately, the reforms that came out of that effort included a dramatic reduction in the number of risk zones from 68 to just nine.[50]

The point, ultimately, of deconstructing the map in this way is not to show that FEMA is mapping flood risk "incorrectly." Nor is it to suggest that there is no reasonable basis upon which to estimate risks. Floods aren't fictions and we want people to know if they are exposed to danger. It's simply to show that the particular process used to assess and map floods *as risk* is shaped by organizational, practical, and political choices meant to solve specific problems: how to produce a tool that will be easiest for users to understand; how to apply national standards and policies to very different local areas; how to establish the relationship between past, present, and future; and how to manage the uncertainty inherent in any process of predicting the future. These particular problems, in turn, reflect a taken-for-granted commitment to the centrality of individual decision-making as a social model for dealing with the problem of flood risk. Actors make demands that the maps be accurate and precise because they are tethered to a very fine scale of decision-making: what to do about an individual property.

A different set of problems and underlying social models might yield a different assessment and visualization of hazards. To illustrate, in the United Kingdom, the particular institutional conflicts and constraints there have yielded different kinds of flood risk maps, some versions of which were made deliberately coarse in order to identify general zones of risk rather than to determine whether individual properties are at risk.[51] There are thus multiple potential visualizations of the "true" risk in an area. They aren't arbitrary, but they necessarily involve judgment and negotiation. The output of the flood map is in fact a compilation of selected data and methods, the choice of which reflects scientific theories about how the world works; it provides "as-if" information in which the 100-year flood behaves as if the conditions and models hold. It is, really, a hypothesis, but it is treated as evidence.[52]

What happens when theories about how the world works have changed? The most recent remapping of New York City's flood risk overlapped with a national-level effort, led by FEMA's TMAC and mandated by Biggert-Waters, to "ensure that flood insurance rate maps incorporate the best available climate science to assess flood risks."[53] The launch of this effort reflected the success of environmental organizations in arguing for a new orientation to the problem of flooding: one that incorporated climate change as a potential major source of loss that ought to be measured, visualized, and costed using improved tools of flood insurance. As the National Wildlife Federation testified in NFIP reform hearings in 2011:

The climate is changing and we are experiencing more intense storms, sea-level rise, and extreme flooding . . . We are already seeing an upsurge in the number of heavy rainstorms and many other impacts. As this Committee looks to reform the NFIP, it is important that we look to the future and not in the rear-view mirror.[54]

This conviction, echoed by other environmental groups, proposed a profound transformation in the way FEMA governed flood risk, changing the assemblage of techniques, data, calculations, and instruments relevant to its assessment. It would involve abandoning the rules of stationarity in order to address the ways that climate change can, for instance, change the relative rates of sea level rise in different places, leading in turn to acceleration or deceleration of shoreline change.[55] Incorporating future conditions, including but not limited to climate change, would mark a significant departure from FEMA's conventional methods of relying on data about the past.

FIGURE 3.2 New York City Panel on Climate Change (NPCC2) map of future 100-year flood zones for New York City, by Lesley Patrick, William Solecki, and the New York City Panel on Climate Change (2014). Courtesy of the Institute for Sustainable Cities, Hunter College.

As Dan Zarrilli's comments at the Rockaway town hall suggested, the New York City government also recognized a connection between flood risk, flood insurance, and climate change. But the new maps were clearly generating hardships for New Yorkers, as the previous chapter described—and eventually incorporating climate change into flood insurance rate maps would likely make the situation look even worse. The challenge facing the city was not simply a technical one of how to take climate change into account; through its own New York City Panel on Climate Change, it had produced numerous maps of what sea level rise would look like locally (see figure 3.2). But the link between such a visualization and its economization by insurance also created moral economy dilemmas related to how and when the costs of climate change would be distributed. Incorporating climate change into assessments and maps suggests that flood risk is in part a function of climate change. But if we understand climate change to be a collectively produced and globally significant problem—not a function of individual decisions about where or how to live—then is it realistic or fair to make individual property owners financially responsible by economizing it through insurance? Put simply: How much should homeowners pay for climate change? This challenge would be worked out on the terrain of technical disputes over measuring and mapping flood risk because the power to define risk is also the power to define responsibilities. Changing the parameters of how risk is assessed, modeled, mapped, and priced can change designations of who has the right, obligation, or ability to do something about hazards.[56]

APPEALING A FLOOD INSURANCE RATE MAP

A few months after the town hall at Beach Channel High School, New York City hired a consulting firm to do its own reassessment of the local flood risk and to produce independent maps of the flood zones and elevations across the city. Six months later, when the results of the study were in, the Office of the Mayor used those results to mount a formal appeal of FEMA's maps. The appeal argued, on the basis of their rival risk assessment costing millions of dollars, that FEMA's models had overestimated water levels by over two feet and unnecessarily mapped 26,000 buildings and 170,000 residents into high-risk zones.

In pursuing this course of action, New York City was participating in an institutionalized phase of flood insurance rate map production and adoption. As Zarrilli's comments to the Rockaway residents suggested, any new map would be subject to various kinds of review by the community it was eventually meant to regulate. FEMA first produces a preliminary flood insurance rate map or pFIRM. The pFIRM is shared with the community in a series of meetings, during which FEMA can explain how the maps were created and what they mean for insurance requirements. FEMA takes public feedback on the maps in two separate phases: a comments phase and then a formal appeals phase. During the comments phase, anyone can submit feedback on issues such as municipal boundaries, street names, and other things that require minor correction. The ninety-day appeals period is more serious and higher stakes. During this period, individuals and communities can contest the technical data and analysis underlying their maps. Individuals can file a Letter of Map Amendment (LOMA) if, for example, they believe that their structure sits above the floodplain, or to show that only an uninhabited portion of the structure is in the flood zone, or if they believe that their entire property has been mistakenly mapped in to the flood zone. Communities can file a Letter of Map Revision (LOMR), in which they ask for an official revision of flood zone boundaries, elevations, or other map features.[57]

In both cases, mounting a formal challenge requires considerable resources; FEMA only considers appeals eligible for consideration if they marshal new information that suggests FEMA's own assessment is scientifically or technically inaccurate.[58] Producing this information, with its supporting documentation, involves hiring engineering firms to conduct additional studies, as New York City did. While in principle everyone has access to the appeals process, the high costs of pursuing it make it hard for less well-off individuals and communities to mount an eligible challenge.[59] As the New York City appeal was just getting started, one city official told me, "Knowing now what the requirements are, I don't see how ordinary people could protest their maps."[60] For those who can afford to appeal, though, their efforts are largely successful. FEMA reports an 89 percent success rate for the roughly 30,000 flood map amendments sought annually.[61] Once FEMA resolves the appeal, a Letter of Final Determination is issued, launching a six-month compliance period before the map becomes the "effective FIRM," with full regulatory force.

As the previous chapter indicated, New York City received its new maps in the wake of Hurricane Sandy, but it didn't receive them *because* of Sandy; the remapping process had been underway for a few years at that point.

Recall also that New York City had been requesting a map update for several years before that—in part, as Bloomberg's *PlaNYC* vision outlined, to help the city adapt to what climate change portended for its waterfront. When those new flood insurance rate maps arrived in the months after the storm, their larger flood zones closely tracked the Sandy inundation line. And in Zarrilli's estimation, as he told the audience at Beach Channel High School, the new maps did reflect the increasing risks facing the city. In brief, New York City didn't need national level reforms or recommendations from a technical committee to take climate change seriously. There was already mounting political will to address the problem, and even a more particular interest in making maps and flood insurance part of that effort. And yet the city eventually argued that FEMA had gone too far, had indeed made the city's flood risk look too bad. It embarked upon a protracted debate with FEMA about the appropriate scientific basis and technical methods for estimating local flood risks.

On its face, the New York City appeal can be read as the familiar story about self-interested homeowners, reckless and greedy developers, and venal city politicians interfering with science. But upon closer examination, the fight over the science of flood risk—in a local context where there is considerable political will to address climate change impacts—shows how narrow technical debates provide a terrain to sort out fundamental political and moral questions related to how to frame and manage the problems of flood loss and risk. The previous chapter uncovered the manifold dilemmas that were generated when new maps hit the ground in the waterfront communities of New York City; the problem was about much more than simply property value at risk of loss from flooding.

At the conclusion of the previous chapter, we had ambivalent New Yorkers, uncertain about what to do today to manage risk and prepare for future flood losses. Yet even though these were individually borne burdens, they were socially shared problems. What might otherwise have remained a diffuse ambivalence and uncertainty across atomized decision-makers was organized through the map itself. When the map laid out the boundaries of the flood zones, it created a new group of people who had something in common: they were, officially, "flood zone homeowners." On Staten Island, one community-based organization launched after Sandy even decided to call itself "Zone A New York," a direct reference to living in high-risk A zones in the city. Significantly, they organized principally not as floodplain homeowners, but as flood *zone* homeowners. The salient issue was less their shared exposure to floods, more their shared exposure to attempts to *govern* flood risk with insurance—attempts that changed how they understood themselves, their futures, and their needs.[62] As Wendy Espeland finds in her own study of bureaucratic rationality in the management of water, interests and identities do not necessarily pre-exist political struggle; they are mutually constituted through encounters between people, and in their interactions with organizational structures and conceptions of rationality.[63] "Misery loves company," Dan Mundy Jr., the president of the Broad Channel Civic Association, told me. "There are going to be a lot more people waking up and they're going to now be forced to understand the details, because they're in it . . . in New York City, where people said, look, I didn't get hit in Sandy, or maybe the house got hit in Sandy but never before in 100 years and now you're telling me I'm in it, and are going to wake up and have to get up to speed on what does this mean? I'm hoping that that collective voice is louder now, to say let's put some minds together here." Even as flood insurance rating individuated policyholders, by assigning prices down to the property level, the map made it possible for them to attach themselves to the shared category of flood zone homeowner.[64]

Some critical risk scholarship has cited and decried the "pacifying" effects that risk technologies like maps have on ordinary people. The idea is that these technologies take what might be properly political questions and make them appear to be "merely" administrative matters of management, which become taken-for-granted. They put important decisions out of view of those so governed, defusing political mobilization. In part due to their technical complexity, risk-based technologies often operate by stealth, obscuring the targets of their interventions.[65]

However, in this case, the flood insurance rate map did not displace or defuse political contestation; it instead helped to activate and organize it. After Sandy's floodwaters receded, flood zone homeowners targeted their representatives on the City Council and in the state assembly and protested at town halls like the one in Rockaway, in local newspapers, and on the evening news, demanding reprieve from flood insurance rather than simply protection from floods. Through their civic associations, and phone calls, emails, Facebook posts, and tweets, flood zone homeowners articulated the moral stakes of the pFIRMs, channeling concerns about fairness, equity, and social and emotional loss, revealed in the previous chapter, to city politicians and administrators. Palmer was one of those homeowners. In an open letter to policymakers posted on Facebook, he raged against "the mind-boggling flood mapping done by incompetents." Flood zone homeowners were citizens and voters and they wanted these types of issues to be known and taken into account. They wanted the city to fight FEMA on the maps.[66]

In pursuing an appeal, however, the city would have to proceed carefully, in light of all the public commitments it had previously made to acknowledge and address the growing threat posed by floods. The language of the appeal had to reaffirm the city's commitment to the risk-based governance of flood, and to the role the NFIP plays in that, particularly in light of ongoing efforts to adapt the city and its residents to climate change. In the appeal's cover letter to FEMA, Zarrilli, whose office led the effort, insisted: "The City takes flood risk very seriously."[67] He cited the city's numerous climate change reports and plans, with their commitments to building upgrades, adaptive infrastructure, and strengthened resilience. But this had to be premised on "accurate" risk assessments and maps. Zarrilli wrote:

The City's goal continues to be to ensure that FEMA's flood maps provide a representation of *current* flood risk based on sound scientific and technical analysis . . . To ensure that we invest wisely in the areas of the City at greatest risk and reach the City's resiliency goals, the City must have a scientifically accurate assessment of flood risk. This assessment starts with accurate FEMA FIRMs.[68]

The technical approach of the appeal was to highlight that unacknowledged degree of epistemic uncertainty around storms that produce floods, even when based on historical data. Given a highly limited historical record of storm events, FEMA's modelers had generated a synthetic record of representative hurricanes and nor'easters—a standard practice—which they ran at randomized tidal cycles. The city's appeal, however, argued that FEMA's models used the wrong number of storms to produce this synthetic record; had a disproportionate number of them washing ashore close to high tide; over-relied on a particular 1950 nor'easter; and mishandled a drag law that showed wind speeds applying too much force to the water. The city's consultants created new models, based on different drag laws, and ran them at multiple tides over a larger series of events.

Rather than view this as a conflict between right and wrong models and maps, we can see how in flood risk assessment, we have an "excess of objectivity," in the words of Daniel Sarewitz. There is a large body of knowledge— storm events, models, drag laws—the components of which can be assembled and interpreted in different ways, as FEMA and the city's consulting engineers apparently did. Doing so yields competing views of the problem and can inform rival claims about how different actors and groups should respond.[69] Divergent technical strategies, made credible due to the epistemic uncertainty involved in assessing flood risk, reflect specific and different interpretations of the relevant information needed for resolving the question of risk.[70] In the city's version of the maps, the flood zones shrank.

Following the announcement of the appeal, Zarrilli told the press that inclusion in a flood zone "can have a devastating impact on neighborhoods." Queens City councilman Donovan Richards observed: "It was necessary for the city to do it, to try to keep that affordability for homeowners . . . But we also have to be cautious, and not shrink the map to the extent that if another storm comes, these homeowners would not have been in the flood zone."[71] The carefully crafted language of the appeal provided a way for the city to be on the side of residents needing access to affordable insurance coverage, while also articulating a commitment to responding to risks expected to worsen due to climate change—based on *more* "accurate," even if less conservative, maps than those initially provided by FEMA.

After over a year of consultation and negotiation, FEMA and the city reached a compromise. But this compromise surprised observers by arriving not at one revised flood map, as is the outcome of other successful appeals, but two. Rate-making in flood insurance for individual homeowners would be based on a flood insurance rate map of *current* risk, incorporating the city's own analysis. FEMA would redo the coastal storm surge analysis on the basis of the city's appeal. The other map—a new, "nonregulatory" and "future-looking" map—would reflect "future conditions that account for climate change," allowing for the depiction of multiple possible future scenarios. Following from the recommendations of FEMA's Technical Mapping Advisory Council, which released the first of its reports while New York City's appeal was underway, FEMA and the city would be codeveloping a "new methodology" that would result in "a new set of flood maps for planning and building purposes that better accounts for the *future* risk of sea level rise and coastal storm surge" (emphasis in original).[72] These maps, incorporating projections of future conditions rather than relying only on historical data, would *not* turn flood hazard into an NFIP insurance premium for property owners. The TMAC, for its part, was aware of and concerned about moral economic controversies in the event that future climate change was allowed to affect insurance premiums. Its report noted: "If future conditions become linked to mandatory insurance requirements, an analysis of the impact to property owners may need to be conducted. Issues of equity and affordability associated with insurance premiums need to be considered." In New York City, the new climate maps would not be regulatory by triggering insurance requirements, but rather advisory. They would tame some of the uncertainty around future conditions in order to guide capital planning and avoid future losses, as well as make clear that the city was not in denial about its flood risk or climate change. In the press release, Zarrilli was quoted:

FEMA's decision to redraw New York City's flood maps, and to work with us to produce innovative, climate-smart flood maps, allows us to begin separating the calculation of annual insurance premiums against current risk from the necessary long-term planning and building we need to do as a city to adapt to rising seas and climate change.

These two maps provide distinct visualizations of risk, framing the problem of flooding on the basis of different technical parameters and, as a result, enacting different political moralities of responsibility. The revised flood insurance rate map, showing current risk, makes individuals responsible for the assessed flood risks to their properties, in the near term. The new, future-looking map makes "climate change" the official responsibility of collective actors, articulated as the city as a whole, over the longer term. The implications of the two-map agreement extend beyond New York City. According to a FEMA spokesperson, it represents the first in "a series of demonstration projects" for a new, national strategy that separates the calculation and depiction of current flood risk from the calculation and depiction of uncertain scenarios defined by the future conditions of climate change. According to the spokesperson, going forward, "new products will be delivered to NFIP communities separately from the FIRMs."[73]

This distinction between current and future is a bit odd. Risk generally, whether officially designated as current or future, implies an orientation toward the future; it organizes problems in terms of probabilities of harms that have not yet been realized. But the distinction here works as a morally satisfying and effectively practical one. It allows the actors involved to solve specific problems of governing, at least for the time being. Contestation over how to define risk produced an outcome that responded to the demands of beleaguered homeowners while also performing a vulnerability to climate change that would allow the city to give at least the appearance of control through evidence-gathering, representation, and planning.[74] In this episode in the life of the NFIP, we see how the accuracy of a flood map is forged in practice, producing a vision of the problem that can be accepted as *reasonable* for the actors involved, in large part because of the particular way it assigns responsibilities for flood risk and loss.

THE PRODUCTION OF AN INSURANCE PREMIUM

Identifying hazardous areas is only the first step in what the instruments of flood insurance are meant to do. The NFIP must also associate a premium with each policy it writes. That mandatory purchase requirement for property owners with mortgages applies in high-risk A and V zones. In low-risk X zones, flood insurance is available but optional.[75] Insurance agents selling on behalf of the NFIP must take a risk class (specified by the zone and its base flood elevation), which applies to many homes in an area, and arrive at a premium that is paid by an individual policyholder. Flood insurance economizes the hazard in order to make the decision of what to do about it one of weighing up costs and benefits at an individual level.

The price of insurance can be determined in many ways and, from the history of the NFIP we have already examined, it's clear that ideas about solidarity and fairness shape decisions of how to do this. Members of Congress in the 1960s recognized a clear moral rationale for subsidizing the flood insurance of property owners occupying the floodplain before their areas were mapped or flood insurance was available. Keeping these presumably high-risk policyholders at reasonable rates was in large part a matter of fairness. Throughout the subsequent decades of the NFIP's operation, the choices of how to manage these persistent subsidies, the addition of zone and elevation grandfathering rules, and whether or on what time scale to increase these below-risk rates, have been conspicuously shaped by moral claims, which are the focus of the next chapter. But here we deconstruct the *actuarial* rate. In public debate about the NFIP, the actuarial rate is often positioned against the subsidized or otherwise discounted rate as the hard-nosed, technically sound, logical, and only fiscally responsible way to price flood insurance; it is needed to capture the "true cost" of flood risk. It is, after all, risk-based, implying it is scientifically grounded. But the choice to economize flood hazards based on actuarial rates, as well as the design of the rate itself, also embeds and reproduces political and normative judgments related to the morally appropriate limits of risk-sharing and to the inculcation of rational behavior to govern the self. The production of an insurance premium, like the production of a map, is not simply a technical process; it requires the adjudication of complex political questions.[76]

What then is an actuarial rate for flood risk, and how is it determined? How does the NFIP engage in its particular economization of flood hazard and decisions related to it? The NFIP defines a full-risk premium rate as one "charged to a group of policies that results in aggregate premiums sufficient to pay anticipated losses and expenses for that group."[77] In other words, there are two main components to an NFIP risk-based premium: there is a part that reflects expected losses, and there is a part that captures other costs associated with transferring risk. The expected losses are calculated as the summed product of (1) the probabilities of floods of various magnitudes (based on a hydrologic model developed by the U.S. Army Corps of Engineers), and (2) the damage, or "loss severity," that would occur at different flood elevations.[78] This expected loss is sometimes referred to as the "pure premium": the cost of coverage associated with paying for losses alone.[79] It is this element of a premium that acts as a "price signal" of risk, increasing or decreasing as the underlying assessed risk does.

But this is not the final price charged to policyholders. There are also costs associated with underwriting risk, which are reflected in adjustments to the premium, called "loading factors." For instance, one loading factor covers the costs associated with figuring out what the losses to a property were after a flood (called "loss adjustment") and any resulting special investigations related to releasing claims payments to policyholders. Other loading factors account for deductible amounts and underinsurance. An "expected loss ratio" adjustment loads rates for Write-Your-Own (WYO) agents' commissions and other expenses; this is what private insurance companies get in return for selling and administering policies for the

NFIP.[80] Finally, a contingency load factors in general uncertainty in estimating risk. Multiple cross-subsidies are also built into NFIP ratings.[81]

When a prospective NFIP policyholder goes to purchase flood insurance, most likely from a private insurance company that has also sold the general homeowners' insurance policy (the vast majority of NFIP policies are sold this way as part of the WYO program), the agent uses an NFIP-issued Flood Insurance Manual to find the price per $100 of coverage. The property owner has to provide the agent with information about the structure (e.g., the year of construction, building occupancy, number of floors, and location of its contents), as well as an elevation certificate prepared by a certified surveyor. The agent uses the flood insurance rate map to locate the property's zone and to calculate the difference between the elevation of the building (i.e., the height of its first floor) and the base flood elevation. This information helps the agent determine which rating table applies to the particular property; the rating table shows the rates for groups of similar risks (based on flood zone and structural characteristics). From this, the agent calculates the price of coverage, based also on the level of coverage chosen by the customer.[82]

Like the production of a flood map, the production of an insurance premium sets boundaries around what is purportedly relevant to the problem at hand—in this case, to the economization of flood hazard. What technical parameters should be allowed to affect the price of insurance and what is left out? Rating practices can and have changed over time, reflecting in part the fact that insurers, both public and private, regularly confront the limitations of their own science and technology for addressing risk. The endeavor to transform uncertainty into calculable, controllable risk is a fragile, contingent, and dynamic one and, as critical insurance scholars have shown, "actuarialism is more art than science."[83] In addition, as with risk mapping, when it comes to pricing insurance, experts understand the task as one of "balanc[ing] complexity against accuracy and precision," as the NFIP's Chief Actuary explained to FEMA's TMAC at a 2015 meeting.[84] Rates are set nationally by zone and are not typically modified locally as the result of a flood episode: "The federal view is that the ultimate goal of the program is to guarantee a financial balance over time at a national level rather than being accurate everywhere at a microlevel (and then compensating negative results in certain areas with positive ones in others)."[85] Even an accurate risk-based rate is circumscribed by judgments of what is practically achievable at scale and with acknowledged limitations in what actuaries can know or find out about risk.

Establishing a price for flood insurance requires assembling and arithmetically relating models and observations, estimations of costs, choices made by the consumer and judgments made by the actuary, information that is social, ecological, and financial. It requires multiple commensurations: the transformation of different qualities into a common (quantitative) metric.[86] The result is a premium. At the same time, this premium reflects the choice to *eliminate* certain factors from rating. Catastrophes, for instance, are left out, excluded from the frame of calculating price, even for full-risk rates. The NFIP does not price policies to be able to pay claims from a catastrophic loss year out of current revenue. Catastrophic losses are losses occurring to many of the insured at the same time, as happened in 2005 with Hurricane Katrina, then again in 2008 with Hurricane Ike and the Midwest floods, then again in 2012 with Hurricane Sandy, and again in 2017 with Hurricanes Harvey and Maria and Irma. These losses exceed the average. Rather than pricing individual policies to reflect such catastrophes, the NFIP is designed to borrow from the Treasury in bad years and repay in good—though with catastrophe after catastrophe, it appears unlikely that it will ever restore its solvency without congressional intervention. A private insurer, by contrast, would include a catastrophe load in insurance rating, in order to cover the costs of building a reserve, purchasing reinsurance, or any other activities undertaken to gain access to capital in high-loss years.[87] All else equal, this would ostensibly result in a higher-than-NFIP actuarial rate. A study by the Property Casualty Insurers Association of America concluded, using 2009 rates, that the NFIP provides coverage on average at half the rate that would be offered by the private sector. Private sector rates would be 23 percent higher for lower-risk properties and more than 200 percent higher in higher-risk areas.[88] In a sense, all NFIP policies are subsidized, relative to what the private market would charge. All this to say that what a true full-risk rate looks like for any given insurer, public or private, will depend upon particular configurations of knowledge and institutional constraints.

In economizing decision-making, the NFIP also decides what and whose *behaviors* can affect the price of insurance. Under its current terms, elevating a home above the base flood elevation or relocation to lower-risk areas count as individual-level measures that decrease flood insurance rates—though other steps might reduce or avoid flood losses. The NFIP also discounts rates if entire communities take specified steps it believes will work toward reducing the risk facing their floodplain occupants. This can include not only infrastructure investments and structural changes to the area, such as building a floodwall or buying out flooded properties, but also measures related to risk communication and even just maintaining flood data or publicizing flood insurance rate maps. In specifying these incentives for individuals and communities, risk-based insurance premiums enact definitions of economically rational and risk-reducing action, in which only a particular set of strategies matter. It's also worth noting that this process does *not* target the behaviors of another set of important actors: the private insurance companies participating as WYO insurers. A 2010 analysis found that in total, more than one-third of premiums collected by the NFIP goes to the WYO participating companies and insurance agents.[89] The GAO has consistently called for closer oversight of WYO practices in order to ensure that payments made to private insurers are reasonable, based on evidence that those insurers are pocketing a great deal more than they spend administering the program and also do not effectively market the policies to improve insurance take-up rates, driving up costs and making the NFIP less fiscally sound. In the GAO's view, FEMA "cannot be assured that the WYO program is achieving its intended goals in the most cost-effective manner."[90] The privatization of FEMA's activities more generally has "increased the amount of public dollars being funneled through government service contracts to private firms," without delivering the promised improvements in services and even, as Kevin Fox Gotham shows in the aftermath of Katrina, worsening conditions on the ground for those FEMA is meant to help.[91] Yet demands for lowering the overall costs of the NFIP tend to focus instead on the perceived shortcomings of the individual homeowners and local communities who rely on the program.[92]

More fundamentally, what is the moral significance of economizing flood hazards in actuarial terms? Risk experts and insurance professionals favor actuarial rating of risks because it is deemed necessary to the financial stability of an insurance system: it secures enough in premiums to pay for expected losses. This is an efficiency argument. There are also two moral arguments. First, rating according to risk prevents the multiplication of opportunistic behaviors, namely, "moral hazard." Again, this is the idea that rational actors (not necessarily "bad" people), when protected from the consequences of their own actions, or if they can avail themselves of financial protection cheaply (i.e., at subsidized rates), will take *more* risks. As we saw, concern about moral hazard animated the design of the NFIP; it was something floodplain managers and economists were particularly worried about. By economizing decision-making in a way that makes risky behavior costly, actuarial rating addresses moral hazard, securing a kind of virtuous, self-responsible behavior. Second, actuarial rating is, at its core, believed to be fair; indeed, actuarial fairness is regarded as a guiding principle of insurance underwriting. Fairness, in this framing, means equal treatment for equal risks. Individuals should assume, through actuarial premiums, the costs of the risks that they "import" to the insurance pool. They also should not have to subsidize those who are higher risks; this is an unfair transfer of resources from low-risk members of the pool to high-risk members.[93] In the context of liberal governance, with its emphasis on individual responsibility, it seems like a natural and essential task to classify people according to risk and treat them on that basis.[94]

Insurance is, however, also a cooperative mechanism. Its essential principle is risk-sharing in order to mutualize the adverse consequences of a loss. When people participate in insurance, they effectively constitute a community of fate, whether or not this fact is salient in their everyday lives (scholars call this "insurance solidarity").[95] In other words, they share responsibility: everyone is affected by what happens to one member of the group. One of the things that makes the NFIP distinct from a private insurer is that no risk can be excluded for being "too bad"; the program is prohibited from denying coverage to anyone in a participating community.[96] In that context, actuarial rating (or any choice of rating principle) sets the limits of that shared responsibility in particular ways. Actuarial rating means that as a general principle, because policyholders living at higher risk of flood are more likely to experience a loss that requires a claims payment, they pay higher premiums than policyholders living at lower risk of flood.[97] There are a number of simplifying assumptions in the economics of moral hazard and insurance that undergird this particular conception of fairness. The first is that flood risk is choice-sensitive, in the way that, say, driving a car over the speed limit seems like a choice-sensitive increase of one's automobile accident risk. Individuals have control over themselves and their property; they have the power to increase or decrease the risk they are bringing to the pool. Another, related, assumption is that people taking care to avoid or minimize risk is effective: if they take the incentivized steps to reduce their flood risk, such as elevating their home above the base flood elevation, they will actually avoid losses to themselves and to the pool. Another assumption is that money compensates for loss, that indemnified individuals will take risks because the money they get from insurance is a satisfactory replacement for what they have lost. Homes, for instance, are financial assets that can simply be rebuilt and replaced.[98]

These assumptions are not in all cases categorically wrong but, at the very least, as we saw in the previous chapter, they may not correspond with the self-understandings of the insured themselves. New Yorkers encountering new flood insurance rate maps did not feel that they had exercised meaningful control over their personal exposure to flood risk, nor did they relate to their homes and neighborhoods in strictly instrumental economic terms. As such, an "actuarially fair" premium felt in many ways unfair. It saddled homeowners with the consequences of a high-risk status that they did not feel they had caused and did not deserve. And in the case of the NFIP, policymakers have regarded cross-subsidization as acceptable, even if actuarially unfair, in order to make it possible for high-risk policyholders to afford coverage—that way, at least they prefund part of their recovery in the event of a loss, lowering the burden of disaster relief on taxpayers.[99] What this underscores is that the price of insurance, though arrived at through a highly technical process of economization, necessarily depends on the ideas of solidarity and fairness that are emphasized, as well as the overall social objectives of an insurance institution. But what is ultimately produced—a premium that commensurates a lot of different elements in order to arrive at a representation of the cost of risk—strips away this context as a basis for judgment.[100]

A different orientation to these issues could lead to a different regime of pricing. For instance, equality of insurance *access* might be emphasized instead, leading to premiums that are not indexed to risk in circumstances where this would put protection out of reach of some needy prospective members.[101] If insurance were imagined not principally as a vector for inculcating personal responsibility but rather as a societal "caring institution," as Deborah Stone has described it, then fairness might require the participation of everyone, rather than only those whose risks can be assessed as particularly high.[102] In sum, in the words of Tom Baker, "Outside formal economic models, there are no purely technocratic, value-free answers to the question of who should pay how much to jump into the insurance pool."[103]

CONCLUSION

Risk, depicted on maps and economized in insurance premiums, provides a framework for modern societies to make decisions in the face of uncertainty. Adding or removing certain kinds of data, modifying an assumption or parameter in a model, moving a line on a map—the ultimate result of these technical changes can alter the costs facing households, the way local authorities plan for the future, how individual and collective resources are allocated, and how communities prepare for coming disasters. When the stakes are high—when the physical safety and financial security of millions of people are at stake—it is no wonder then that a diverse set of actors and institutions are preoccupied with the design, operation, and effects of the instruments of risk management. "Risk definition is, essentially, a power game," in the words of Ulrich Beck.[104]

The contentiousness of flood mapping and insurance rating is no secret in the life of the NFIP. It has been widely remarked upon. But this chapter has offered a perspective on this contention that does not treat politics as separate from science. What this demonstrates is that politics is not something that happens after the engineers, modelers, and actuaries have completed their work. As sociologists of science have long been arguing, politics is not a matter of "distorting" the outcomes of an otherwise value-free science.[105] Politics is instead bound up with risk assessment, which is to say, bound up with any effort to symbolically represent and materially alter the present in anticipation of a particular vision of the future. We see this in the way that flood insurance rate maps and actuarial premiums frame the problem of flooding, and what to do about it, in particular ways. They take the form they do because scientific processes and technical capabilities always interact with organizational decisions, institutional constraints, and professional judgments. The choice to include or exclude some factors, and not others, from analyses and calculations reflects not only the public policy objectives such instruments are meant to help accomplish, but also social models and moral commitments embedded in professions, governance institutions, and the culture at large.

In the story of New York City's appeal of its flood insurance rate maps, calls for map accuracy, and technical debates over what this consists of, provided a terrain for negotiating and navigating complex considerations related to who bears responsibility for what and when. Introducing climate change as a potentially relevant parameter for assessing flood risk and pricing insurance complicated already thorny matters of what homeowners were or could be held individually responsible for. It was not simply a question of figuring out how to measure future conditions or technically relate them to existing scientific methods. Rather, the situation signified a larger question about the terms upon which new understandings of what might cause future losses could be connected to the burdens and benefits facing homeowners today. The two-map solution provided a settlement that assigned responsibilities in ways that a variety of stakeholders could accept as reasonable.

If there is no separating politics from science, then perhaps we have to accept that science cannot resolve some of the irreducibly political and normative questions related to how we live with uncertainty, hazards, catastrophes, and loss. Technocratic faith in models, maps, and prices tempts actors to continue to fine-tune these instruments, but no estimate of risk alone can tell them what they *should* do. With this in mind, some scholars advocate moving away from discourses about true or real risk in favor of an approach that recognizes the socially constructed nature of risk and models of it. In this view, the objective of producing risk knowledge should be one of establishing shared understandings rather than definitive estimates, acknowledging that there are many participants who may have conflicting views. This would enlarge the dimensions of risk recognized in social debate in ways that could lead to more robust—because more broadly legitimate—decision-making.[106]

Such an approach also addresses the fact that these technical and often arcane risk instruments may be far from pacifying in their effects. In this case, through the operations of classifying risk, New York City's flood map itself constituted a social group that was defined by their relationship to the flood insurance rate map and to flood insurance more broadly. This group mobilized politically to attempt to influence how the instruments of flood insurance were designed and deployed. One of the ways in which risk definition is made a power game is not only through the mobilization of preexisting interests and identities, but also through the constitution of new ones through processes of risk definition and delimitation.[107] The inextricably political nature of assessing and pricing flood risk creates the possibility of these kinds of "looping" effects, where calculating risk does not simply represent an underlying, objective reality (that we get more or less right), but rather generates new kinds of real effects, which loop back into the knowledge practices through which risks are calculated, visualized, economized, and distributed in insurance.[108]

The simplifications that made a high-risk zone in New York City comparable to one in Missouri, or California, or Florida, also united homeowners in all of these places in a bigger fight over the terms of physical and financial security. About 100 miles away, in Toms River, New Jersey, another flood zone homeowner was fighting his new flood insurance rate map and this legislation he had heard about as he was rebuilding after Sandy: the Biggert-Waters Flood Insurance Reform Act. George Kasimos took his fight to Congress, with homeowners from floodplains around the country behind him.

Chapter Four

SHIFTING RESPONSIBILITIES FOR LOSS
National Reform of Flood Insurance

George Kasimos did not want to meet in a coffee shop. "I'm not a sit-down-and-drink-tea kinda guy," he told me. Instead, whenever we met up, he would pick me up in his blue Ford F150 pickup truck at the train station in Newark, New Jersey, and we'd drive around, stopping to check on the different home reconstruction projects he was managing for his business and to pick up supplies at Home Depot. Kasimos talked quickly and loudly, in a booming voice suited to his former linebacker's frame, about elevation certificates, V zones and A zones, mitigation grants, claims adjusters, and Congress, pausing just long enough to take a drag off his cigarette and ask, "OK, so what questions do you have?" His answers to those questions rarely seemed to follow in a linear way, but then the ins and outs of flood insurance seemed to him labyrinthine. He didn't yet fully understand how it all hung together or why things seemed to work the way they did, but he was sure of one thing: homeowners like him, who had played by the rules, who had done nothing wrong, were paying for problems they hadn't created. "I don't mind paying a couple bucks extra," he told me. "But you know, we've got to do it the right way."

During one of our drives, en route to another errand, Kasimos took a phone call from a lawyer in Tampa who had questions about the latest developments in flood insurance; she had seen stories in the newspapers about New Jersey and New York residents being unable to afford new premiums, but would this affect Florida? "This is a national issue," Kasimos assured her. "Everybody's rates are going up. Is it going up 10 percent or is it going up 2000 percent, that's the issue . . . Everybody's going to suffer, it's just a matter of how much they're going to suffer."[1] He had been trying to spread the word about the changes to flood insurance since February 2013, when his neighbors gathered in a local deli to talk about this obscure new legislation: the Biggert-Waters Act. "We gotta let people know that everybody is going to be affected," he told the group. Kasimos did not think of himself as a political person; he didn't even vote in every election. But when, as he began mucking out his flooded house after Hurricane Sandy, he found out he was in the "dreaded V zone" on a new flood insurance rate map and that his flood insurance could go up to tens of thousands of dollars a year if he didn't elevate his house—which he could not afford—he said he had to do something. In the months since that first meeting, he had spent his own money printing red, white, and blue bumper stickers emblazoned with the name of his growing network: "Stop FEMA Now." Underneath, he put: "Save our homes." His truck sported two of them.

So far, we have traced issues of moral economy in flood insurance, moving across time and scale. From its earliest days to its operations in the present, flood insurance has shaped and been shaped by negotiation over the right or fair distribution of burdens and benefits when insurance governs flood hazards. From experiences on the ground to debates at the city level, we have seen residents, officials, and experts experience and evaluate flood maps, insurance prices, and public policy in light of their normative understandings of how risks should be shared, who should be held or made responsible and when, what a fair price for accessing financial security in the face of future losses looks like, and the perceived fairness of the NFIP's effects. In this chapter, we move back to the national scale in order to focus squarely on the legislation that had George Kasimos so unsettled: the Biggert-Waters Flood Insurance Reform Act of 2012. This major overhaul of the NFIP passed in between Hurricanes Katrina and Sandy, when the NFIP was $18 billion in debt to the U.S. Treasury. This debt transformed the relevant issue of compensation from one of restoring individual fortunes after a loss, the preoccupation of policymakers in the 1960s, to one of an apparent conflict between the NFIP's obligations to compensate policyholders and its dependency on the collective resources of taxpayers when its own fund could not meet those obligations—a conflict that many expect to persist and worsen with further effects of climate change. Biggert-Waters set in motion the kinds of local dilemmas described in chapter 2, which, as we will see here, reverberated up to policymaking at the highest levels and shaped the next phase of the NFIP's life. The flood zones on the maps not only linked the identities, fates, and claims of New York City's flood zone homeowners, as chapter 3 discussed; they also helped Kasimos to unite homeowners across the nation's flood zones, under the banner of Stop FEMA Now. Stop FEMA Now and its allies took local dilemmas and aired them on a broader, national stage, making and responding to moral claims about fairness, obligation, and deservingness.

This chapter tells the story of Biggert-Waters in three acts, following the advocacy that led to reform, the backlash to reform, and the "reform of the reform" that was ultimately passed. Supporters and opponents of Biggert-Waters alike cited and agreed upon various NFIP failures. They also shared certain sentiments: a belief that good science was essential to the legitimacy of the NFIP and the expectation that individuals should take responsibility for their actions. But they disagreed about what constituted a fair and effective path forward. The chapter examines the claims made by participants in flood insurance reform, on both sides, to justify and oppose proposed changes to the NFIP's various technical characteristics. Of particular importance were claims about *deservingness* and *choice*, which we will see mobilized to justify arguments for changing the balance of individual and collective obligations—what individuals must face alone versus what risk pools and taxpayers will support together. Who deserves help, and what kind, if natural hazard risks can be individually assessed and foreseen? Are individuals to blame for their vulnerability to natural disasters? How should flood insurance manage the incentives and choices of the insured?

These particular questions reflect legacy tensions in the NFIP between the solidaristic features that made it resemble a social insurance program, and the actuarial features that emulated private insurance techniques— tensions that were designed into the program in the 1960s, as chapter 1 described. On the one hand, the impulse to create the NFIP reflected an understanding of the flood-afflicted as blameless victims of acts of God, for whom the government could socialize the risk as it did other risks through social insurance programs. With the establishment of a flood insurance program, the federal government in a single act transformed flood from uninsurable to insurable risk, protecting property owners by spreading flood risks nationwide and providing more reliable compensation. Further-more, in providing subsidies that decoupled some premium levels from risk, providing guaranteed coverage (such that no flood risk is too bad to insure, even for properties that repeatedly flood), and, after 1973, mandat-ing coverage, the NFIP resembled other social insurance programs, estab-lishing solidaristic terms that socialized risk and provided protection to those who needed it.

On the other hand, flood insurance at the same time transformed floods into scientifically foreseeable, patterned events that can ostensibly be planned for by individuals on the basis of probabilistic risk assessment. As the previous chapter explained, the technologies of flood insurance econo-mize flood hazards, and behavior concerning those hazards, at the individ-ual level. The program was meant and expected to be, eventually, fully actuarial in the way it priced insurance. Rates based on assessments of flood risk would, in the view of the NFIP's architects, create "much stronger" price incentives that individuals would incorporate into choices about whether to buy or build in a flood zone. The outlines of the NFIP codified expecta-tions regarding individual choice, dependent on the availability of scien-tific risk assessment that would produce both information and incentives. The NFIP in these ways emulated a private insurance institution in classi-fying risk and assigning individual contributions on that basis, oriented toward incentivizing particular kinds of decision-making.

The controversies examined here, and the language in which they were fought out, also reflect how flood insurance is situated in American politi-cal culture and its moral economy of social provision more broadly. As dis-cussed in the book's introduction, scholars have demonstrated the histori-cal and ongoing relevance of ideas of deservingness, choice, and fairness in a variety of policy domains conventionally associated with the welfare state: employment, health, injury, and old age. Political sociologists and political scientists have connected the scope and generosity of social pol-icy in these domains to the articulation and mobilization of "categories of worth," particularly whether policymakers and the public perceive recipi-ents as "deserving" or "undeserving." Such distinctions serve discursively to justify the balance of individual and collective obligations and to institutionalize programmatic boundaries between categories of beneficia-ries. In the United States, this normative distinction has been especially powerful.[2] The deserving are generally believed not to be to blame for the adversity they face, whereas the undeserving are often narrated in policy debates as those who have made poor choices; they are in some way personally responsible for their own troubles. Claims of deservingness thus implicate judgments about the existence and meaningfulness of individual choice. This implication has been apparent in the last several decades of American social policymaking, where deservingness has not always been explicitly invoked by political elites.[3] Instead, arguments for cutting back on spending, adding requirements, or reducing eligibility have been premised on ideas about choice, not only as a way of attributing blame (i.e., past choices create present suffering), but also as a strategy of governing. Policymakers seek to manage the choices of beneficiaries, scrutinizing the "perverse incentives" that disincline the target population from taking personal responsibility and that keep them dependent. The concerns that people have about flood insurance, related to deservingness and choice, are very much of a piece with more general imperatives and disputes in the politics of social provision. Yet we don't typically pay as much attention to how these designations do important political work in the context of natural hazards and disaster policy.[4]

With the establishment of the NFIP, the federal government forged a new kind of social interdependence in the face of this particular natural hazard. With the design and implementation of its technical and contractual features, it sets the *terms* of that social interdependence: who pays how much and for whose security, what kinds of conditions accompany access to coverage, and the incentives to which insureds are expected to respond. When the NFIP faced financial crisis after Katrina, stakeholders debated matters of deservingness and choice in pursuit of divergent visions for how those terms of social interdependence should be reset: the particular ways in which flood insurance should individualize or socialize the problem of flood loss and whether the NFIP should prioritize actuarialism or affordability going forward. The distinctions that emerged from this debate discursively and institutionally reorganized arrangements for managing the costs of flood loss.

ACT I: CHOICE AND DESERVINGNESS IN BIGGERT-WATERS

What ultimately became the Biggert-Waters Flood Insurance Reform Act was the result of seven years of House and Senate committee meetings on flood mitigation, catastrophe insurance, and the federal budget.[5] Biggert-Waters, named for the then-subcommittee chair, Representative Judy Biggert (R-IL), of the House Subcommittee on Insurance, Housing, and Community Opportunity, and its ranking member Representative Maxine Waters (D-CA), was the most comprehensive reform of the NFIP since its establishment. In the context of the NFIP's $18 billion debt ($16.1 billion of that from Hurricane Katrina alone), it was intended to put the program on a path to fiscal health, namely, to restructure the program to bring in enough in premiums to cover the nation's flood risk over the long term.

The key provisions of Biggert-Waters targeted the NFIP's core functions of mapping and pricing flood risk. It recommitted resources to fund flood risk studies and maps for the sake of providing up-to-date and accurate scientific risk assessments and risk-based insurance rates. As the previous chapter described, this part of the reform also mandated that FEMA, through its Technical Mapping Advisory Council, study how to incorporate "the best available climate science" into its flood risk mapping. If the NFIP was going to improve its maps, it needed to do so in a way that was explicitly geared toward preparing the country and its residents for climate change. The more dramatic immediate change following the reform was the elimination of premium discounts from a gradual phase-out of subsidies and the immediate end of grandfathering in favor of new actuarial rates, program-wide, that would better reflect the individual insured's true cost of risk coverage. The loss of subsidies would affect about 20 percent of policyholders across the country, concentrated in states with large populations: Florida, California, New York, and Texas, as well as flood-prone areas of Louisiana, New Jersey, and Pennsylvania. The loss of grandfathering would affect an unknown number; at the time, FEMA did not have the data to determine which policies were based on grandfathered rates.[6] The legislation also toughened the penalties on lenders who failed to enforce the mandatory insurance purchase requirement; mandated that FEMA study the effectiveness of building codes and made grants available for building code enforcement; and mandated that FEMA study the affordability of actuarial rates—but did not indicate that this study should come *before* FEMA increased rates as it implemented the rest of the law.

Much of the energy behind Biggert-Waters came from a coalition of environmentalists and conservative, libertarian, and taxpayer groups called SmarterSafer. Member organizations have come and gone over time, but on the environmental side, American Rivers, the National Wildlife Federation, and the Sierra Club were among the first to sign on. Member organizations have also included the Coalition to Reduce Spending, the R Street Institute (a free-market think tank that split off from the Heartland Institute, a major forum for climate change skeptics), the National Taxpayers Union, Taxpayers for Common Sense, and the Taxpayers Protection Alliance. In the context of contemporary American politics, such a coalition is otherwise unlikely, but these groups agreed that the NFIP was in need of drastic reforms that would have policyholders pay risk-based rates.[7] For environmental groups, risk-based rates, premised on enhanced maps that could incorporate the effects of climate change, would yield environmental protection, acting as a control over real estate development in hazardous and sensitive natural terrains. For right-of-center coalition members, risk-based rates corrected a problem of low-risk policyholders and taxpayers being forced to support high-risk policyholders financially for the expensive consequences of their choices. Removing discounts and increasing premiums would also open up the possibility that private insurers, some of which were now in a position to underwrite flood risk, could compete for business and sell their own products to profitable segments of the market. This would make flood insurance more like a "free market" and potentially lead to the government exiting altogether, the ultimate goal of some member groups. Insurance industry interests also supported reform for this reason, as well as because higher premiums would also mean higher commissions for the Write-Your-Own (WYO) private insurance companies, who earn a percentage rather than a flat fee. The Reinsurance Association of America, Liberty Mutual, USAA, and Swiss Re, as well as the National Association of Mutual Insurance Companies (NAMIC) all signed on to support Biggert-Waters. In the context of the NFIP's massive debt, Smarter-Safer's advocacy for this particular kind of reform also had a compelling fiscal dimension: the NFIP needed to bring in more in premiums to meet expected losses. By 2011, SmarterSafer had begun working closely with the House Subcommittee on Insurance, Housing, and Community Opportunity to draft what became Biggert-Waters.[8]

In March 2011 congressional hearings on legislative proposals to reform the NFIP, witnesses (including representatives of SmarterSafer member organizations) and members of Congress connected the apparent impossibility of NFIP debt repayment to "the persistence of federally subsidized premiums," in the words of Representative Robert J. Dold (R-IL).[9] Keeping these subsidies was also, in the words of a witness from the Association of State Flood Plain Managers (ASFPM), "help[ing] people ignore their risk," by not sending a clear signal through risk-based insurance prices. Instead, the NFIP should "enable market-based financial decisions." The ASFPM witness went on: "It is very important that the people who are living at risk, know the risk and share the—and be part of paying for their risk. It is, we feel, inappropriate to externalize that risk to the rest of the taxpayers, the Federal taxpayers."[10] This was particularly true in the case of severe repetitive loss properties, which had been rebuilt again and again. The chairwoman of NAMIC testified: "Quite simply, American taxpayers should not be forced to subsidize a small subset of NFIP policyholders who continue to rebuild in high-risk areas."[11] This was, she later stated,

simply not fair to the American taxpayer. There are folks who wish to [rebuild]. If they wish to rebuild in these areas, they need to be charged actuarially sound rates. If they want to absorb that risk, they need to pay for that risk. They need to pay for it, not the American taxpayer.[12]

A representative from Taxpayers for Common Sense testified about the importance of homeowners' engaging in some "decision-making to deal with about where their home is, or mitigation measures they could take that would reduce the cost or reduce their vulnerability." The issue was, in his words, about "trying to remove that risk off the back of the taxpayer and putting it back on to the policyholders where it logically belongs."[13] In written testimony, added to the official record, Taxpayers for Common Sense argued, "taxpayers deserve to have those who choose to live in harm's way pick up their share of the tab."[14] In May 2012 Senate hearings on NFIP reauthorization, a Montana floodplain administrator testified:

The American taxpayer is increasingly unwilling to provide financial support for those who have time and time again received handouts post-flood who then do absolutely nothing to prevent future damages as they know Uncle Sam will be there check in hand to quite literally bail them out again.[15]

Neither were taxpayers willing to support irresponsible NFIP policyholders: "Gone, too, are the days that the taxpayer will support those who knowingly choose to live in areas and in homes with severe flood risk." In the same Senate hearing, a representative from the Heartland Institute submitted a statement urging that "the federal government should not encourage the choice to live in harm's way" through below-risk insurance rating and outdated flood risk assessments and maps.[16] Experts at these hearings were asked to address how an actuarial shift would affect low- and middle-income policyholders. They suggested voucher programs, like those administered by the Department of Housing and Urban Development (HUD) for housing, or separate appropriations for supplementing insurance payments.

Taken together, these reformers sought to motivate policy change in large part by emphasizing the knowability of flood risk, which carried with it obligations surrounding individual choice and what flood zone policyholders thus deserved vis-à-vis taxpayers. Floods were not calamities that hit people unaware; for decades now they had been understood as scientifically assessed risks, visualized on maps. The availability of risk information seemed to make flood risk choice-sensitive: policyholders put themselves at risk when they chose to buy or build in the flood zones and they were therefore not blameless in the event of a loss. They could have seen it coming; they could have made a different choice. The scale of economization— the way a risk-based premium could be assigned to an individual policyholder—worked against a sense of broadly shared vulnerability. Your premium, your risk. This bolstered the argument that taxpayers who had made the choice *not* to expose themselves to high flood risks ought not be made to pay for the risks of others.

A reformed NFIP would not only enhance fairness based on prior choices, but also enact a more sensible risk-based calculus of choice going forward—one that had long been promised but not delivered because of subsidization and grandfathering. The prudent future role of the NFIP was not to provide support in the form of subsidized insurance; that was feeding an ongoing moral hazard that invited development in the floodplains. Rather, echoing earlier arguments related to the NFIP and in other arenas of policymaking, individuals needed *information*—visualized on maps and transformed into a price signal—that would allow them to make the best choices for themselves. Reform needed to involve some restructuring of the incentives of the insured, with individuals taking more responsibility for exposure to and for managing their risks.

The Biggert-Waters bill won bipartisan enthusiasm, passed both houses of an otherwise highly polarized Congress (373–52 in the House, 74–19 in the Senate), and was signed into law by President Barack Obama in July 2012. Under the law, subsidized policyholders would see a 25 percent increase each year until premiums reflected the full-risk rate. The end of grandfathering would affect all policyholders as soon as their maps were updated—a dynamic that began playing out first in the greater New York City area, when it received new maps after Hurricane Sandy. Properties that had been intentionally built outside the flood zones could find themselves mapped in and subject to flood insurance purchase requirements for the first time—at actuarial rates. Or, if new maps showed that a property was now at higher risk, or if the property was sold, the policy would not be able to stay at the earlier (lower) rate. FEMA began implementing the law without completing the affordability study.

ACT II. BACKLASH TO BIGGERT-WATERS: DISPUTED CHOICE AND DESERVINGNESS

What started with George Kasimos in a New Jersey deli ultimately grew into a nationwide network of floodplain homeowners, mobilized to protest Biggert-Waters. Stop FEMA Now—eventually called a "grass-roots political juggernaut" in the pages of the *Wall Street Journal*—grew quickly through social media, with new chapters forming first in Sandy-affected New York City, and later in coastal and riverine communities nationwide.[17] Stop FEMA Now reached and organized residents across the political spectrum. "WE DON'T CARE IF YOU ARE A DEMOCRAT, REPUBLICAN OR INDEPENDENT," Kasimos insisted in an email to subscribers. "WE JUST WANT TO SAVE OUR HOMES." Members included suburban and urban residents, retirees and young parents. Across a considerable diversity of experience and identity, Stop FEMA Now drew on the NFIP's own risk classifications to mobilize this new political affiliation of flood zone homeowner. Members shared emotional stories over email about facing the loss of their homes due to the pressures of flood insurance increases (see figure 4.1).

Kasimos's kids helped him get Stop FEMA Now on YouTube, Twitter, and Facebook, where he urged homeowners to write and call their representatives in Congress, and to tweet politicians and journalists with the

FIGURE 4.1 A home for sale in Broad Channel, Queens, with a homemade Stop FEMA Now poster in its window. Fieldwork photograph taken by the author.

hashtags #stopfemanow, #saveourhomes, and #fixflood.[18] He used social media to develop ties between Stop FEMA Now and other grassroots home-owners' insurance reform groups and networks, which had formed in recent years to protest increases in private wind and other homeowners' insurance rates.[19] The Homeowners' Hurricane Insurance Initiative (HHII),[20] a church-based insurance reform initiative that began in Alabama, cross-posted Stop FEMA Now content on its Facebook page, along with pictures of church marquees reading, "PRAY FOR THOSE WITH FLOOD INSURANCE" and words of spiritual encouragement: "With the Lord all things are possible!"[21] For HHII, the insurance struggle they shared with Stop FEMA Now was a matter of justice; in the words of one its Face-book group members: "The Lord hates an unbalance [sic] scale."[22] These were apparently not problems of public insurance alone; changes to private insurance also spawned controversies about the fair terms of risk-sharing. Kasimos himself eventually began traveling around the country to speak about flood insurance at other homeowner-organized insurance events.

Stop FEMA Now also gained more powerful allies in the National Association of Realtors, the National Association of Home Builders, the American Bankers Association, and the U.S. Chamber of Commerce. Eventually, Stop FEMA Now also affiliated with the larger Coalition for Sustainable Flood Insurance, led by Greater New Orleans Inc., a regional economic development alliance, that applied significant pressure to members of Congress. These were groups who shared an interest in the continued economic viability of floodplains for home construction, property transactions, and commerce.

Stop FEMA Now reopened questions about what homeowners could or did choose, and what homeowners in risky areas deserved when it came to managing the rising costs of flood risk under Biggert-Waters. In its efforts to make increasing insurance rates morally and politically indefensible, and to preserve the affordability of flood insurance, Stop FEMA Now articulated a set of NFIP implementation failures that, it argued, made meaningful choice over exposure to risk effectively nonexistent. The failures had chiefly to do with the way the NFIP maps and communicates risk, which both Stop FEMA Now and reformers agreed was a major weakness of the program. Stop FEMA Now did not argue that the flood risk facing an individual property *couldn't* be assessed scientifically. Rather, it argued that FEMA was bad at producing and communicating those scientific assessments. This had two important implications, in Stop FEMA Now's view. First, it meant that many homeowners did not and could not know their "true" flood risk when they moved into their neighborhoods. As New York City had most recently dramatized with its maps from 1983, many of the maps were long outdated and therefore unreliable visualizations of current risk. For any given community, the many years between reassessments would compromise the basis of sensible zoning that should keep residents out of harm's way. In addition, some local and state regulations did not require previous owners or realtors to disclose a property's history of flood losses or insurance claims to prospective buyers. Homeowners had not recklessly moved into, or rebuilt, in areas of prohibitively expensive risk exposure. To the extent that high-risk flood zone homeowners were creating burdens for taxpayers at large, they were doing so unwittingly.

Second, for Stop FEMA Now, the weaknesses in FEMA's maps also meant that actuarial premiums could not be established on a sufficiently legitimate scientific basis. In a video posted to YouTube in the early days of Stop FEMA

Now, called "The Truth About Flood Insurance," Kasimos told viewers: "If the flood maps are mess, we can only assume that the actuarial side of the flood insurance program has some problems, too." Stop FEMA Now urged homeowners to fight new maps on the grounds that they "overestimated" risk whenever possible. As the previous chapter described, even if maps were up to date, their scientific and technical accuracy could be contested, through FEMA's formal appeals process, on the basis of competing assumptions, data, and models. This was important too for thinking about what, if anything, the coincidence of Sandy with Biggert-Waters, new maps, and higher insurance premiums had to do with climate change. "It's all about that," Kasimos told me. "But I guess you can have an intelligent argument with FEMA and say this is what we feel it's going to rise." There was unavoidable uncertainty as to whether decisions should be made on the basis of higher or lower projections and, if homeowners were going to foot the bill, there ought to be some more definitive "national number," in Kasimo's words, for inches or feet of future sea level rise.[23] Such a thing is, we saw in the last chapter, impossible to establish authoritatively. Stop FEMA Now argued that homeowners would take responsibility for their individual risk. But because of what they saw as weaknesses in mapping, policyholders could not trust that the risk was itself legitimately established, whether it was based on "backward looking" assessments of flood risk or on projections of future climate change. The president of the Broad Channel Civic Association, Dan Mundy Jr., who also urged his neighbors to fight Biggert-Waters, told me:

We're not trying to say we shouldn't look at risk, and we're trying to dodge things here, but we want it to be accurate. And if you're going to tell someone you're going to lose a huge value on your house based on Biggert-Waters and maybe somebody won't invest here, or maybe you got to raise your house for 100,000 dollars, we said to them, we don't want it 99 percent correct. What you're already telling us is, it's not even 80 percent correct. We want 100 percent correct.[24]

Stop FEMA Now also claimed that the NFIP had not communicated to subsidized policyholders that their rates did not in fact reflect their risk. Indeed, in the case of most subsidized properties, the "true risk" rate could not be estimated on the available data; FEMA did not have complete records of property elevations that would make such estimates possible.[25] Because of these technical and communication gaps, Stop FEMA Now argued, there had been no effective signal that would allow homeowners to exercise choice and control over their personal flood risk. Several officials who have audited the NFIP backed up this claim; as one of them put it, it is "not inconceivable that people have no idea what their risk actually is" and "people didn't even know they were subsidized to begin with."[26]

Stop FEMA Now and its allies also worked to highlight histories of floodplain development spurred by economic pressures for growth and facilitated by public officials and policymakers who deferred to developers. We saw in chapter 2 how local actors in New York City interpreted the new flood insurance rate map through the lens of this history, which shaped their own understandings of the fairness of their new map's effects. Such concerns were raised to the level of the national conversation about what, if anything, Congress ought to do next. In December 2013, Columbia University Law School convened a panel discussion called "Soaring Flood Insurance Rates: Should Congress Step In?," gathering flood risk and insurance experts, New York City officials, and representatives from Smarter-Safer. Kevin Boyle, then-editor of Rockaway's local newspaper *The Wave*, was there to provide his firsthand experience of the changes. He referenced the question of risk and choice, with visible irritation:

The other thing is, we've been in the communities—you know, you talk about the original flood insurance program and why it was enacted, well you know a lot of things can be argued the same way and you can pick holes in them now . . . there was a compact, a promise somewhat; they encouraged coastal development. And I bought my house with flood insurance, and other people built the community with a subsidized program in place. It's changing the game a little late for a lot of people.[27]

To the extent that homeowners in the nation's floodplains had chosen to live in high-risk areas, their choice was facilitated not only by flood insurance implementation problems, but also by the interests of powerful actors, inside and outside government, who encouraged real estate development (some of whom were now political allies of Stop FEMA Now). In the words of Mundy, the Broad Channel Civic Association president:

The government made a program, it was the stated policy of the United States government from '68 on, is that [flood insurance] will be available, and it will be affordable. It wasn't because oh, we want to help these people out. Maybe part of it is. It was because of the fact that all of these neighborhoods around here, back then, were looking, "Do we build around here?" And of course the government's always been building and creating these areas! And it's been a huge tax return for the government in general, and for the American people.[28]

For black homeowners, the experience of this history of floodplain development intersected with legacies of discriminatory housing policy and predatory real estate practices that have produced combined ecological and economic precarity. Flooding disproportionately harms black neighborhoods, which are often located in low-lying areas unprotected from flood defenses and without green spaces that absorb water—areas in some cases "discarded and unwanted by whites." Even after the official end of redlining (the practice of denying home mortgages and other financial services in predominately poor or black areas), inclusion in real estate markets has come on highly unequal terms. For instance, black and Latino homeowners were targeted for, and disproportionately received, subprime mortgage loans during the housing boom, even when they could have qualified for prime loans. In areas hit by Sandy, and in floodplains nationwide, these homeowners would be some of the most adversely affected by intensifying flood hazards and increasing flood insurance premiums. They had achieved and held onto homeownership despite tremendous political, economic, and environmental obstacles, and flood insurance would make that achievement more tenuous.[29]

In highlighting these histories, homeowners in effect agreed with SmarterSafer and other supporters of Biggert-Waters that the federal government *had* allowed or even encouraged habitation in areas that should perhaps never have been developed. As described earlier, FEMA had not ensured that local communities were complying with the land-use requirements that were supposed to be a condition of accessing the NFIP, despite early and consistent warnings from the Government Accountability Office (GAO) and other experts.[30] Communities were getting protection—and individuals were getting subsidies and grandfathered rates—but local officials were not actually restricting or regulating development in the flood zones and were thus contributing to putting more people and property at risk. But Stop FEMA Now drew a different conclusion from this history, arguing instead that the problem and its solution were to be found not in the incentives facing insured individuals, but rather in the collective failures and contradictions of public policy related to natural hazards and economic development.

Another of these failures was to be found in the way the NFIP had structured the WYO program, through which private insurance companies sell and service NFIP policies and receive a commission while bearing no risk. Stop FEMA Now argued that these commissions, which were factored into the premiums paid by policyholders through "loading factors" in rate-setting, were excessive and wasteful. They had driven up the costs of the program and had more to do with the financial precarity of the NFIP than did the choices of individual homeowners. "Everybody's eating like a pig at the trough," Kasimos told me.[31] These commissions were like "kickbacks" and they should be capped; it was the same paperwork, whether the premium was $500 or $5,000. In emails to members and in its outreach, Stop FEMA Now attempted to redirect blame to the private insurance companies and to the politicians who bended in the face of their deep pockets and lobbying.

Stop FEMA Now had complicated the argument about past choices, asserting that homeowners were not to blame for the present crisis facing the NFIP, their individual at-risk situations, or their troubles in the face of actuarial rating. They were indeed still victims—not of an act of God flood, but rather of policy failures and contradictions—deserving of sympathy and solidarity. By late in the summer of 2013, it was clear that the mobilization had the attention of the national media and of politicians. Senators Mary Landrieu (D-LA), David Vitter (R-LA), Robert Menendez (D-NJ), and Charles Schumer (D-NY) vowed to address the concerns of Stop FEMA Now and reopened discussions of flood insurance in Congress.

Supporters of Biggert-Waters had reason to worry about the longevity of the reform; they ramped up their media outreach to explain and justify Biggert-Waters. In their attempts to wrest control of the public perception of Biggert-Waters, environmentalists and scientists continued to stress the importance of risk-based rating for the purposes of planning and individual decision-making.[32] At the Columbia University Law School event with Boyle, a representative from the National Wildlife Federation assured the audience: "By no means is it the goal of the National Wildlife Federation to cause people hardship. Our goal is to send market signals—not a market shock—but a market signal that's going to encourage the good behavior I just described," that is, shifting (re)building away from "pristine environments" that provide natural protection from floods.[33] Particularly in the context of climate change, the general picture painted by the science was unambiguous; these were tough but nevertheless urgent and necessary changes, meant to protect sensitive ecologies and to make individuals more resilient. As one environmental journalist described it, higher insurance prices would serve as a "wake-up call" for floodplain residents, forcing them to confront the costs of climate change.[34]

Some defenders of Biggert-Waters confronted the deservingness of homeowners by turning to arguments about whom the shift to actuarial rating would really affect. There were "truly needy" policyholders, as witnesses, including members of SmarterSafer, had testified in congressional hearings, but in the wake of the backlash they called any retreat on NFIP reform a "beach house bailout." Taxpayers were being asked to continue to support the owners of vacation homes and luxury condominiums. The president and chief economist of the Insurance Information Institute (III), an industry organization, argued that below-risk premiums were subsidizing millionaires:

I mean, it was subsidizing vacation homeowners, businesses, properties that have been repeatedly flooded. Is this a good use of taxpayer money in this time of austerity? Probably not. Does it make sense at all for people to be subsidizing for people to live on the beach? My answer to that is no. And I think, unless you're one of the people who's receiving that subsidy, the answer is generally no. . . . Why on earth should the federal government be providing subsidized coverage to millionaires to have a beach house? There's no rationale for that.[35]

The notion of the beach house bailout also steered the argument for reform out of the potential trap of entrenched sympathy for and solidarity with disaster victims. Biggert-Waters' implementation had, after all, coincided with Hurricane Sandy. In the national media, the optics of the backlash to Biggert-Waters centered on how its changes were affecting areas devastated by the storm, where Stop FEMA Now had its origins. Stories in the press showed families, standing in the wreckage of their homes, describing how even if they could rebuild, they might not be able to afford to insure and thus faced displacement. These were sympathetic figures: they had just suffered catastrophic loss, only to face a new source of financial strain. They were also often white. The most visible activists with Stop FEMA Now were white and many of the stories about the effects of Biggert-Waters centered on white and working- or middle-class families. They were the same people who have always been treated more generously by disaster relief and social policy. The suffering of people of color in disasters has not historically attracted the same resources or redress.[36]

The slow and complex process for settling claims after Sandy, described in chapter 2, also made the NFIP appear insufficiently responsive to the plight of those who had paid in, attracting the ire of members of Congress. Stop FEMA Now devoted a share of its advocacy work to these compensation issues, as well, publicizing errors in loss adjustments—in some of the most notorious cases, the result of fraudulent engineering reports—which served to further the sense that homeowners were victims of a program that was treating them unfairly.[37]

Defenders of Biggert-Waters argued that despite the optics, these homeowners were *not* representative of who was really going to be affected by the changes to the NFIP. The NFIP needed reform because the majority of the people who were benefiting from a subsidized system could afford *not* to be subsidized. They did not deserve the sympathy of the public, or the support of taxpayers, because they could and should take responsibility for living on the water. One of the founders of the SmarterSafer coalition, from a libertarian think tank, distinguished those who deserved sympathy from those who did not:

First, the places that have been hit the hardest so far [by Biggert-Waters] are non-primary residences—second homes—and severe repetitive loss properties that taxpayers have already rebuilt. The affordability issue? I don't care, and I don't think anybody else should, either. Nobody's entitled to a second home, and almost nobody is entitled to have the taxpayers rebuild their house more than once . . . In the case of severe repetitive loss properties, there are a handful of people who are maybe old or long-term incumbent homeowners, who you do have to feel sorry for . . . Yes, there may well be pain to them. But I don't understand how or why there's a public responsibility to subsidize somebody to live in a particular house in a particular place. There's some public responsibility to house people. People like to live near water. The houses facing the highest rates are the houses right near water, which are expensive. To me, there is an affordability issue, but it's actually reasonably small.[38]

A reformed NFIP would withdraw support from the undeserving wealthy: a group that was receiving an unneeded and unjust subsidy. The editorial board of the *Wall Street Journal* concurred, describing flood insurance as "a classic example of powerful government aiding the powerful, encouraging the affluent to build mansions near the shore," in a December 2013 editorial.[39]

Stop FEMA Now argued instead that Biggert-Waters was affecting a population deserving of solidarity: ordinary, hardworking families, trying to hold onto a piece of the American dream through homeownership. In our conversations, Kasimos was quick to clarify that a "subsidy" in this case was not about avoiding one's "fair share"; it was not welfare, for the affluent or anyone else. "I'm not down with welfare," he told me. "I like to pay my own way. And I don't mind paying a little extra if I have to, to help the next guy."[40] But the increases under Biggert-Waters were so unaffordable that they would force people out of their homes and economically devastate their communities. Here again the local effects of new maps and insurance prices were mobilized into the national effort targeting congressional action. On September 28, 2013, three days before some of Biggert-Waters' rate increases were to go into effect, protests took place across ten states, all under the banner of Stop FEMA Now. At the rally in Queens, New York, a resident of Hamilton Beach told the crowd that his neighborhood consisted of

mostly single-family homes. Most of our residents have family ties to our community, having grown up there and later purchased their first homes there. The homes are modest but they are *our homes*. Homes that would become unaffordable if the flood insurance rates are allowed to skyrocket. Homes that would become virtually unsellable if the buyer is required to carry an outrageously high flood insurance premium.[41]

When Eric Ulrich, the Republican New York City councilman who represents several flood zone Queens neighborhoods, spoke at the rally, he framed redress on flood insurance as a matter of obligation to the middle class. He invoked the federal response to the 2007–2008 global financial crisis and the housing market collapse, which had bypassed the needs of ordinary Americans. Many of his constituents still felt the effects of the crisis and they would now be facing more hardship as the result of flood insurance:

You cannot send the message to the American people that it's OK to bail out the auto industry, that it's OK to bail out the banks and the big insurance companies, but you're not going to bail out the middle class. You're going to force people out of their homes because you're going to force them to purchase flood insurance they can't afford. It's not right. And members of Congress have a moral obligation to do it, and we have a moral obligation to vote them out of office if they don't.[42]

In an open letter to Congress posted to Stop FEMA Now's website in February 2014, Palmer, who had joined the group and organized his neighbors in Rockaway, wrote:

Although some groups lead you to believe that all flood policyholders and people who live by the water are multimillionaires, nothing could be further from the truth. In reality we are police officers, firemen, teachers, nurses, sanitation men, and soldiers, also senior citizens and retirees greatly devastated by ruinous flood premiums. We are also families who must live by the water for our livelihood: fishermen, oil workers, engineers, sailors, etc. We are people who have survived for years living in areas that have never been flooded. Now a manmade disaster—the Biggert-Waters Act—will destroy our neighborhoods, causing the unthinkable prospect that we will lose our homes . . . This is about wonderful, hard-working tax paying citizens. But most importantly for me it is about my family, friends and neighbors.[43]

The man-made disaster of Biggert-Waters would push out workers and families on the basis of risk assessments and insurance prices. NFIP policyholders deserved support and solidarity because actuarial rates would have unequal and economically catastrophic effects for the many policyholders who could not afford them. These policyholders were also, in Palmer's words, "hard-working tax paying citizens," whose tax dollars went to compensate uninsured losses from not only floods, but also other natural disasters that were more common in other parts of the country. "I'm American, I want to help them," a Stop FEMA Now member told me. "We see sometimes tornadoes, forest fires, horrible things happen. It seems to me that there's times that different areas of the country suffer from natural disasters, and we step in and we help them."[44] Flood zone homeowners were owed solidarity because of their own participation in other collective mechanisms for redistributing resources to those in need.

Flood zone homeowners were also, by their own interpretation, environmental stewards. Perhaps they were not engaged in the specific kind of "good behavior" identified by the representative of the National Wildlife Federation, but residents stressed that they took care of the waterways that they lived near. As Kasimos put it, "If you're a tree hugger, and you want to get everybody out—look, I live on the water. I fish on the water. I pick up garbage that's floating around ... because that's what I love, I love that ... We appreciate it more than anybody."[45] He told me about taking to the water on his jet ski to clean up debris after Hurricane Sandy. Residents of Rockaway and Broad Channel, in New York City, described similar acts of care, not only related to cleanup from Sandy but also to longer histories of involvement with local environmental groups and advocacy with city environmental authorities.

In truth, property owners of highly varied resources have benefited from subsidized flood insurance—luxury condominium developments and vacation homeowners, along with working-class communities.[46] A July 2013 GAO study of 715,000 subsidized policies found that "counties with higher home values and income levels tended to have larger percentages of remaining subsidized policies compared to those with full-risk rates." However, when the GAO looked at the policies themselves, they found that "remaining subsidized policies generally carried smaller NFIP coverage amounts than nonsubsidized policies in SFHAs [high-risk flood zones], a possible indicator of lower home values."[47] In the wake of Biggert-Waters and Sandy, opposing sides of the reform issue staked a position as to whether NFIP policyholders deserved redress by strategically foregrounding different rhetorical figures of who stood to lose when subsidies and grandfathering disappeared. What emerged discursively from the contestation between the two was a notion of deservingness as determined around an axis of *ability to pay for risk exposure*—ability to take responsibility on the basis of risk and its price. Those who deserved sympathy and support were those who truly could not financially support their exposure to risk.

ACT III. REFORMING THE REFORM

In response to the controversy, in October 2013, Representative Maxine Waters (D-CA), whose name was on the original bill, organized a bipartisan congressional group to begin work on new flood insurance measures in the House and Senate. Her office issued a statement:

I am outraged by the increased costs of flood insurance premiums that have resulted from the Biggert-Waters Act. I certainly did not intend for these types of outrageous premiums to occur for any homeowner. When I agreed to coauthor this legislation, our goal was to create a bipartisan solution to repair our National Flood Insurance Program. Neither Democrats nor Republicans envisioned it would reap the kind of harm and heartache that may result from this law going into effect. Plainly put, I am committed to fixing the unintended consequences of the Biggert-Waters Flood Insurance law.[48]

In March 2014, again with bipartisan support, Congress passed the Homeowner Flood Insurance Affordability Act (HFIAA), also called Grimm-Waters for Congressman Michael Grimm (R), who represented Staten Island, and Maxine Waters. Kasimos was invited to the capitol for the signing to represent Stop FEMA Now.

The HFIAA did not repeal Biggert-Waters, but it did delay the most dramatic premium increases while FEMA completed its affordability study and produced a framework. The terms of the HFIAA made further technical adjustments to the NFIP that reflected the arguments made in the wake of Biggert-Waters. The HFIAA maintained Biggert-Waters' resource commitment to flood risk assessment and mapping; the NFIP must produce up-to-date, accurate scientific information to rate insurance and to provide a sound basis for individual choices going forward. This reaffirmed personal exposure to flood risk as something individuals could and should play a proactive role in understanding and managing. The HFIAA also reinstated grandfathering. Homeowners would return to paying the rate they had been quoted at the time they purchased the policy—when they made a choice on the best or only information available to them at the time. Now, although most subsidized or grandfathered homeowners could return to below-risk rates, they could expect their premiums to increase by as much as 18 percent every year, moving gradually toward actuarial rates. Severe repetitive loss properties, however, would continue to see up to 25 percent annual increases as required by Biggert-Waters, as would nonprimary residences and businesses.

Congress also addressed the issue of deservingness as it had been framed in the backlash to Biggert-Waters. The two sides had disputed whether at-risk homeowners really deserved sympathy, the key contention being whether or not these homeowners could actually afford to pay actuarial insurance premiums: were they beach house millionaires or ordinary folks? With its new legislation, this time explicitly an "affordability act," Congress indicated that FEMA first needed to identify and institutionalize methods for telling the difference. The HFIAA made it clear that any support should be offered in consideration of a policyholder's income or wealth, providing "targeted assistance to flood insurance policyholders based on their financial ability to continue to participate in the National Flood Insurance Program."[49] FEMA needed to define criteria for treating policyholders differently in order to avoid unduly harming homeowners when rates increased.

This task would begin with reports from an affordability study committee, convened by the National Academy of Sciences (NAS) and comprising social scientists, flood experts, and statisticians, who solicited input from federal and state agencies, nonprofit and trade organizations, and research organizations. At the committee's second meeting, just days after the HFIAA passed, a representative from HUD described the negative and uneven impacts of a "pure cost, risk-based approach," with specific reference to hardships in New York City as sea levels rose:

High point in the Rockaways is 14 feet . . . You get to Breezy Point, and they're right on the beach . . . Put a meter of sea level rise into that—the problem is not going to be the storm, at that point. At that point, it's going to be high tide, and it's going to be coming from the bay side . . . But what do you do with 80,000 people? Cops, firemen, teachers. They've lived there for generations. So we tell them they have to move tomorrow? We're not going to allow them to live there? There are people who will live in risky areas, who can afford to do that. We're not going to see a migration out of the Hamptons. We are not going to be able to price these people out of the market. They want to live there, they'll live there. They can afford to rebuild; they'll build it up; they'll do whatever. But in working-class communities, we can price people out of that market. We can drive them out of it. And we will destroy those communities.

A director at a civil engineering firm responded:

I'm getting the impression that all change is bad . . . Are we really doing justice to allow people, just because they've been there, to continue to live in some of the riskiest areas? Or, do we help them to do something else? Do we really want the population that is most vulnerable to live in the most vulnerable areas?. . . At some point, it seems like we'd want to break that cycle.

The losses facing these vulnerable populations in vulnerable areas might be justified. The representative from HUD agreed. But, he asked, "Where are they going to go, and who's going to pay for it?" He went on:

You don't have to tell them they have to move today, but we have to start talking to them about where their kids are going to live, and where *their* kids are going to live. . . . And you've got to do it now, because in thirty years, we are going to be a situation where we have to move people . . . We want to help people decrease their risk. There are some people who will do that on their own, if we give them the right information. And there are some people who we're going to have to give them the right information so that they decide that it's important that they do it, and then we're going to have to give them some help in order for them to do it . . . We can't look at everyone the same.[50]

Though the mandate of the committee was to devise technical strategies for assessing the affordability of premiums and policyholders' ability to pay, the discussion involved unavoidable moral dilemmas about both what was fair and what was in the best interests of vulnerable homeowners, particularly given expectations that flood losses would worsen due to further effects of climate change.

The next year, in March and December 2015, the committee released two reports to guide the design of an affordability framework. The committee pointed out that introducing an affordability framework would require the NFIP to collect and use new kinds of data, never previously collected, on its policyholders: their income, wealth, and housing costs.[51] In addition, the committee noted, even once FEMA was able to tell its policyholders apart, introducing means testing to the NFIP for the first time would require difficult political decisions regarding eligibility: Who counts as truly needy of continued federal support in order to afford flood insurance? This was not a technical question that the study committee could answer.

Whereas these kinds of distinctions are common in housing and public assistance, they represent a significant change in the particular context of natural hazards and disaster policy, where means tests and need-based considerations are not so familiar. After natural disasters, for instance, federal relief is damage-based, not income-based.[52] In their first report, the NAS committee looked to other federal agencies and programs that use means tests, including HUD's housing vouchers, the Supplemental Nutrition Assistance Program, Medicaid, and the Children's Health Insurance Program for potential methods of distinguishing eligibility and determining attendant support.[53] Following the release of the NAS reports, a February 2016 GAO study determined that depending on the eligibility threshold used, 47 to 74 percent of subsidized policyholders would likely be eligible to receive some form of assistance.[54]

In April 2018, FEMA released *An Affordability Framework for the National Flood Insurance Program*. Based on consultation with other federal agencies (HUD, along with the Departments of Energy and Agriculture, the Federal Housing Finance Agency, the Small Business Administration, the Office of Management and Budget, and the GAO) and academics, it outlined a set of different flood insurance affordability program design options, specifying the advantages and disadvantages of each. Having done so, FEMA and the NFIP now await further congressional action before any one or number of them can be funded and implemented.

CONCLUSION

Through governance of natural hazards and disasters, states play a central role in keeping people safe and in helping them recover economically in the event of catastrophe. In doing so, they establish a kind of social contract, determining what will be collectively managed and what will be individually borne. This much was evident in the origins of the NFIP, examined in chapter 1. From this close examination of ongoing contestation around the terms of flood insurance, we see that *how* that balance is renegotiated depends, in part, on the relative strength of moral claims for solidarity from fellow citizens and taxpayers. The effort to reform the NFIP, to address its massive deficit and restore its fiscal stability, was waged as a debate about the fair terms of social interdependence. How should individual responsibility determine each policyholder's contribution to the risk pool of the NFIP? Who gets to live how and where and at what cost to whom? Supporters of Biggert-Waters argued that flood risk was choice-sensitive, since risk information has by now long been available, and that many of those affected by Biggert-Waters were affluent vacation homeowners who did not deserve support that they didn't need anyway. The NFIP thus ought finally to adhere to its actuarial aims, underwriting risks more tightly so that individuals are responsible for the risks they bring to the pool and for understanding and managing the true cost of living in the floodplain. Opponents of Biggert-Waters argued instead that homeowners had not been able to exercise choice over their risk exposure and that it was ordinary, hardworking Americans who would suffer under a fully actuarial regime. Flood insurance premiums thus needed to remain affordable, with reasonable contributions to the risk pool. The controversy surrounding Biggert-Waters arrived at a definition of deservingness around ability to pay for risk exposure: those who could afford their full-risk rates should pay them; those who could not should get some form of assistance. Subsidies were unwarranted and unjust, and should be withdrawn, *if* they were going to those who could afford to go without them. In other words, if in the 1960s policymakers had been worried about flood victims and homeowners generally, it now mattered *who* was receiving assistance and on what terms: rich and poor alike might face flood risk, and find themselves at some point underwater, but deservingness of sympathy and support could not be assured on that basis alone. Michele Landis Dauber concludes from her history of U.S. disaster relief that "disaster victims have escaped any serious scrutiny as the able-bodied recipients of large, long-standing federal transfer payments," but debates over flood insurance reframe their deservingness along a different axis.[55]

As Barbara Kiviat argues, in a study of contentious classification in car insurance pricing, "people use causal theories as a tool of moral adjudication. Some theories pass moral muster and others do not."[56] In the context of flood insurance and in controversy over Biggert-Waters, given the historical failures of the NFIP to communicate risk, it became difficult to assign blame for *past* choices, to defend politically the idea that flood zone homeowners had been the primary agents in causing their own difficulties. Stop FEMA Now and its allies had persuasively argued that people weren't getting what they deserved with the shift to actuarial rating, because the lack of quality information and other failures of the NFIP had precluded meaningful choice. Homeowner claims about the morally justifiable limits to their own individual responsibility were made in part by blaming the government for failing to live up to its own responsibilities. By creating the NFIP, and by premising the whole thing on flood maps, the government had in a sense taken on responsibility for keeping those maps accurate. If the government was derelict in this responsibility, then expecting more from homeowners who had already acted as they ought to, by buying houses out of the flood zones or at high enough elevations, seemed to violate a kind of contract. For Stop FEMA Now, the causal theory that the financial strain on the program was attributable to homeowners choosing to live at risk did not pass muster.

The ultimate outcome with the HFIAA, however, enshrined choice on the basis of actuarial price signals as central to the moral economy of flood insurance going forward. Defining deservingness around ability to pay for risk exposure makes the designation not about blame for the choice but about who can bear the costs of it. And as in other arenas of social policy-making, this definition undergirded the institutionalization of changes to natural hazards policy: with its affordability framework, the NFIP has pursued methods and criteria that will make such distinctions practically possible in the administration of flood insurance as it makes its actuarial shift. Everyone who participates in the NFIP will be expected to show the particular kind of "good behavior," described by the representative from the National Wildlife Federation. But actual contributions to the risk pool will be attenuated by a consideration of means, drawing a line internal to the program in order to adjust obligations to those who can and cannot afford to cover their personal exposure to risk.

The incorporation of need-based considerations in the NFIP qualifies an individualization of responsibility for addressing the problem of flood loss. Given the hybrid public-private characteristics of the program, this individualization takes a particular form. The NFIP does not individualize responsibility by excluding the highest-risk property owners from the community of fate, leaving them completely on their own, as a truly private system might. Instead, it individualizes responsibility in two different but related senses. It makes all policyholders more *accountable* for their own risks through the gradual program-wide shift to actuarial premiums, as well as responsible for managing their own exposure to risk by modifying their consumer choices on that basis. Stop FEMA Now's achievement, in the end, was to blunt the negative distributional effects of this individualization, through reinforcing a commitment to provide assistance to those who cannot afford to be fully accountable for the risks they bring to the pool. This outcome protected those homeowners for whom the income shocks could be catastrophic, and Stop FEMA Now counted it as a win. But the price of flood insurance is still going up. As flood risks spread and worsen—as FEMA itself expects they will under further conditions of climate change—insuring them will require more and more of household budgets, with households having to find ways to manage the pressure on their finances.

Fundamentally, the core presumptions are that individuals are the source of risk—to themselves, to the risk pool, and to taxpayers—and that greater individual responsibility on the part of those facing high risk, expressed as a form of market-based financial decision-making, can effectively manage our collective relationship to catastrophes and the losses they create. A certain faith in individual incentives remains, despite the evidence that a combination of factors has prevented them from working the way they are expected to, not least of which is policymakers' persistent aversion to acting on that faith. This testifies not only to the enduring and broadly shared appeal of tropes of personal responsibility in American political culture, but also to the institutionalization of economic styles of reasoning in policymaking.[57] It seems proper, taken-for-granted, that individuals should evaluate their own behavior and that of others with respect to economic calculation. With Biggert-Waters, Congress did toughen penalties on mortgage lenders who fail to enforce the mandatory purchase requirement and provided resources to strengthen enforcement of land-use regulations and building codes. These measures address important and persistent implementation challenges, but it remains to be seen whether they can withstand the enduring pressure for local growth and development that have compromised such efforts in the past. As of this writing, the program remains in debt, bringing in total premiums that will likely be insufficient to cover liabilities that are only expected to grow.[58]

The outcome reached here is far from the last word on what the NFIP will look like and how it will work. This particular re-reform of the NFIP represents a tentative political resolution to the competing demands made on the program—tentative because it must be reauthorized every five years, when these arrangements can change again. Existing law maintains the actuarial status of the NFIP, insuring natural hazard risk much like a private insurer in order to manage the incentives and responsibilities of individuals. However, it maintains its solidaristic commitment to providing guaranteed coverage and to keeping it within financial reach—no longer through subsidies based on risk, but through some new form of targeted assistance based on means. Some flood insurance experts have observed that actuarialism and affordability in the NFIP, given its embattled history, may be economically and politically incompatible.[59] In high-risk flood zones truly actuarial rates will be or become unaffordable for too many people, especially with climate risk accounted for, and every move in that direction has been and will be met with opposition, even as some communities face a future in which they will almost certainly be underwater. In March 2019, the Trump administration announced another proposed reform of the NFIP that would tie premiums to individually assessed flood risk, calling it "Risk Rating 2.0"—a move that climate advocates cheered. The plan would use private sector data to calculate the flood threat even more finely to each home, rather than relying on broad rating classes. About the proposal, FEMA's deputy associate administrator for insurance mitigation told Bloomberg News: "The new rating plan will help customers better understand their risks . . . Our effort is to improve our product and price it more fairly," the suggestion being that the fairest way to underwrite risk is to base it on individual circumstances. Reformatting risk assessment in this way could have the effect of reformatting the politics around it, by eroding the shared category of flood zone homeowner. But we may or may not find out; just a few months later, FEMA announced it was delaying the introduction of Risk Rating 2.0 "to conduct a comprehensive analysis of the proposed rating structure so as to protect policyholders and minimize any unintentional negative effects of the transition."[60] SmarterSafer and Stop FEMA Now remain active, watching congressional action on the NFIP closely and continuing to line up supporters on their respective sides of these issues.

Whether existing forms of flood insurance, disaster relief, and other natural hazards and disaster policy can organize a social response that adequately protects people in a world of increasingly intense and destructive hazards is an unsettled question. The NFIP is still in a perilous position, which was cast into sharp relief when claims from Hurricanes Harvey and Irma in 2017 again overwhelmed its claims capacity, driving it further into debt. In the wake of these catastrophes, public commentary on the NFIP also addressed larger existential questions about the physical and financial futures of America's floodplain communities. Should the state provide financial security for homes that private markets would never underwrite? What places, ways of life, and communities will, must, or should be lost, and what role will insurance play? We turn to these questions in the next chapter.

Chapter Five

FLOODPLAIN FUTURES

Trajectories of Loss

The problem of how to manage the costs of disaster losses is an old one. But today, in the face of a succession of catastrophic storms and floods, along with growing awareness of the prospect of even worse losses as climate change continues, we have reached a moment of ferment over the role of public and private insurers in managing shifting and intensifying hazards of all kinds. When Hurricanes Harvey, Irma, and Maria hit one after the other in the late summer of 2017, the combined claims drove the National Flood Insurance Program (NFIP) even further into debt. In the wake of these catastrophes, public commentary on flood insurance returned to a familiar set of flood insurance shortcomings—inaccurate maps, underpriced risk, continued (re)building in harm's way—but this time also addressed larger existential questions about the physical and financial futures of American communities. Climate change will undoubtedly continue to transform the nation's floodplains. This may make some places no longer livable in their current form, regardless of what happens with the NFIP. How should insurance then operate to govern human activity and decision-making in the present, in light of expectations for this kind of future, one in which the ground beneath our feet literally disappears? What role, if any, will or should insurance play in determining how and when retreat from the coasts takes place? How will evolving understandings of climate risk, shaped in large part by instruments like flood maps and insurance premiums, depreciate property values and erode the economic prosperity of individuals and communities in the nation's floodplains? Is insurance actually working to camouflage a climate change bubble in the housing market that, once recognized, could suddenly collapse the value of real estate investments and set off another financial crisis tied to housing? These questions reflect, fundamentally, a curiosity and an anxiety about the contours of loss in a climate-changed world: what will disappear, when and how; which areas or forms of habitation will be abandoned; who will be affected first and worst by loss; and how losses are linked together in ways that connect the fates of individuals, institutions, and even entire economic systems.

The normative questions about what insurance and other institutions of finance and governance *ought* to do in this context will be hotly contested in the years to come. This chapter examines the evidence so far on some of the empirical questions: Where are climate-related economic losses starting to appear, and who is beginning to feel the financial pressure? This evidence is just emerging and its implications are still taking shape. On the basis of this emerging evidence, the chapter outlines a few trajectories for floodplain futures and addresses the role that the NFIP, and insurance more broadly, might play in each of them, based on what we have learned about the social significance and moral economic stakes of flood insurance thus far. Each trajectory discussed here reflects different orientations to loss: the extent to which it is viewed as inevitable, manageable, or acceptable. These trajectories are not mutually exclusive or exhaustive and the developments that take place in different geographies will necessarily vary. But in any and all cases, there is nothing deterministic about how climate change will affect local economies and ways of life. Areas like floodplains face real threats but, as Kasia Paprocki argues, the anticipation of future climate crisis can sanction destruction (or protection) in the present. Climate change adaptation in pursuit of "ideal futures" can license material interventions that affect people's lives as profoundly as the threats themselves.[1] In the domain of insurance, the effects that are realized will reflect, in part, how political actors configure insurance to achieve different aims; how authorities respond to claims of what is fair or right in the face of collective, if unevenly experienced, perils; and how different interests mobilize imaginaries of climate change in pursuit of their desired outcomes.

CLIMATE-RELATED ECONOMIC LOSSES IN U.S. FLOODPLAINS

In the controversies surrounding the NFIP traced so far, we've seen home-owners and other stakeholders alarmed about the *possibility* of widespread declines in property values as flood hazards worsen and are reassessed and economized in insurance. They outlined the catastrophic effects of such declines in order to make claims about the fairness and appropriateness of insurance arrangements. But are these declines in fact already underway? What do we know about the relation between changing climatic conditions and the financial landscape in U.S. flood zones? Early evidence seems to show that floodplain property values in some areas are indeed already show-ing depreciation due to sea level rise and its effects on flooding, particu-larly in vulnerable coastal areas. In Miami-Dade County, Florida, for instance, researchers have found that the correlation between elevation and price appreciation of single-family homes has grown stronger since 2000; the appreciation in value of lower elevation homes has not kept up with the appreciation of higher elevation homes. The researchers interpret this as an early signal of a growing preference for properties perceived or observed to be less vulnerable to the "nuisance" or "sunny day" flooding that has begun to plague Miami-Dade.[2] Residents are getting sick of normal tidal flooding causing water to pool in streets and on sidewalks, overrun drainage sys-tems, snarl commutes, and complicate the normal rhythms of daily rou-tines. Another study of Miami-Dade found that the real estate market there lost $465 million in value from 2005 to 2016 due to tidal flooding from sea level rise, controlling for other economic trends like the housing crash that began in 2007 and the Great Recession that followed.[3]

While Miami-Dade is one of the most threatened metropolitan areas in the world, what's emerging there may reflect a more general trend. The researchers who looked at declines in Miami-Dade's total home value later applied their methodology to cover 9.2 million real estate transactions across Florida, South Carolina, North Carolina, Virginia, Georgia, New York, New Jersey, and Connecticut, and reported that $14.1 billion has been lost in home value across these states due to sea-level-rise flooding since

2005.[4] Another study of coastal counties nationwide concluded that properties within a quarter-mile from the coast and exposed to sea level rise sell for approximately seven percent less than otherwise similar properties. The "sea level rise discount" for these exposed properties has increased significantly over the past decade. It is also highest for non–owner-occupied homes, suggesting that it is investor-owners, looking for second (or third, or fourth) homes—not ordinary people in their primary residences—who are really starting to account for expectations of future losses due to climate factors. In counties that show high levels of "climate change worry," however, exposed owner-occupied properties also sell at an 8.5 percent discount.[5]

County-level data collected by Attom Data Solutions, a real estate data tracking firm, and made available to the New York Times also showed that in 2016, median home prices in high-risk flood areas were still 4.4 percent below where they were 10 years before, while home prices in low-risk areas were up 29.7 percent over the same period. Home sales in flood-prone areas also grew less quickly. The Times attributes this in part to the cost of flood insurance; local real estate agents in Atlantic City, New Jersey; Norfolk, Virginia; and St. Petersburg, Florida reported that increasing flood insurance premiums were already hurting home prices in their markets.[6] This may indeed be the case in the floodplains of New York City. Researchers looked at residential property transactions from 2003 to 2017 in order to study how Biggert-Waters (which increased premiums), Hurricane Sandy, and FEMA's new flood insurance rate maps affected home prices there. All three factors decreased sale prices, with the largest decreases on homes that were mapped in to the expanded high-risk flood zones, where flood insurance is mandatory for homeowners with mortgages. There, prices of homes that did not flood during Sandy but that were in the new flood zone fell by 11 percent.[7] A RAND study of flood insurance affordability in New York City, commissioned by the city government after Biggert-Waters, examined a range of scenarios related to property values and found that "the decline in value of some property in the current high-risk zone is so large that the property is almost worthless." Even in less extreme cases, "most affected homeowners are likely to see significant drops in the value of their home." New risk maps with corresponding increases to flood insurance premiums would represent "a significant financial loss to most homeowners" in the city's flood zones.[8]

WHO STANDS TO LOSE?

In American towns and cities, revenues that fund local public schools, road-building and maintenance, parks, public transportation, cops, and fire-fighters are raised in large part through property taxes, which in turn depend on property values. Given this connection between private property values and public life, when property values decline in an area, the losses ripple out to affect everyone. But who is affected directly? Who is paying more for insurance? Whose housing, and housing wealth, is threatened? The empirical answers to these questions have symbolic significance. As we saw in the previous chapter, while property owners of varying means were affected by the loss of subsidies, the politics of insurance turn largely on public perceptions of who stands to lose and whether they deserve sympathy and redress as a result. Will these increasing risks and costs going forward be a mere nuisance to rich beachfront homeowners, or are they a serious economic threat to ordinary Americans? Are we talking about people losing their second homes or their only homes?

The answer is that we're talking about both. Geographies of vulnerability and risk reflect locally specific histories of planning, land use, economic development, and housing policy. When we examine the areas facing the most serious threats from climate change—both hazards themselves and their economization through insurance—we are addressing the fates of both the privileged and the marginalized. Miami Beach, with its luxury high-rises, experiences flooding, but so do lower-income places like Canarsie in Brooklyn and the Kashmere Gardens neighborhood of Houston—areas that also have historically had relatively high rates of black homeownership. Coastal flooding affects second homes on the beach, and inland flooding often affects poor and working-class neighborhoods in industrial towns and cities that developed to take advantage of waterways.[9] About 72 percent of all NFIP policies are written for primary residences, meaning people's homes rather than investment or rental properties.[10] Among severe repetitive loss properties (properties that have been repeatedly rebuilt after floods), located in some of the most dangerous areas, 81 percent are single-family homes and 75 percent are modest, valued at less than $250,000, according to a 2017 analysis of FEMA data.[11] While both rich and poor places will be visited by the effects of climate change, the difference is in if and how they can respond. Some property owners can afford to modify their homes, to withstand higher floodwaters, stronger storms, more precipitation, and rising insurance premiums. Those who cannot are financially tied to houses that are at greater and greater peril. They can't afford the property-level risk mitigation that would save them money on rising NFIP premiums (recall that elevating a freestanding home in New York City costs about $100,000) and, if they can't sell those homes for any kind of financial return and move on, they are quite literally stuck in place, bracing for the next flood.

When it comes to the NFIP, recall that FEMA had to answer this question of who would be affected by a program-wide shift to actuarial rates that would "price in" worsening flood risks and higher expected losses. Who could afford these risk-based rates and who would need continued financial support of some kind? This commitment to finding an "affordability framework" for the NFIP was the outcome of the contestation examined in the previous chapter. Though this is new for the program, we have seen that since the NFIP's establishment, policymakers have always been interested in the affordability of flood insurance, in order to keep financial protection accessible to as many Americans as possible. Yet the operations of the NFIP were never indexed to what people earned or could spend; FEMA had never before collected data on how flood insurance was situated in the context of its policyholders' individual finances.

It ultimately did so by conducting a series of analyses that examined the intersections of U.S. Census data, Special Flood Hazard Areas, and NFIP policyholder data, to develop a picture of who is at risk and who has insurance, in terms of both income and mortgage status. The resulting April 2018 report found that generally incomes are lower inside high-risk flood zones than outside them, with the exception of a few states.[12] FEMA also determined that inside those flood zones, about 26 percent of NFIP residential policyholder households and 51 percent of nonpolicyholder households are low income, as defined by the U.S. Department of Housing and Urban Development (households with income less than 80 percent of their area median income). Twelve percent of homeowners with NFIP policies in high-risk flood zones are housing-cost-burdened, with a ratio of mortgage principal and interest payments, property taxes, and insurance (including flood insurance) to household income that exceeds 0.4, a standard used by the lending industry to assess housing affordability. In high-risk flood zones, more nonpolicyholders own their homes outright than have mortgages—meaning they are not legally required to have a flood policy in place. Yet they also have significantly lower incomes than their policyholder counterparts. What this suggests to FEMA is that a lot of people in flood zones are lower-income families who have either inherited their homes down the generations, or who are retirees. They are the people who are "particularly sensitive to the financial burden of flood insurance," according to FEMA. Flood insurance affordability is thus a particular concern for households that do not currently have flood insurance but who do face flood risk. On the basis of these findings, the report concluded, "The affordability of flood insurance represents a challenge for a greater number of households as FEMA moves closer to risk-based rates for currently discounted policies."[13]

Every state has communities that participate in the NFIP, but the highest numbers of policies are concentrated in the Atlantic and Gulf coast states, where there are large populations and significant lengths of vulnerable coastline. It's worthwhile to take a closer look at the socioeconomic dimensions of insurance for some of the communities in these states, where climate change and its insurance economization could dramatically transform the tenability of homeownership. We saw in chapter 2 the ways that changes to flood insurance would burden, in particular, communities of working-class families in New York City. Similar patterns emerge in other locations with high NFIP participation. Florida has the highest number of NFIP policies in place—around 1.5 million as of 2015—and in Miami-Dade, where researchers have observed property values changing in ways correlated with assessments of climate risk, geographer Zac J. Taylor has concluded that it is already cash-strapped families who are bearing higher-than-average financial burdens stemming from the insurance economization of hazards facing their homes. With a sociospatial analysis of the intersection of insurance costs and housing precarity, Taylor finds that some high housing-cost burdened municipalities already pay relatively higher rates for flood coverage. For instance, Miami Gardens, a largely black area, saw median household incomes decline by nearly 12 percent between 2011 and 2016. But households there pay the highest percentage of their income to flood insurance. Miami Gardens will have a hard time adapting as risks and insurance change. Much of Miami Gardens is at only three feet in elevation, below the six feet of sea level rise projected for the Miami region by 2100. Its housing stock is relatively old, too: more than 77 percent of properties were built prior to 1980, before land-use planning and building standards took effect, and the housing there is difficult to retrofit. In the case of both hurricane and flood insurance, some of the highest cost burdens are falling on communities where incomes have declined or recovered below the national average from 2011 to 2016. More generally across the area, Taylor finds significant overlap between zip codes with the highest rates of cost-burdened owner-occupied households (meaning households that spend more than 35 percent of their income on housing, inclusive of insurance) and those that have costs of insurance well above the state average. People of color are disproportionately residents of the neighborhoods where high insurance costs overlap with high housing costs for mortgage-holding households. Taylor also finds that wealthy- and second-home–dominated barrier island communities (with some of the highest coastal exposure) actually pay relative low average NFIP rates, which they note may reflect that residents in these areas are largely not relying on the program for coverage.[14]

Texas also has a high number of NFIP policies. In the Houston-Galveston region, Earthea Nance has found that increasing flood insurance rates, authorized under Biggert-Waters, indeed triggered real estate market devaluation, as experts expected and residents feared. But the areas facing the most significant impacts were disproportionately poor in Harris County and disproportionately poor and minority in Galveston County.[15] Beyond devalued homes, higher costs of insurance can act as a barrier to homeownership in the largely nonwhite areas that have suffered from legacies of discrimination in housing markets. The impacts of Biggert-Waters on some policyholders were, as we know, ultimately slowed down by further reform. But severe repetitive loss properties are already seeing large increases in premiums year-on-year, and risk-reflexive rating is the general direction of travel for the NFIP more broadly, and for private insurance for other natural hazards. Nance's analysis confirms that under such conditions it is the already marginalized who suffer first and worst. Compounding impacts of climate change, the expanding risks, enlarging risk zones, rising costs of premiums, and eroding property values work together to reinforce and reproduce existing patterns of inequality, hardship, and exclusion.

This evidence is just emerging and we have to interpret these results with caution. As with scientific understandings of how climate change transforms our physical and ecological world, precise economic estimates of changes in value and price, and their effects for different geographies and people, depend on how datasets are defined and delimited, variables and measures (like property values) are constituted, and assumptions are operationalized. The overall picture, however, is one of geographically and socially uneven change. Some market actors, situated in some property markets, may be internalizing information about and experience of climate risks in ways that erode the appeal of what might otherwise be considered an amenity: living near the water.[16] The attendant hardships will be most burdensome for those whose housing and economic security are already relatively precarious, in less affluent geographies where we are already seeing the financial pressures of rising insurance costs play out.

TRAJECTORIES OF FLOODPLAIN FUTURES

What are the possible trajectories for floodplain futures? In this section, I outline some trends and expectations, some changes that are already underway, and their emerging or expected effects, at scales ranging from individual livelihoods to the national economy. Some trajectories are premised on a vision of the future in which certain kinds of losses are inevitable. For instance, property devaluations and massive sell-offs *will* take place as markets, described almost "naturally," price-in more regular experiences of flood loss, estimates of current risk, and projections of future scenarios. Some areas simply must be depopulated and abandoned because they will be ruined: the waters are coming for them. Market actors will become increasingly cognizant of that and will act accordingly. Insurance is an institutional mechanism of that vision of transformative loss; diminishing insurance affordability and availability, reflecting worsening climatic conditions, means some floodplain futures will not be economically sustained. There will be loss and pain, but this cannot be avoided. In other trajectories, these losses are outcomes that must be resisted; land and property values must be defended and the appropriate strategy is to adapt in place, to rebuild and reengineer for resilience to further impacts of climate change. Insurance plays a role in this transformation, as well—by providing the incentives and resources to fund such investments. Understandings of what *should* happen are bound up with expectations of what *will* happen, with insurance occupying an ambiguous position and tethered to divergent commitments related to the acceptability and inevitability of certain kinds of loss. In reality, we are already beginning to see a mix of outcomes.

Systemic Loss: A Climate Change Real Estate Bubble Bursts—or Doesn't

Consider an expensive beachfront house that is highly likely to be submerged eventually, although "eventually" is difficult to pin down and may be a long way off. Will the value of the house decline gradually as the expected life of the house becomes shorter? Or, alternatively, will the value of the house—and all the houses around it—plunge the first time a lender refuses to make a mortgage on a nearby house or an insurer refuses to issue a homeowner's policy? Or will the trigger be one or two homeowners who decide to sell defensively?

These were the ponderous concluding questions of a short report titled *Life's a Beach*, posted to the website of Freddie Mac, the government-sponsored enterprise that purchases, guarantees, and securitizes mortgages, in April 2016. Taking as a premise that rising sea levels and spreading floodplains would destroy billions of dollars of property and displace millions of people, the question was then how systems of housing finance were implicated in and exposed to the resulting losses when the climate change bubble bursts. Freddie Mac likened the conditions facing lenders, servicers, insurers, investors, taxpayers, and homeowners to those that proved catastrophic during the most recent housing crisis and subsequent Great Recession. Specifically, home equity is still at the center of many Americans' economic security. Home construction, sales, and home-related expenditures still act as significant contributors to the national economy. Mortgage debt is still entangled in broader networks of financial risk transfer. In this context, if or when climate change vulnerability gets priced in to insurance premiums, property values, and real estate transactions—in other words, when a climate change housing price bubble pops—it could have ripple effects for the entire economy.

This time, however, the resulting economic losses and social disruption "are likely to be greater in total than those experienced in the housing crisis and Great Recession," in the view of Freddie Mac. Home values in the riskiest areas wouldn't just decline; they could plummet to zero. And unlike the last housing crisis, their owners could have no reasonable expectation that the value of their homes would ever recover. Entire areas might be "climate redlined"—deemed too risky to insure at all. Anecdotal accounts of would-be buyers spooking at high insurance costs would become more common across the United States. In the "inevitable sell-off," those who manage to get out early fare well enough. Those who do not get out in time will see huge destructions of wealth.[17] There is evidence that in recent years banks have increased the share of their mortgages in areas hit by hurricanes that they sell to Fannie Mae and Freddie Mac. Banks make loans in risky areas and move them off their books, in the process shifting the risk to taxpayers who back up Fannie and Freddie.[18] As a 2016 *New York Times* article put it: "Like a game of hot potato, builders, homeowners, banks, flood insurers and buyers of securitized mortgages try to hand off risky properties before getting burned. Developers erect houses and sell them typically within a couple of years, long before their investments depreciate. Banks earn commissions even on risky home loans before bundling these mortgages into securities and selling them to large pension funds, insurers or other buyers."[19] Taxpayers would potentially be in the position of bailing out the financial industry yet again. The physical effects of climate change would be locally devastating, but the potential economic losses would be nationally calamitous. In this way, floodplain futures are national futures.

If, when, and how this systemic loss manifests depends on a complex mix of interacting conditions. One piece of this relates to the vagaries of individual cognition and unevenly evolving perceptions of the threat climate change poses to homes; as Freddie Mac wonders, when, if ever, will a large number of market actors question the fundamental value of assets located in harm's way? The temporal ambiguities of climate change itself make this hard to know. Individual and collective market actors operate with their own notions of how seriously to take climate change in the context of real estate decision-making. Those who expect significant sea level rise within the time horizon of a conventional thirty-year mortgage, for instance, will likely draw different conclusions about the viability of life and investment in a coastal floodplain compared to those who think of climate change as a problem of 2100, or to those who don't believe in it at all. Confidence in the ability of governments and engineers to solve the problem, either through mitigating climate change's worst effects or investing in adaptive infrastructure, may also buoy expectations in ways that prevent or forestall the bubble from bursting—or even cause it to grow.

Another element at play is the activity of the real estate industry, which structures how other market actors receive and interpret information about the value of property generally and how this might interact with climate conditions specifically. Some states have pushed to impose rules on real estate agents and property sellers that obligate them to disclose climate-related damage to properties for sale, but in others the burden of discovery falls entirely to the prospective buyer, who may not know what information to ask for, or to ask at all.[20] For privacy reasons, FEMA does not reveal a property's flood insurance claim history to anyone other than the owner. Local authorities also do not disclose the addresses of repetitive loss properties.[21] This may explain the finding noted earlier, about investor-owners being the first to price the effects of expected sea level rise exposure. Economists view such buyers as more "sophisticated"; they are more likely to have enlisted expert professionals whose job it is to assess prospective transactions for these and other kinds of risks. They know what to look for and can find, and pay for, the hard-to-gather information. Where information about previous flood or other climate-related damage is obscured, however, conditions prevail that allow some buyers to continue investing in homes that may be underwater, physically or financially, before too long. The economists who produced that study concluded that the "absence of a current house price discount in less sophisticated market segments raises the possibility of a large wealth shock to coastal communities."[22]

In a vision of floodplain futures in which the climate bubble bursts, the federal government continues to move toward actuarial rating of flood insurance and, in coastal areas vulnerable to catastrophic storms and hurricanes, the costs of private wind insurance policies also continue to rise in line with views of increasing risk. In other words, insurance functions as economists expect it does and believe it ought to: as a relay of objective information about risk to markets. It is a fundamental force in the devaluation of coastal and other vulnerable property, on however uncertain a timeline. However, we know now, of course, that policymakers intervene in ways that blunt the force of property devaluations. This has been a dynamic endemic to the NFIP, most conspicuously in recent history with the controversy over Biggert-Waters and its mandate to phase out subsidies and end the grandfathering of below-risk rates. In these periodic battles over flood insurance, homeowners and local and state officials make other kinds of claims about what insurance is and ought to do. They articulate more solidaristic insurance imaginaries that foreground the role of insurance in providing economic security and sustaining communities' continued economic vitality, to argue in favor of arrangements that keep premiums affordable. Pricing people out, even when they are in danger of being washed out, registers almost as an illegal taking of property, in a broader political and cultural context in which homeowners have always relied on the government to protect homeownership and investments in property.[23]

In the context of private insurance for other climate-related perils, like wind damage from storms and hurricanes, policymakers also have a track record of taking measures that preserve the affordability of private insurance for consumers, while at the same time maintaining the desirability of at-risk property for private insurers and reinsurers. In Florida, for instance, Taylor shows how a variety of public policies work to sustain and even grow private risk capital flows, which taken together keeps insurance underwriting and builders building in hazardous flood- and hurricane-prone areas. The state acts as a central market-maker, performing norms and adopting regulations that place the use of insurance-linked securities and other risk capital products at the center of its risk management practices. It has worked actively to source risk for private markets, while also securing that risk by maintaining public backstops to socialize the costs of any market failures that might occur as a consequence.[24] Other researchers have also documented how Florida policymakers have intervened at the level of catastrophe modeling and rate-making in order to adjust how, whether, or the extent to which intensifying risks can be telegraphed to homeowners, taxpayers, and consumers through increased insurance premiums. The devastating hurricane seasons of 2004 and 2005 led catastrophe risk-modeling firms to change the way they projected future hurricane losses, but the cost and political implications of intensified risk estimates in Florida ultimately led the state to push for multiple risk models, set at multiple time horizons, allowing different models to be used for different purposes (similar to the multiple maps we saw in New York City in chapter 3), ultimately preventing dramatic price hikes on constituents.[25] At the same time, the Florida legislature passed a bill that not only limited consumer rate increases, but also required the state's public insurer to extend coverage to homeowners who were refused private policies, in this way using the public insurer "as a means to deflect market judgments of risk when they threaten the state's economy."[26]

In short, the interconnectedness of housing finance, of which insurance is a major part, with larger financial systems indeed means that the bursting of a climate bubble in housing prices would send shockwaves through regional economies and potentially beyond. In this scenario, insurance effects this transformation through assimilating information about changing risks, economizing hazards to and decisions about property, and operating only in markets where losses can be financially managed. However, this almost naturalistic understanding of how the logic of insurance does or should play out is belied by, first, the activities of a number of powerful actors and institutions which militate against the bursting of a climate bubble, or at least might manage it into a slow deflation rather than a pop. This preserves something like a status quo in which housing and real estate can continue to act as a major economic engine. Second, we know also that policymakers and officials often respond to moral economy claims about the fairness of losses in ways that circumscribe the operations of risk assessment and economization.

As in the crisis of 2007–2008, highlighting the systemic economic losses of climate change can obscure high degrees of variation in individual outcomes. Decreasing insurance availability and affordability will be punitive for property owners in the middle and working class who need mortgage approval to acquire assets and build wealth over time. They will be squeezed out of housing markets if they can't afford or access the insurance necessary to get such approval. For the rich, however, the ability to buy in cash exempts them from these requirements and, should they want insurance, their ample resources assure they can access it at any price (a small but growing private flood insurance market does exist, with much of the business focused on underwriting especially valuable properties). They can continue to buy and (re)build. In major coastal cities especially, building booms on the waterfront are fueled in part by wealthy global elites from all over the world, whose cash can transform neighborhoods in ways that make them luxury part-time hangouts, at the expense of longtime residents and communities.[27] This outcome is one manifestation of another trajectory: something scholars, journalists, and activists have started to call "climate gentrification."

Loss of Community: Climate Gentrification

Houston was still in ruins after Hurricane Harvey when signs advertising buyouts for flooded homes first started appearing in some neighborhoods. If you were the owner of such a home and you called the phone numbers for more information, you were likely offered terms of sale at dimes or pennies on the dollar. But the promise of immediate cash for structures in any condition, even houses that were then uninhabitable, could be a tempting proposition, especially if you lived in one of the lower-income neighborhoods that the buyers targeted. These buyers were a combination of small and large investors: some local residents-turned-house-flippers and some Wall Street speculators, all of whom saw economic opportunity in rain-lashed subdivisions, even those expected to experience similarly destructive floods in the years ahead. They could buy these ruined homes, fix them up to a higher flood-resilient standard (and advertise this feature as an amenity), and sell them for a tidy profit—or rent them to former homeowners. In the process, they reasoned, they were helping homeowners who could no longer afford to own property there to "move on," while also providing the financing to redevelop Houston to withstand future floods.[28] Important and desirable social good, with some financial upside for the savvy and entrepreneurial, could be reaped from this landscape of loss.

Further effects of climate change can work to effect, hasten, or exacerbate socioeconomic transformations of floodplain areas that redistribute wealth, change the distribution of affordable housing, and push lower-income and longtime residents out. In other words, climate change interacts in complex ways with existing patterns of gentrification. What happened in the days and weeks following Harvey is one pathway of climate gentrification: a major disaster provides a catalyst for turnover in housing ownership, the destruction of housing wealth—particularly for those whose homeownership was already precarious—and the displacement of existing residents in favor of wealthier ones. But such changes can also take place in the absence of the major destruction of property that comes with catastrophic weather events. Jesse Keenan, Thomas Hill, and Anurag Gumber, who found the evidence of faster appreciation of higher-elevation homes in Miami discussed earlier, identify three pathways to climate gentrification. In the first, lower-risk properties surge in value, fueling migration from high-exposure areas and attracting capital, and causing displacement in those lower-risk areas. This is what the researchers suspect is happening in Miami: increasingly common nuisance flooding in Miami Beach is driving real estate developers to higher elevation inland areas like Little Haiti, home to Afro-Caribbean and Latino residents who were historically excluded from once-enticing beachfront areas through decades of discriminatory real estate practices. Now, with new developments coming in, rents are rising, making it less livable for both longtime residents and new waves of immigrants who would normally settle there.[29] Something like an NFIP flood insurance rate map can be influential in these circumstances, redirecting flows of people and money through its visualization of risk and its classification of different geographic zones. The rich move to avoid loss and dispossess poorer people in the process.

In the second pathway to climate gentrification, living in high-exposure areas gets so expensive, only relatively rich people can continue to live there. Areas that were once mixed-income become more exclusive. A number of factors can contribute to this and, again, insurance is of crucial significance. Rising premiums for flood and wind insurance can push annual household costs beyond what some lower-to-moderate income families can feasibly sustain. Stricter building requirements, often tied to insurance as conditions of coverage, can make homes more expensive to construct or retrofit in order to maintain compliance with codes. Local governments may also increase taxes in order to raise revenues for climate change adaptation and protective infrastructure. As some families leave, their homes may be replaced with climate-resilient homes that only the wealthy can afford.[30] As we saw in chapter 2, this may be what is taking hold in parts of New York City, where the city government has offered to buy out floodplain homeowners, while reserving the right to redevelop the land. Houses have been knocked down and new luxury condo developments have gone up in some of the riskiest flood zones. Owing to post-Sandy building requirements, these developments incorporate features like storm surge buffers and absorbent green space, features that offer "more individuated building-level defensibility and longevity." In the process, the neighborhoods become less affordable and it's not clear where those who sold to the city can afford to move next.[31]

The third pathway to climate gentrification involves the unintended consequences of public investments in infrastructure, which can work to increase land and property values and wind up displacing populations. This pathway resembles what some scholars have described as "green gentrification" or "environmental gentrification," whereby the creation of urban parks and green space, the planting of trees, and the adoption of other "sustainability" amenities attract an influx of affluent residents.[32] Climate-resilience investments may be a new breed of such amenities.[33] As cities like New York, Boston, New Orleans, and San Francisco invest in flood defenses, the areas protected by them become more attractive places to live, driving new waves of demand that can price out poorer residents. Here, too, insurance is playing an emergent role. In a study of urban resilience initiatives in U.S. cities, Stephen Collier and Savannah Cox find that public authorities work with private insurance companies to access otherwise elusive financing and expertise for planning and undertaking initiatives related to retrofitting, disaster recovery, and new climate change adaptation infrastructure of various kinds.[34]

In a given floodplain, these pathways may combine with each other and with the other long-standing patterns of development, investment, neglect, and marginalization that have fed local manifestations of gentrification more generally throughout the United States. And like gentrification more generally, the floodplain areas facing these potential trajectories are places that can generate or maintain some appeal—in this case, in spite of their escalating hazards. People want to live on or near the beaches of Miami. They want the views afforded by the waterfronts of New York City. Miami and New York City will not be lost, but their constitutive neighborhoods will be transformed as some residents lose connections to their communities, with little in the way of high-quality affordable housing available elsewhere, in favor of new developments and new residents. In areas without these amenities, increasing exposure to hazards and increasing costs of insurance may not be met with the same kinds of investments to make vulnerable areas livable for at least a little bit longer, albeit only for some. This orients us to other possible floodplain futures, defined by difficult decisions related to who or what can be protected and what should or must be lost.

Loss of Place: Retreat from the Floodplain

Climate variability and environmental change, or their manifestations in changing economic realities, can lead people to abandon places. Another floodplain trajectory is one in which waterfronts and floodplains become active sites of destructive transformation, depopulated before they are permanently underwater. In some cases, this will feel coercive and traumatic. In recent years, media outlets have started telling the stories of American "climate refugees," once a designation reserved only for poorer people living in poorer parts of the world and fleeing extreme forms of deprivation, starvation, and ecological collapse.[35] In 2018, *The Guardian* declared: "America's era of climate mass migration is here." The article and others like it have told the stories of Americans abandoning their repeatedly flooded homes. They are sick of the water, can't access insurance or comply with its requirements, and lack the personal resources to make themselves safer. Their communities aren't investing in flood protection, either. These dispatches convey the sense of mourning that comes with feeling pushed out of one's home and away from cherished places, as well as the desperation of having to figure out what to do next when you are largely on your own.[36]

The situation can be just as difficult to bear under circumstances of "managed retreat": coordinated, collective efforts to move away from soggy—and increasingly expensive—areas. Residents of Isle de Jean Charles, Louisiana, a narrow strip of land that is one-tenth of the size it was less than fifty years ago, received the first "climate resilience" grant—$48 million—to resettle on drier land. Many of the residents are indigenous people of the Biloxi-Chitimacha-Choctaw tribe; their tribal chief had been pushing for relocation for nearly twenty years by the time the grant was awarded. About the impending move, one resident told the writer Elizabeth Rush: "I mean really we are talking about having to choose to move away from our ancestral home. I know a lot of people figure we would be celebrating, to be moving to firmer ground and all. But it's not like I threw a party when I heard about the relocation. I'll be leaving a place that has been home to my family for right under two hundred years . . . We're actually leaving the place where we belong."[37] In 2020, the Trump administration started pushing evictions from flood zones, by tying federal aid to requirements that local governments use eminent domain to take and demolish private property facing high risk—making managed retreat mandatory rather than voluntary.[38]

The loss of place can, however, take on a different emotional valence, one of noble sacrifice in pursuit of a greater good. Loss of place may indeed always be a hard experience because change is hard, but in the context of climate change not every managed retreat is traumatic and not every loss of place is met defensively. In several Staten Island neighborhoods devasted by Hurricane Sandy and where flood insurance premiums were on the rise, for example, local residents organized for their own community's dispersal, mobilizing to unbuild their own homes. They worked actively to produce their own loss, according to economically and morally acceptable terms. Staten Islanders successfully pushed the governor of New York to implement and expand a buyout program that would purchase and demolish their homes, with the condition that new structures could not be built in these hazardous areas. In her ethnography of the buyouts, Liz Koslov describes how retreating residents felt they were the agents who would finally and prudently undo the "costly and destructive mistake" of building on the Island's wetlands in the first place, "righting past wrongs regardless of what the future had in store."[39] Though they faced loss, the Staten Island buyout groups made meaning out of the experience in which they were heroic and responsible. They would be doing a greater service to their "forgotten borough" by taking on the challenges of relocating, as the restored wetlands would provide more natural protection from future floods for those residents who remained. Their place would be lost—sacrificed, really— to protect or promote other cherished things and ideals.

However, the Staten Islanders' sense of honor and of being left whole, even as they lost, as well as their ability to plan in this way for a climate-changed future, was structured in important ways by the willingness of politicians to extend generous terms to this largely white, politically active, middle-class, property-owning enclave.[40] Buyouts, like other forms of disaster assistance, can work to reproduce or even worsen existing racialized inequalities between residents and communities. Researchers have found that Houston-area participants in FEMA's hazard mitigation program following Hurricane Harvey were able to use buyouts as an opportunity to pursue racialized projects of social mobility, using the resources to move to nearby areas that were on average 34 percent whiter and 32 percent wealthier than their old neighborhoods.[41] Another study of 40,000 voluntary FEMA-funded buyouts across the country found that those buyouts were disproportionately located in more populous and prosperous counties; the authors attribute this to wealthier counties having the resources and expertise to make it through an intense series of bureaucratic requirements to participate in the program.[42] This results in lengthy waiting times for a buyout to be complete—more than five years for most FEMA-funded buyouts—which lower-income residents in flood-prone areas cannot easily withstand.[43] In other vulnerable floodplains, like those that are home to indigenous Alaskan native communities, people have been unable to move, despite repeated and resounding community support for doing so. One of these communities, Shishmaref, has voted to relocate but can't afford its local share of the moving costs. And the vote to move has justified further neglect and disinvestment in the community, compounding its vulnerability to future disasters.[44]

The mobilization on Staten Island was borne of the devastation of Hurricane Sandy, but also by the pressures of flood insurance. As discussed throughout this book, the NFIP treats flood risk as, in some respects, a problem that can be individually "owned" and addressed at the level of individual properties. Rather than pursue uncoordinated "sell-offs" motivated by insurance-led devaluation of their homes, Staten Islanders turned the combined experiences of many homeowners facing agonizing individual choices into collective claims for resources and redress. Though it was directed toward a different end, this was the same dynamic that characterized the efforts of Stop FEMA Now. Insurance as a governance tool can't help communities of homeowners make sense of a loss, but from these examples we can see how, in some floodplain futures, insurance arrangements might lead those facing private struggles to articulate and mobilize flood loss—and sometimes climate change more broadly—as a public problem. In Staten Island's floodplain, the solution to that problem was sacrifice. In others, it may be to defend or even grow in the floodplain.

Refuse to Lose: Defending and Growing in the Floodplains

While Staten Islanders retreat from the waterfront, other floodplain communities may find, in the sum of many individual grievances, a persuasive rationale for spending money on flood protection and other mitigation measures meant to keep the water at bay.[45] The NFIP itself rewards these initiatives through its voluntary Community Rating System (CRS), which provides community-wide discounts of up to 45 percent for all policyholders if the community institutes one or more of a set of FEMA-approved floodplain management policies. Over the last few years, New Haven,

Connecticut, for example, built seawalls and invested in maintenance of its storm drain system in order to save its residents money on their flood policies.[46] Several communities in New Jersey enrolled in the CRS after Hurricane Sandy and after it received new flood insurance rate maps.[47]

In this trajectory, certain kinds of losses are unacceptable and are not inevitable if only money can be found to create the conditions—physical and economic—that will allow people to stay where they are, at least for a while. The fates of different floodplains diverge. Communities, like their residents, have different fortunes, different amounts of revenues to spend on financing their own resilience. Municipalities with wealthier tax bases— that is, municipalities that can raise higher revenues—can avail themselves more easily of the expertise and technical capacity that are often needed in order to plan and build complicated engineering projects that can protect high-risk areas. Poorer communities, by contrast, may have to cut other public services or take on crippling debt to fund risk mitigation and adaptation. Some communities will be attractive to private (re)insurance companies looking to sell catastrophe or resilience bonds and other forms of financing; others won't.[48] Even within the same cities, communities and neighborhoods will fare differently. In New York City, a $1 billion floodwall to protect Lower Manhattan—with its high concentration of extremely valuable commercial real estate—is under construction. In the outer borough neighborhoods of Coney Island and the Rockaways, money hasn't gone toward long-term mitigation or storm protection at anything close to the same scale.

When communities go looking to the federal government for financial and technical support, they find that there is no clear national policy for who gets help, or what kind, to protect their floodplains or to adapt in place. For instance, Congress chooses which Army Corps of Engineers projects to fund on an ad hoc basis, and many more projects get approved than are ultimately funded and built.[49] Cost-benefit analysis is central to determining the feasibility of projects and their eligibility for funding, which means there is a lot at stake in determinations of what qualifies as a cost versus a benefit, and to whom. In another extremely vulnerable Louisiana village, Jean Lafitte, which is sinking into the Gulf of Mexico, the mayor has tried to game these calculations by securing so much public investment that Jean Lafitte would "eventually become too valuable to abandon." But it is unclear if he will succeed in attracting federal support to defend his 7,000 constituents from encroaching waters. Historically, the Army Corps' priority has instead been to protect New Orleans, its West Bank suburbs, and Louisiana's ports, essential to the country's petrochemical production. Feasibility studies have repeatedly concluded that defending Lafitte was "not economically justifiable."[50] In a language of economic common sense, cost-benefit analysis directs federal resources for defense toward some floodplains and away from others, and some communities have a harder time making the case for the value of their continued existence as they face intensifying threats of loss.[51]

In some floodplain futures, the vision is one of not only protecting what is already there, but also of continuing to grow and (re)develop. In New York City, for instance, even as Staten Island was unbuilding, 12,350 apartments, in about 150 new residential buildings, were under construction or planned to be built elsewhere in the city's riskiest flood zones as of July 2018, following more than 9100 units built in the past four years in those zones. Over 97 percent of the new buildings under construction in the floodplain are in areas that were underwater during Hurricane Sandy.[52] This kind of new building in the floodplain appears to be emblematic of a broader national trend. Across the country, tens of thousands of houses have been built in areas at risk of chronic future flooding. From 2010 to 2016, housing growth rates were faster inside coastal risk zones than outside, in more than half of the country's coastal states.[53] While some floodplains depopulate, others may become denser than ever. Such a trajectory corresponds to observed historical patterns. Following "billion-dollar" storms in the early 1990s, disaster zones experienced significant demographic and housing growth.[54] Research has shown that greater property damage from natural hazards tends to accelerate local land development. This can unfold as an "uneven redevelopment" that fortifies affluent neighborhoods and shores up high-end industries, while neglecting and deepening the disadvantage faced by low-income, disproportionately nonwhite communities, workers, and small businesses.[55]

These building booms may seem counterintuitive, even reckless, on their face. But they can be an intelligible strategy given the prevailing structure of public revenue arrangements in states and cities, which may encourage growth *in order to* avoid catastrophic future losses. Public revenues, which could be allocated to building or retrofitting infrastructure for climate change adaptation or resilience, often rely heavily on property taxes.

Florida, where there is also no state income tax, is in some ways the most extreme example of this. In order to raise revenue, policymakers there either have to raise property taxes—never a popular measure—or continue to build more and more expensive real estate that can then be tax-assessed.[56] These revenues are essential for precisely the kinds of major infrastructure investments that are needed to protect people and property from the already observed and coming effects of climate change. Taylor calls this a "grow to defend" climate adaptation finance model.[57] Building more is what not only allows states, towns, and cities to finance mitigation, but it also limits the extent to which residents are burdened by those costs. And if new developments are built with "flood-proof" features that can then be marketed as amenities, then the real estate industry profits while local officials also get to brag about the new climate resilience bona fides of their towns and cities. This sustains a vision of floodplain futures premised on continued growth and real estate development, even as the climate changes.

Insurance is a key institutional mechanism of transformation in this floodplain future, as well. While the NFIP is ostensibly meant to discourage building in harm's way, the broader world of insurance technologies and commercial products can operate toward opposite ends. As briefly mentioned, financial innovations in (re)insurance, particularly the creation and proliferation of insurance-linked securities (ILS), has made possible the continued underwriting of property and the building of new developments, even when exposed to considerable hazards. ILS instruments do this by securitizing property catastrophe risks and transferring them to capital markets, where they are sold to capital market investors like pension funds. Securitization transforms insured real estate risk into a lucrative asset class—making climate change a market opportunity rather than a peril. At the same time, as Taylor analyses in the Florida context, by transferring the prospect of major real estate devaluation from (re)insurers to global risk capital markets, securitization also facilitates the reproduction of risky real estate. (Re)insurers go looking for risky properties to underwrite *in order to* pass them on in the form of catastrophe bonds and other alternative risk transfer products. They "underwrite to securitize," in much the same way that mortgage lenders "originated to securitize" in the run-up to the global financial crisis. More building in floodplains and hurricane zones means more risk that can be commoditized, securitized, and sold. The resulting built environment is secured, at least insofar as it has insurance policies in place for future losses, but this security is necessarily selective—those places and properties deemed undesirable for these types of capital transactions will not be able to access private networks of indemnification.[58]

CONCLUSION

Again, these floodplain futures are not mutually exclusive, and we find evidence of each of them taking hold in different areas of the country. In many ways, these trajectories are linked. Considering them together provides a way to inform a preliminary sense of the roles insurance might play in a climate-changed future. The fact that there are multiple roles for insurance, and the possibility of their realizing contradictory ends, highlights that insurance is not one coherent thing that works in only one way. In some visions of the future, insurance shapes a climate-changed world by acting as a signaling mechanism of ostensibly objective risks to property, revealing a climate change bubble, influencing market transactions, redistributing people and capital across vulnerable landscapes, and gentrifying neighborhoods in the process. In other visions, insurance provides the political animus to make collective claims for retreating from or defending the floodplain. It offers the resources and incentives to continue growing. Actors can look to insurance to format and organize climate-related loss in different ways, harnessing it to interventions that target individual and collective security as the climate continues to change. Social struggles over floodplain futures will be, in part, fights over the legitimate arrangement of insurance costs, protections, incentives, and regulations. There is nothing inherent in insurance that indicates the kind of political project in which it is enlisted. Rather, actors relate to new costs and changing property values in light of their understandings of what can or should be sacrificed, and what can or must be defended, and the rightness or wrongness of doing either.

CONCLUSION

What Do We Have to Lose?

The storm shattered the state's rainfall records. The National Weather Service issued an advisory notice warning of "life-threatening storm surges" and "catastrophic" flooding. Homes, roads, schools, and churches were engulfed, trees toppled and cars were carried blocks away from where their owners had parked them. People all over the state lost power and utility companies were not sure how long it would take to restore it. Neighbors with boats took to the muddy, polluted floodwaters to conduct impromptu rescues. Everyone seemed to be saying they'd never seen anything like it before.[1]

Eventually, the storm passed. The rain stopped. As residents returned to the barely recognizable ruins of what had once been their homes, as they mucked out, stripped moldy walls and carpets, took inventory of all the possessions they had lost, many would find that they did not have the resources to recover. Only a small fraction had a flood insurance policy in place at the time of the storm. Many were not in officially designated high-risk flood zones and so were not required to carry an NFIP policy. Some could not afford the premiums. Others did not know about the flood risk facing their homes.[2] Disaster relief would surely come—given the way it has become practically a right of citizenship for homeowners in the wake of catastrophic floods—but the average payout per resident was likely to be a few thousand dollars, a drop in the bucket relative to what was needed.[3] People would have to raid college funds, retirement savings, borrow from friends and family. Homeowners worried about continuing to make their mortgage payments. Some would consider selling, but their property values, even for a repaired and rebuilt home, had taken a hit. They were no longer physically underwater—the floodwaters had receded—but their homes might soon be financially underwater.

This reads like a summary of the events chronicled in this book. But this is not a description of the aftermath of Hurricane Sandy; these were the outlines of Hurricane Florence, which battered the Carolinas six years later, in September 2018. We could also be describing Hurricanes Harvey, Irma, Maria, and Matthew in the years in between: all historic storms that produced catastrophic floods, physically and economically devastating their victims. And in their aftermath, a familiar variety of bewildering considerations related to current risk and future conditions, recovery, and rebuilding, weighed in relation to the way the NFIP manages flood risk and loss.

The catastrophes keep coming; the losses keep mounting. While climate scientists are reluctant to attribute any single event to climate change, they agree that global warming has taken place and that increases in air and water temperatures have led to rising sea levels, stronger storms, higher wind speeds, and heavier precipitation. Hazards have already worsened. In a climate-changed United States, the NFIP has established a particular distribution of responsibilities for loss, without actors in that world consistently having to mobilize climate change as such. Something like observed (rather than projected) sea level rise can be accounted for even in "backward facing" risk-reflexive insurance tools when a flood insurance rate map gets updated to reflect changes to an area's topography. Since Palmer's neighborhood was first mapped by FEMA in the early 1980s, sea levels have risen several inches.[4] The NFIP is in this way a kind of financial first-responder to climate risk, already working, however inconsistently and haltingly, to price in changes to the landscape and pass them on to property owners. Americans may remain divided and in denial about climate change or what to do about it, but the bill for insurance premiums comes due every year. This book has argued that if we want to understand how climate change is and will continue to impact people, communities, and governments, we need to understand and trace the contested operations of insurance institutions.

What then have we learned about loss and climate change from analyzing flood insurance? In a potentially traumatic and watery world, the destabilizing losses that individuals, families, communities, cities, and countries face have to do not only with the land literally disappearing beneath our feet, or storm surge knocking down our homes; these losses also issue from the economic arrangements societies have in place to manage worsening hazards. There are losses due to floods, when things get drenched and destroyed. And there are losses due to being priced out of a risky neighborhood, or seeing a decline in property values, or having one's expectations and obligations upended. These losses—experienced or expected—interact to shape the demands that people make on the institutions that govern their lives and, as a result, how and with what effects insurance programs assess, economize, and distribute the burdens of living with natural hazards and disasters. Climate change will undoubtedly generate losses of various kinds, but not in a deterministic fashion. When people contest and reconfigure insurance technologies, practices, and terms, they shape the course that those losses can take. And they do so on the basis of claims about what is fair, prudent, just, deserved, or equitable. From the story of the NFIP, we learn that when people interact with insurance, they are grappling not simply with technocratic problems of risk: with how to measure it and price it, or how to make—or get others to make—rational decisions about it. Though it is these issues that are the recurrent focus of commentary and reform, this book has shown that when actors experience insurance and encounter its technologies, they are facing broader and more troubling political and moral questions. The issue is not chiefly one of taking flood risk seriously or of wanting to make individuals and communities more secure, physically and financially, in a world where hazards worsen. People often agree about that as a general principle. Instead, it is a challenge of sorting out everyone's roles in preparing for that world, a world where some individual and collective fortunes may decline, in which some beloved places may disappear when they become too dangerous or too costly to protect or insure, in which our prevailing social contracts for distributing risks and responsibilities, burdens and benefits, face new kinds of strain. In brief, though flood insurance is often treated as principally about the problem of how to live with water, I've shown that at its core, flood insurance is about how we live with each other: the terms upon which we organize our interdependence.

The NFIP long predates the appearance of climate change in public discourse and policymaking. But from its history, we can appreciate that dealing with mounting losses due to climate change will mean dealing with unavoidable issues of moral economy. This is true even when we are thinking about loss the way that flood experts and insurers do: as the destruction of assets and the costs of protecting and replacing them, the kinds of losses that are measured, costed, and compensated in dollar terms. We saw this in chapter 1, when the magnitude of flood loss became a public problem that demanded new kinds of national responses. Policymakers and flood experts worked to fashion an insurance program that could, in theory, efficiently and cost-effectively compensate those who had lost, while at the same time working to stem overall flood losses over time, by acting through the economic calculations of individual decision-makers. Even when they spoke in hard-nosed technocratic language of efficiency and objectivity, they sought to inculcate particular ethics of individualized rationality, prudence, and taking care, held up as desirable and virtuous behavior. Policymakers had to evaluate those plans, and design the terms of the new NFIP, in light of other commitments related to what was owed to existing floodplain residents and what could be fairly expected of them. They arrived at a new settlement of responsibility for loss, in which causal understandings of floods changed, as did mechanisms of accountability. The federal government took on responsibility for producing and providing information about floods, now assessed in terms of risk and cost, and individuals and local communities were expected to make rational calculations on that basis.

By following the NFIP out of the halls of Congress and onto the streets of New York City, we saw in chapter 2 that when people interact with insurance, they also confront other kinds of real and potential losses. Insurance provides a terrain not simply for working out whether, how, and when the loss of a house can be dealt with financially, but also one for facing losses that can never be recouped, from which people feel they may never recover. The changing arrangements of the NFIP raised the possibility that some New Yorkers would be priced out of neighborhoods they loved, severed from connections that were sources of security, meaning, and identity. The values that felt imperiled were not only financial, but also social, emotional, and moral. Flood risk was also not the only thing that threatened them with loss; in fact, flood insurance itself became a recognized potential source of loss as new flood insurance rate maps came to seem "scarier than another storm." These vernacular experiences and understandings of loss shape how people respond to changing landscapes of flood risk and its cost, what they seek to protect, and whether they feel more or less secure as climate change unfolds.

Loss is of course a very real experience, of serious material consequence to individuals, communities, and governments. But loss is also defined as a problem on the basis of particular knowledge practices related to risk and its expected cost. Conventional treatments of the NFIP, and discussions of climate risk more broadly, tend to treat flood risk and its cost as straightforward measures: representations of the scale and spatial location of the problem of loss that need to be made as objective and accurate as possible. Chapter 3 dispensed with the taken-for-granted character of risk and cost, getting into the production of flood insurance rate maps and insurance premiums in order to examine how they produce knowledge about loss and format particular actions, such as elevating a home or relocating, by particular actors, as meaningful responses. The actors who design, produce, and deploy these technologies encode judgments about the parameters that are relevant to their estimations and leave other factors out. People may make divergent judgments, on the basis of equally technical or scientific data and methods, as we saw with New York City's appeal of its new flood insurance rate maps. The maps also helped to organize political identities; the boundaries of the flood zones drew lines around a constituency of flood zone homeowners who mobilized to shape practices of risk assessment and economization. When it comes to accounting for climate change in the parameters of how we define and know loss, the outcome of two maps, which do different kinds of political work, illustrates that these technologies do not simply reflect changing conditions of loss, more or less accurately. Instead, they establish a vision of loss that various stakeholders can accept as reasonable, in light of how it aligns with expectations about who should do what and when—in other words, who is or can be made responsible for loss.

In chapter 4, we saw questions of responsibility for loss take center stage in the national-level controversy over flood insurance reform. This discussion of what to do next about the NFIP became a larger conversation in which environmentalists, right-leaning political groups, homeowners, and insurance and real estate interests debated issues of public liabilities and collective resources, obligations to compensate flood victims and protect homeowners, the significance of socioeconomic differences among policy-holders, and the government's ability to map and price risk. Stop FEMA Now organized variegated and complex experiences of loss on the ground, of the type that emerged in New York City after Hurricane Sandy, into polit-ically potent claims for revisiting the new terms of flood insurance set in motion by NFIP reforms. At stake were competing ideas about whose losses mattered, whether it was the so-called deserving or undeserving who were facing loss, as well as about the extent to which individual homeowners had been agents in their own losses, through the choices they made. Parties to the reform, on either side, did not dispute the reality of flood risk or the idea that the NFIP was failing to govern it effectively. Rather, they had dif-ferent moral visions for how the burdens of flood loss should be interpreted and distributed going forward. The outcome of this attempt at reform rein-forced the centrality of individual decision-making, on the basis of eco-nomic calculation, to collective security in the face of intensifying hazards and mounting losses.

When we look to the future, there are indeed multiple potential trajec-tories of loss, which we examined in chapter 5. Examining them together illustrates that there is nothing foreordained or inevitable about how chang-ing ecological and climatic conditions in floodplains will unfold to pro-duce, shape, and distribute losses, or our ways or knowing and acting on those losses. It remains to be seen who the losers—and who the winners—will be, and which areas will be built up and defended while others are sac-rificed or abandoned, as the climate continues to change. Insurance fea-tures across these different trajectories, taken up by actors to motivate and make possible particular visions of transformation in anticipation of loss. The work of individuals, groups, communities, powerful interests, and insti-tutions shapes the course of loss, producing divergent outcomes in terms of who loses what, when, how much, and with what results.

Over five decades of flood insurance and the catastrophes keep coming; the losses keep mounting. Even still, today, many stakeholders, scholars, and commentators believe the NFIP, and risk-reflexive insurance more broadly, ought to be an important part of how individuals, communities, and the federal government adapt to climate change's effects, so long as we can assess, map, and price risk accurately and get the incentives right. But this takes for granted that objective risk and its true cost are the chief issues with which we must grapple in order to make the NFIP work the way it was designed to, to manage and reduce people's exposure to flood risk, and the way some hope it might, to deliver adaptation to climate change. It confines discussion of the NFIP to its performance as an environmental and land-use program, one that should make it possible for us to rationally engage flood risk as a problem of dollars and cents. This conventional understanding of the NFIP and its problems operates with an unduly narrowed vision. It misses the bigger story about flood insurance and the important stakes for the role insurance plays in shaping our climate-changed present and future.

If we zoom out from U.S. flood insurance specifically, we see an increasingly active intersection between other kinds of insurers and climate change, particularly in the private sector. Far from consigning climate change to a category of uninsurable catastrophic risk, private insurers, and particularly reinsurers, have found new ways to assess risk and do business even at the frontiers of their risk knowledge.[5] The industry has in recent years self-consciously carved out a central role for itself in the financial management of climate change—and, in the process, shaped collective imaginaries of what climate change is and what can be done about it. Reinsurers hire climate scientists and publish climate science reports, the findings of which are taken up in the media and widely publicized. Insurers and reinsurers offer innovations in climate modeling that help publics and policymakers to know climate change in particular ways. Having encountered limitations in conventional actuarial techniques for dealing with catastrophic losses, they have created new products (such as microinsurance, parametric insurance, and insurance-linked securities) and sold them to sovereign nations, U.S. states, and even school districts, establishing new circuits of financial flows for addressing climate change's impacts.[6] These developments have been met with excitement about their seemingly apolitical character and their commercial possibilities, with headlines like "While Politicians Debate, Munich Re Innovates," "Insurance Gains Clout as Climate Change Solution for the Poor," and "The Catastrophe Bond Business Is Booming."[7] The United Nations Intergovernmental Panel on Climate Change includes chapters on insurance in its reports, linking it to the financing of recovery from natural disasters, adaptation of the built environment, and the enhanced resilience of individuals and communities. Much like the architects of the NFIP in the 1950s and the 1960s, people who see this role for insurance promise better outcomes on the basis of probabilities and prices, a vision in which information and incentives drive desirable social change. Through these activities of modeling, pricing, and commercializing weather- and catastrophe-related risks, insurers and reinsurers objectify and commodify climate change. The (re)insurance industry "gives climate change a shape and presence," framing it as uncertain, yet simultaneously manageable and even profitable, at least to some extent, for some actors, under particular circumstances.[8] At the same time, major insurance and reinsurance actors are sounding alarms about how climate change might impact ordinary policyholders as and when risk-reflexive pricing is adjusted to match the threats. In March 2019, upon the release of a major report on how climate change is affecting the reinsurance industry, Munich Re's chief climatologist told *The Guardian*: "If the risk from wildfires, flooding, storms or hail is increasing then the only sustainable option we have is to adjust our risk prices accordingly. In the long run it might become a social issue." In response to the report, a representative of Insurance Europe, which represents 34 national insurance associations, directly referenced matters of obligation and deservingness: "The sector is concerned that continuing global increases in temperature could make it increasingly difficult to offer the affordable financial protection that people deserve, and that modern society requires to function properly."[9]

The struggles we have seen in the context of the NFIP should lead us to far less tentative expectations of social issues "in the long run." Such issues are already with us. Though public insurance programs like the NFIP perhaps more conspicuously implicate the state, policymakers, and citizens in overtly political confrontations, the issues of moral economy excavated here can apprise us to the complexities, contradictions, and conflicts attendant on using insurance, public or private, to govern a volatile world. The NFIP itself participates in, and can orient us to, the moral economy of climate change, specifically key dimensions of how societies define, distribute, and respond to its associated losses. Again, this is not *limited* to matters of insurance, but when people debate, use, and reorganize insurance institutions, practices, and technologies, they work out the answers to important questions. How should moral commitments shape who pays for risk and for protection, how much, and on what terms? How does insurance itself come to enact moral commitments related to what individuals, taxpayers, and governments ought to do, support, or defend as we see further effects of climate change? What is lost and what is protected? In the story told here, climate change has at points appeared conspicuously on the agendas of various actors, as it did in New York City when municipal authorities navigated questions around the role that FEMA's flood insurance rate maps could or should play in preparing the city and its residents for climate change. For the environmentalists involved in Biggert-Waters, flood insurance reform was also essential because of the threats posed by climate change. At other points, climate change receded from view or was ambiguously connected to flood insurance, as it was for New Yorkers trying to interpret what new maps and insurance premiums signaled, if anything, about climate change, what they should do about it, and when. But whether actors are talking explicitly about climate change or not, insurance provides the terrain for establishing how different groups of people will fare in a climate-changed world.

INSURANCE AND THE MORAL ECONOMY OF CLIMATE CHANGE IN THE UNITED STATES

How then can flood insurance help us to see and analyze elements of the moral economy of climate change in the United States? The often-arcane details of how insurance programs are structured have outsize social implications: they reflect contestation over, and themselves institutionalize, interrelated moral commitments about responsibility for loss, justification of loss, and compensation for loss. From the story of the NFIP, we can see how debates about insurance, along these dimensions, can reconfigure the terms of interdependence in a world of increasingly severe perils, with significant material effects.

To the extent that the federal government and local communities rely on risk-reflexive and risk-differentiating insurance (public or private) to govern climate change's impacts, this makes the costs of climate change's effects something that have to be proactively understood and managed, in particular by individual insureds. This form of insurance individuates policyholders as owners of calculated shares of the risk: they are responsible for knowing, securing, and, where necessary, mitigating that risk—which depends upon the assumption that they *can* meaningfully mitigate risk. This connection between individual responsibility and risk mitigation is, we have seen, an important component of the logic underpinning the NFIP. It also forms the basis of some arguments that insurance should be harnessed to climate governance. Efforts to inscribe climate change into the NFIP, through legislating changes to its flood maps or connecting it to urban adaptation policies, reinforce a normative commitment that climate change ought to be governed in part through shaping the calculations of individual decision-makers. Even with all of the debate and disagreement surrounding the particulars of the NFIP, the fundamental idea that taking *some* personal responsibility for loss is a morally worthy undertaking persists, across stakeholders. Recall the insistence of homeowners, even as they sought reprieve from rate increases, that they want to take responsibility, that they're willing to pay a bit more, that they're "not down with welfare." What that personal responsibility looks like in practice—what it requires of different actors in terms of money spent and actions taken—depends in large part on how blame and accountability for loss are widely understood. We saw this from the start of the NFIP. If floods were not acts of God, but hazards that could be probabilistically assessed and anticipated, then losses were a failure of decision-making that needed to be better informed and incentivized, on the basis of accurate science and price signals provided to decision-makers by the government. We saw it decades later, when Stop FEMA Now challenged the idea that individual policyholders could or should be held accountable for the shortcomings of the NFIP by introducing other blameworthy actors, inside and outside the government.

Climate change sits in an unsettled and contestable position relative to prevailing notions of blame and accountability as they relate to flood loss. Claims that connect flood loss to climate change can recast attributions of responsibility. For instance, attributing loss to climate change can implicate fossil fuel companies that have obfuscated the issue; national governments that have shown insufficient ambition in mitigation; and the relatively affluent, writ large, whose carbon-intensive consumption practices disproportionately contribute to emissions. If climate change is understood to be the principal cause when a house floods (or burns down or blows over), and these other actors are to blame for it, then where are the limits to what individuals can feasibly and fairly be made responsible for? And given the available climate science, what can people and governments reasonably be expected to know about it, and to do about it, if they are to make rational decisions about where or how to build and live?

The answer to these questions, the NFIP teaches us, depends in part on claims as to whether losses—from disasters themselves or from the way those disasters are managed by insurance—are justified or deserved. Pricing people out of floodplains that will see more intense disasters may seem to be all for the greater good, over the long term. But concerns about who those people are, and whether they're being treated fairly, shape the action that actually takes place in the present to set such processes in motion. Such concerns can circumscribe how authorities use available risk technologies to govern the present and anticipate the future, as we saw when New York City and FEMA officials agreed on two maps to stipulate different arrangements of responsibility for current flood risk and future climate change. Those concerns are also reflected in settlements of a "fair" price for securing against loss. In flood insurance, a fair price is one that signals risk, but with the weight of that financial obligation indexed in some way to a person's ability to pay—the outcome enshrined by the Homeowner Flood Insurance Affordability Act. Participants in insurance debates confront each other with tropes, familiar in other public policy arenas, about hard work, playing by the rules, the American dream, taxpaying citizenship, and making good choices. To the extent that these tropes remain affectively resonant and politically persuasive, the claims that they sustain will work to shape the precise ways that insurers and governments can define and distribute climate risk as a matter of political practice. To manage climate change's impacts, insurance programs and products may apply standardized methods of economization across centrally managed individuals, but the story of the NFIP shows that actors seize upon the social differences between those individuals—who they are, what they did or can do, and what they're owed in the face of loss—to make them into politically meaningful distinctions in how they can be treated.

Finally, the NFIP provides a window into how claims about the failure of insurance institutions in the face of climate change, and the subsequent changes to insurance such claims motivate, have a great deal to do with issues of compensation for loss. Compensation looks straightforward from the point of view of individual contracts: you pay a premium, you get claims paid in the event of a loss. But compensation becomes morally weighty when the obligation to compensate policyholders runs into the limits of what a risk pool can sustain, which happens with the kinds of catastrophic losses we expect more of due to climate change. When the NFIP goes into debt, it draws on its borrowing authority with the U.S. Treasury. For private insurers, too, catastrophic losses can mean the increasing importance of and demand for public backstops. When catastrophic loss happens, compensation draws in other collective resources, implicating taxpayers and political groups who have questions about what that compensation is or should be making possible, in light of what they believe to be fair or prudent. Insurance claims are meant to restore property, but in a climate-changed United States, restoring property, at least in a particular place, might well be the very thing the public and policymakers no longer want to enable. They may believe this ought to be avoided because it seems to reward bad behavior at the expense of those who have shown good behavior, or because it stands in the way of making sensible transitions in the built environment. Indeed, we've seen elements of both appear in the claims made about the appropriate future of the NFIP.

Compensation becomes morally and politically troublesome in other ways. Insurance is necessarily a limited tool when it comes to experiences of loss because it can only offer indemnity for the loss of a specific form of capital. Insurance makes it possible to treat the losses of climate change as a matter of asset value at risk and calculations of dollars and cents, as the New York City comptroller's report suggested. But it cannot fully encompass what people will lose and what they seek to protect. The loss of a house is underwritable, but the loss of a *home* may indeed be incalculable.[10] Furthermore, policyholders feel that they have been failed when insurance itself seems to generate losses that cannot be compensated, making them feel insecure and uncertain rather than made whole. In dealing with insurance in a time of climate change, when high premiums or collapsing property values may force people to confront major changes to their lives, commensurating disparate values and impacts so that they can be governed in economic terms "may distort the stakes of a decision for different groups," as Wendy Espeland puts it. Doing so can preclude the expression of things people deem worthy of protection, but thereby magnify their significance.[11] In response, people make claims about the justice of what they have lost or may lose, beyond what can be accounted for in dollars and cents. Such claims may actually establish the grounds for material redress or compensation, helping to secure economic conditions that minimize the impact of loss by making it politically difficult for politicians to introduce changes that produce "harm and heartache," as Representative Maxine Waters put it when she vowed to revisit Biggert-Waters. People are capable of thinking with and combining multiple registers of value, which together inform their understandings and experiences of loss, and the forms and amounts of compensation they desire, seek, and find acceptable.

Didier Fassin writes that moral economies characterize the manner in which a social issue "is constituted through judgments and sentiments that gradually come to define a sort of common sense and collective understanding of the problem."[12] These matters of responsibility, justification, and compensation are dimensions along which the problems of loss, bound up with climate change, are constituted and addressed. Their specific empirical contours, related to what constitutes responsibility, fairness, or value, can change. Fassin also cautions that moral economies pertain to a "particular historical moment and a specific social world." Common sense and collective understandings about loss and climate change are subject to change with and as policymakers and other interested actors renegotiate the design of the NFIP, in interaction with developments in insurance and risk rationalities more broadly, and as ecological conditions change. This is one reason this book explored a variety of potential floodplain futures. We can and should expect existing settlements to be upset as debates recur and, when they do, we can return to these three dimensions of the moral economy of climate change—responsibility for loss, justification of loss, and compensation for loss—in order to understand their stakes and significance.

Thorny questions of what people owe each other, and the terms of accessing insurance protection as the climate changes, are not confined to the management of public programs like the NFIP. They are also at stake in private insurance for other kinds of natural hazards, as George Kasimos found out when he found allies among homeowner groups who were protesting increases in private wind insurance. Fire risk is also privately underwritten in the United States and these stakes have become conspicuous in California where, according to the state's wildfire disaster agency, climate change has worsened wildfire conditions and extended wildfire season. There, increased wildfire risk has driven up private insurance premiums, putting comprehensive policies out of reach of many homeowners. In some cases, insurers are "defensively underwriting," dropping policyholders altogether (something a public program like the NFIP is not legally allowed to do); from 2015 to 2018, insurance companies dropped more than 340,000 homeowners from wildfire areas.[13] Insurers can also hollow out policies to reduce their coverage. After huge fire losses in the November 2018 wildfires, many small private insurers went out of business altogether. As a result, more homeowners have come to rely on the state as an insurer of last resort. In California, this is called the "FAIR plan" and it provides only very basic coverage.[14] "Protection gaps" will grow between those who can afford to buy their way into private networks of risk-sharing and those who cannot.[15] During those wildfires, Kim Kardashian and Kanye West had a private fleet of firefighters protect their $50 million mansion, a benefit of their high-end private insurance policies.[16] As the world warms, they and their rich and famous friends will always have access to insurance protection; they can pay any price for it. The residents in trailer parks outside of Santa Rosa, which also burned, may not. As in the context of flood insurance, in the wake of these catastrophic fires, a flurry of debate kicked up over what these at-risk homeowners deserve in terms of broader support as the climate changes. Many of the same questions were asked. Should we continue to make insurance and disaster relief available if it allows people to rebuild and live in risky areas? What should insurance cost? Should we provide the resources for those homeowners to move on, out of harm's way? Should we take measures to protect the economic security of the most vulnerable residents? Should we, more radically, rethink or abandon real estate capitalism and the particular kinds of land development it has fueled? Following the controversies in the life of the NFIP allows us to see how claims related to fair prices, the deservingness of different groups of people, and the appropriate roles of the state, the market, and individuals, can shape the course of developments in private insurance markets, too. It awakens attention to how insurance innovations—such as private firefighting teams—meant to manage intensifying losses will necessarily run into moral economic concerns that can shape how they are taken up and used.

These moral economic dimensions revealed in natural hazards insurance are themselves situated in a broader American political and moral economy of social provision. Though this kind of insurance is not typically named as part of the welfare state architecture (the way programs like Social Security and Medicare are, for instance), because homeownership underpins economic security and wealth creation in the U.S. context, changes to flood insurance, or to private insurance that affects the purchase and ownership of residential property, are also highly consequential for the near- and long-term economic security of individuals and communities. If we look at the bigger picture, for many Americans facing impacts from climate change that may increase their financial burdens, life has become more precarious in other ways. Some scholars have observed a general tendency, over the last several decades, toward increasing risk segmentation, with the unpooling of risks in both private and public insurance.[17] The appeal of domestic social policy that spreads risk and protects more people has also given way to a preference for policies that embrace risk as an incentive that can reduce individual claims on collective resources—policies that often upwardly distribute wealth in the process.[18] Jacob Hacker has chronicled what he calls "the Great Risk Shift" toward greater individual risk bearing over the last 30 years: a "massive transfer of economic risk from broad structures of insurance, including those sponsored by the corporate sector as well as by government, onto the fragile balance sheets of American families."[19] A variety of policy adjustments—often subtle changes to eligibility requirements and implementation rules—have together served to pare back and fragment the welfare functions of the state, leading it to offer increasingly incomplete risk protection.[20] Risk privatizations across pensions, health care, income, and employment affect a homeowning middle class that has long resisted reductions in its own safety nets, even as many of its members show enthusiasm for reforms that curtail benefits targeting the poor. Other scholars have provided their own accounts of risk shifts, privatization, or individualization (in the United States as well as Europe), documenting the adverse outcomes of often subtle changes to state policy, and public and private insurance, that have changed the balance between collective and individual responsibility.[21] At the same time as these protections and provisions have eroded, we have seen divestments in the kinds of public goods, like education and infrastructure, that help people to live safe and secure lives, in good times and bad.[22]

This is the world in which the NFIP operates and the context in which any (re)insurance response to climate change will be lived and experienced in the United States. Compared to countries in Europe, for instance, the United States is trying to deal with increasing disaster losses in a context of high relative poverty rates.[23] When an actual disaster strikes, many Americans are now simultaneously worried about job insecurity, burdensome health care costs, and precarious retirements. And when that disaster strikes, Americans living in other parts of the country are quick to come to the aid of the suffering people they see on the news. They send money or donations of basic supplies; sometimes they even show up in person to help rebuild houses and schools. But the last several decades of American policymaking have not matched this compassion and solidarity with an institutionalized commitment to collective flourishing.

CLIMATE CHANGE AND THE POLITICS OF LOSS

We are used to seeing ruminations about, analyses of, and political demands around climate change framed in terms of sustainability. Such a framing focuses attention on which elements of the status quo (in environmental conditions, in economic systems, in lifestyles) can be preserved, reproduced, even enhanced, while citizens and governments work also to mitigate the worst impacts of climate change and adapt to the effects we cannot avoid. Of course, loss is the other side of that coin. As Miriam Greenberg writes in her critique of sustainability thinking, "Sustainability asks us to define those things of greatest value in our present that ought to be sustained in order to achieve this utopian vision of the future. Simultaneously, it forces us to consider those things that are not of value, and should not be sustained."[24] Yet we don't typically start from loss; it is the more melancholy counterpart to the utopian pretentions of sustainability. I have done so here because it's not the case that all the interesting social and political work goes into the sustaining bit, and everything else simply falls away. Experiences, understandings, and expectations of loss have to be actively produced and given meaning, and insurance is centrally implicated in that.

Starting from loss helps to examine the ways in which some moral economies of climate change are and will continue to be forged, in part, by the politics of those who have something to lose: economic rents and returns on investment, as well as cherished places and connections to communities. These are losses that accrue not only to the elites and powerful industries that benefit most from commodified housing, but also to the property-owning middle and working classes. When land disappears or property values in risky areas collapse, people and political groups forge new connections in order to reestablish conditions of security in the face of such losses. This is made possible in large part through the very techniques and instruments of insurance, as illustrated by the way lines drawn around flood zones on the NFIP's maps articulated a new collective political identity—flood zone homeowner—and united residents who shared that identity in blue and red states, working-class neighborhoods and beachfront vacation areas. This new political actor then became an active force in shaping subsequent developments in flood insurance. It made common-cause with realtors and home builders—whose lobbyists have long cultivated relationships on both sides of the aisle[25]—while at the same time identifying them as some of the bad actors who had created their problems to begin with. When Stop FEMA Now took its grievances to Congress, it earned the solidarity of some of the most progressive and conservative senators and representatives, who stood shoulder-to-shoulder at press conferences and vowed to respond to their needs. On the other side formed that unlikely coalition joining libertarian and taxpayer groups with environmentalists. These strange bedfellow alliances around the NFIP apprise us to potentially surprising (re)alignments in the politics of responding and adapting to climate change, where partisanship, class, region, and environmentalist values don't play the roles that they historically have or that we expect them to.

In other words, when it comes to negotiating the moral economy of climate change, insurance creates "climate publics," in an unusual or even accidental sense. These publics unite people who may or may not care about climate change per se, who may be otherwise at different ends of the political spectrum, but who share what it is they have to lose in a world of rising seas, devastating storms, shifting precipitation patterns, and widespread wildfires. They can secure protection from such losses without talking about climate change, and instead by talking about the economic arrangements and public policies that govern its effects.[26] Policies and programs have politics. They shape who people are, what they want, and how they organize.[27] David Garland argues that the centrality of insurance rationalities to contemporary governance, particularly welfare state governance, means that that key historical actors are not so much social classes as *risk categories*: "social groups defined by their relationship to a particular policy such as social security, old age pensions, or health care"—and flood insurance.[28] From the NFIP, we see how insurance arrangements—through grouping people into risk categories, through changing meanings of risk, through the assertion of particular values—will contribute to constituting the actors and ideas of political and moral life in a time of climate change.

These are climate politics and climate publics that leave some issues and people out. Recall the town hall in Rockaway, with both ends of the peninsula coming together to deal with unresolved issues related to Hurricane Sandy. The storm and flood had drenched and devastated both homeowners and renters, landlords and public housing tenants. The social theorist Ulrich Beck wrote that such shared experiences, characteristic of climate change, forge a kind of "enforced cosmopolitanism," across wealth and region, compelling "communication between those who do not want to have anything to do with one another."[29] But the residents who turned up at that town hall were there to prosecute very different concerns. To the extent that fights over climate change, what's fair and unfair, and determinations of who will fare better or worse, happen through insurance contestation, they are fights over preserving perquisites and privileges for only those who can and do participate in property ownership. Homeowners will not necessarily make common cause with other populations whose economic security or survival chances will be compromised by climate change.

Indeed, Stop FEMA Now did not. In mounting a set of claims about choice and deservingness, the Stop FEMA Now homeowners did lay open some of the public policy contradictions that left individuals responsible for managing risks that were collectively produced, imperfectly understood, and constantly changing. But in its activism, it did not put forth a vision of broad collective responsibility or mutual aid that would have, perhaps, led it to make common cause not with home builders and realtors, who pass risks onto residents, but instead with environmental justice organizations and community-based groups who have mobilized resources and organizing power to advocate for the needs and priorities of low-income people, communities of color, immigrants, and workers in recovering from floods and preparing for climate change.[30] Stop FEMA Now is a homeowners' organization and confined its attention to the issue of what homeowners stood to lose; their insurance solidarity, dramatized by the maps, was central.[31] After Sandy, public housing residents in the outer boroughs of New York City—neighbors of some of the activists in Stop FEMA Now—went without power or heat for weeks and, over four years later, over a dozen public housing sites were still using temporary boilers. Renters affected by Sandy, more likely to be poor and people of color, reported increased rents, displacement from their pre-Sandy homes, overcrowding, and dangerous and unsanitary housing conditions.[32] They struggled to recover without the benefit of the many policies and programs that target homeowners. Forms of assistance that are designed to restore property, like flood insurance, work to shore up the wealth of those with property and with the money to insure it. Junia Howell and James R. Elliott have shown that the more disaster aid an area receives from FEMA, the more wealth inequality grows, along lines of not only homeownership, but also race and education. "Natural hazards do not just bring damages, they also bring resources," Howell and Elliott note. But people are not equally positioned to take advantage of those resources. "Equal aid is not equitable aid, especially when it is systematically designed to restore property rather than communities."[33] To the extent that insurance plays a central role in how societies manage the impacts of climate change, this is a strategy that will reproduce conditions of relative privilege and deprivation based on property.

American political culture and welfare state politics have imbued homeownership with a kind of moral superiority over other forms of housing tenure.[34] American social policy is geared toward promoting and protecting it, much of it indirectly through tax incentives, loan guarantees, and credit programs.[35] But the status of this presumed life goal, or even right of citizenship, seems less secure in a world of rising sea levels, shifting precipitation patterns, growing floodplains, and "sunny day" flooding, in a world where those investments might soon be underwater. Human settlements will have to change in such a world, but precisely when they will, how they will, and with what effects can follow any number of trajectories. From the moral economic controversies around flood insurance, we can see that climate politics around issues of adaptation may be powerfully driven by how homeowners confront the possibility or reality of loss, and how other political actors respond. In the context of debating flood insurance reform, though Stop FEMA Now largely did not engage the points raised by environmentalists about preparing for climate change, its activism was ecologically consequential. It defended an existing social order in which the incumbency of existing homeownership warrants protection. Where protection means softening the effects of new maps and higher insurance premiums, this in a sense can preserve and reproduce a status quo in which homeowners manage to stay put, in carbon-intensive housing and property landscapes, at least for a little longer. In some communities, protection has also taken the form of new commitments to structural flood protection and community resilience: floodwalls, funding for home and street elevations, green infrastructure, and so forth.[36] Controversies around insurance have in these ways already motivated a set of material changes to the landscape. Whether they connect their own struggles to climate change or not, the activism of homeowners and other participants in insurance politics, as they negotiate the terms of responsibility for loss, acceptable compensation for loss, and whose or which losses are deserved or justifiable, is ecologically decisive for whether or how radically carbon-intensive and hazardous arrangements of housing, property, and infrastructure can change—as well as who will win and who will lose when they do.

All of this suggests that sociologists who study climate change and climate justice ought to broaden their view beyond the policies, social movements, protests, and programs that are explicitly oriented toward emissions regulations, climate resilience, energy efficiency and transition, environmental protection, and so forth, and cast an eye toward the array of insurance, housing, infrastructure, and natural hazards policies that economize both threats and behaviors, and that shape how people live with loss. As Liz Koslov argues, "practices and forms of mobilization that promote mitigation and adaptation exist beyond the expected sites and styles of climate action."[37] There is more work to be done to assess how these various policies, with the constituencies, preferences, and channels of influence they have created, will act as key sites at which moral economies are negotiated and the social conditions of a climate-changed future are determined.

WHAT DO WE HAVE TO LOSE?

The world of people thinking about the present and future of the NFIP is dominated by experts—economists and actuaries, engineers, and climate scientists—who are keenly attentive to how the technical arrangements of the program might be adjusted to make the program work the way it is supposed to. Today the NFIP is still in massive debt, even after a significant chunk of that debt was forgiven in 2018. It appears ill equipped to absorb the catastrophic losses wrought by the kinds of storms we have seen in recent years and that we expect to see in the future. The ideas for fixing flood insurance are varied and numerous. For some, the only reasonable path forward is to bare down and see through actuarial reforms, allowing the price of flood insurance to rise in order to signal the risk without a subsidy or grandfathering, and to find some other way to deal with the disproportionately negative effects on lower-income homeowners. For others, the incentives of FEMA's Community Rating System ought to be expanded and better publicized, so that communities have the option of taking steps that bring premiums down for all their policyholders. Many have called for increased funding for retrofitting homes, such as paying for home elevations, and for massive expansions of buyout programs for repeatedly flooded properties. These steps would help homeowners avoid getting back to a dangerous normal and would relieve the NFIP and taxpayers of some of the burdens of supporting flood-prone properties in the process. There is a great deal of consensus behind the idea that the production and dissemination of flood insurance rate maps need to be fully funded and technically upgraded. Building codes and outright land-use regulation could be strengthened, the interests of the real estate and construction industry be damned. Some have argued that the federal government needs to get out of the flood insurance business altogether, to leave this to private insurers who now claim they are capable and willing to underwrite flood risk more efficiently.

Which, if any, of these proposals is taken up and tried out in the coming years will undoubtedly be accompanied by vigorous debate. All of them are oriented toward the question of how we manage our relation to the water as it rises and rains down. In this book, I have argued that attention to moral economies and their implications for how Americans experience and manage loss reveals the ways in which flood insurance is not merely an environmental policy. Understanding the core dilemmas of the NFIP as not simply technical, but more fundamentally political and moral, opens up new vistas for thinking about how it, and insurance more broadly, might be reimagined to reshape the ways we live together and meet the challenges of climate change.

As we have seen, the design and operations of the NFIP reflect and institutionalize a particular vision of how people live together, premised on concerns about moral hazard and the idea that insurance shapes outcomes principally through the ways it incentivizes decision-making and action. In this vision, when people are separated from the full costs of their actions, bad things happen: they take less care to avoid loss, they create burdens for others. From this standpoint, the challenge is one of managing demands on collective resources that would otherwise spiral out of control. As Tom Baker has shown in his genealogy of moral hazard, the general lesson is that less is more: insurance institutions can achieve desirable outcomes only by limiting the amounts of coverage and carefully managing the conditions of accessing it. If we are given more safety, security, and welfare, then we will take advantage.[38]

However, the calculative rationalities of risk that are bound up with insurance can become attached to different sets of purposes and political programs.[39] The political scientist Deborah Stone invites us instead to think about "insurance as moral opportunity." She observes that, through its effects on political culture and collective political action, insurance expands our sense of what we consider adverse and worthy of collective responsibility, and produces social benefits in the process—benefits that the conventional economics of insurance, and the styles of political reasoning it informs, often ignores. Participation in a risk pool means agreeing to impose costs on yourself, not only for your own benefit when you incur a loss, but also for the benefit of others who might suffer from loss when you do not. The moral opportunity created by insurance is then "the opportunity to cooperate with and help others," underpinned by "motives of charity, compassion, civic responsibility, and justice."[40] Insurance does not reflect or respond to our individual (selfish) nature so much as it actively sets norms related to mutual aid, inclusion, and individual and collective well-being. As the NFIP has made plain, in Stone's words, "Insurance influences how individuals behave, not so much by dangling incentives in front of them one by one, but rather by offering arenas for collective moral deliberation and political action."[41]

What then is the moral opportunity of flood insurance as we face intensifying climate change? If we refocus from aggregating individual calculations to deliberate collectively about our unavoidable interdependence, then we can perhaps let go of some well-worn and historically unproductive preoccupations. We might let go of the idea that people can meaningfully own calculated shares of risk or exercise meaningful control to avoid the kinds of immense losses that may be coming. Rather than engage in political debates about what people in flood zones did or ought to choose, and whether those choices turned out well or badly, we might instead see the coming floods, which we have scientific reason to believe will affect more and more people, as requiring, economically and morally, a broader sharing of the burdens and gains of social interdependence. Economically, spreading the risk more widely protects more people and brings more revenue into the NFIP, helping the program cover the losses of the next flood and keeping it on firmer financial footing. After all, floods have never stopped short at the borders of the official flood zones, beyond which disaster relief continues to compensate uninsured losses. Already, over 20 percent of flood insurance claims come from losses outside of currently mapped high-risk zones. FEMA itself warns: "Everyone is at risk—due to weather systems, land development run-off or regional events." Major current and future flood risks are not just coastal, but riverine, as dramatic flooding across the Midwest demonstrated in the spring of 2019.[42] And yet only a subset of residents is paying into the program. It's like having a health insurance program for only the sickest members of the community. If it stays that way, insisting on an actuarial basis may well be impossible; the costs will simply be too high for those individual households to bear. According to a 2013 report commissioned by FEMA, individual premiums per NFIP policy are projected to increase by 10 to 70 percent in 2010 dollars by 2100, if they are to offset the projected increase in flood losses.[43]

Morally, spreading the risk treats the coming disasters as a shared challenge, the costs of which we have a duty to share broadly—not because they are an act of God, but because no matter how much we know about the risk, no matter how precisely or at how fine a scale we think we can map and price it, collective and systemic failures both create flood hazards and expose people to them. Those hazards reinforce existing disadvantages as they intersect with economic inequality, structural racism, and fraying safety nets.[44] They destroy things that are fundamental to well-being and that societies generally deem worthy of protection: not only a secure place to live, but also our health, stable work and employment situations, and connections to our communities.[45] All of the controversy over classifying, as precisely as possible, who is at how much risk and what each person's risk should cost, can obscure the more fundamental question of why so much attention is given to how individuals, rather than larger social systems, must change to be made more secure in a climate-changed United States. If our attention were focused on those collective failures, we might instead, for instance, pursue an approach to land use and housing that conspicuously regulates in the public interest, rather than trying in vain to align urban development and hazard risk through the subtle operations of incentives for private actors—an approach that has, historically, worked to enrich the powerful real estate and financial industries. This is a vision that Suzanne Mettler describes as one of government operating not through inconspicuous individual "nudges" in the right direction but instead through a politics that "reveals" who wins, who loses, and who participates.[46] As Mettler argues, this kind of politics may sacrifice the promises of efficiency that come with bureaucratic administration (promises that have not, in fact, even been realized in the case of the NFIP), but offers gains in the quality and impact of political citizenship because we can then better appreciate how policies structure our and others' opportunities and outcomes.

Using insurance technologies and practices, and the economic calculus of risk they offer, to govern climate change may seem to offer a dispassionate way to decide what to do but,[47] as Brian Wynne notes, "the very term *risk* is laden with political and moral implications." Another moral opportunity of insurance is to treat risk as "an essential part of democratic life," open to negotiation and redefinition, rather than assumed to have a singular, basic, universal meaning which we either succeed or fail at estimating, understanding, and acting upon.[48] Charles Perrow has similarly argued that "sensible living with risky systems means keeping the controversies alive, listening to the public."[49] This does not consign us to interminable debate that provides no basis for action. It simply reflects that, for all the reasons explored here, more "accurate" technical measures of risks and costs cannot definitively settle controversies. Where representations of the environment are concerned, people demand "not only objectively claimed matters of fact but also subjectively appreciated facts that matter," in the words of Sheila Jasanoff. We can understand flood risk in a way that deals explicitly with how that risk is historically produced, unequally felt, and connected with ideas about how the world is or ought to be.[50] The alternative ambition is therefore not to arrive at one persuasive account of the hazards risk we each face, or a technically satisfactory economization, or a version of calculation that can tame all the inevitable overflows. Rather, it is to enlarge the dimensions of risk recognized in social debate—to acknowledge and validate the relevance of multiple forms of value, as well as concerns about equity, membership, and compassion, to how we organize risk-sharing and manage loss.

Finally, the moral opportunity of insurance is also one of creating the political conditions for debating more transformative desires for a climate-changed future. When we run into the apparent limits of what flood insurance in its current form can do, to prepare individuals and communities for a wetter future, we have the opportunity to contemplate more radical departures from the status quo in how we live with nature and with each other. The important failures to address may not be of programs and probabilities and prices, but of imagination. We could reconfigure risk-sharing and repurpose risk information in our social and political fabric. For instance, we can reexamine whether financial and physical security ought actually to be delinked from the vastly unequal perquisites of home-ownership, or whether basing so much of social provision and wealth creation on the commodification of housing even makes sense when its financial value may collapse if and as climatic conditions worsen. We could rely on information about increasing risks and costs not chiefly to influence individual decision-makers, who then have to manage their own resilience, but rather to inform massive investments in decarbonized, safer, and affordable housing for all. The moral opportunity of flood insurance is one of recognizing our fates as connected and reconsidering the political and economic arrangements that make the losses of climate change something we each have to weather individually.

METHODOLOGICAL APPENDIX

In the introduction, I provided an overview of how the project of this book unfolded: how questions that emerged in initial stages of research led me to new questions and new sources of data, which I then followed up, yielding still newer questions requiring yet more data collection and analysis. Here I provide more information about the methodological choices I made along the way, the reasons for making those particular choices, and the journey of writing this book.

Underwater began as the dissertation for my PhD in sociology at the University of California, Berkeley. My interests as a graduate student had developed at the intersection of the environmental and the economic. I was interested in how ordinary people experienced environmental problems as economic realities, as well as in how economic practices and techniques became seemingly sensible solutions to certain environmental problems. But I certainly never set out to write a dissertation on flood insurance. Indeed, I had prepared and nearly completed a prospectus on an entirely different project having to do with market-based environmentalism and American environmental organizations. That project was (and remains) intellectually interesting to me. But when events began unfolding in New York City after Hurricane Sandy, I felt I had to change course (just a few weeks before my prospectus filing deadline, no less, and with the merciful indulgence of my very understanding dissertation committee). What was taking place there—a flood disaster, and then an economic disaster—scratched my same intellectual itch about the environmental and the economic, but it also compelled me emotionally. In a very general sense, the dilemmas facing ordinary people resonated more strongly with me than did the strategies of organizations.

As I describe in the introduction, what was just beginning in New York City and in other areas affected by Hurricane Sandy appeared to be the first instance of changes that were down the line for National Flood Insurance Program (NFIP) communities around the country. Biggert-Waters was meant to roll out nationally, but Hurricane Sandy expedited local processes of remapping flood risk and communicating increases in flood insurance to those who were making decisions about how or whether to rebuild following the storm. It seemed that how things went in New York City would be consequential for how things went for the rest of the nation's floodplains. My sense of things was ultimately borne out; the local controversies that sprang up in Sandy-affected areas led to national mobilizations and subsequent reforms to the NFIP. The two-map solution developed and piloted in New York City also constitutes a model for how FEMA will deliver climate risk information to NFIP communities going forward. New York City is also the largest floodplain in the United States by population. The challenges this major global city faced in adapting to changing flood risks and their costs could be illuminating for other cities in an urbanizing country and world. There were strong analytical reasons to begin the project there.

There were also strong personal reasons. If we are reflexive about our research methods, we have to acknowledge the ways our biographies inevitably end up shaping the issues we want to take up and investigate. My mother grew up in the Bronx and, though she raised me and my brother in the suburbs of Washington, DC, her New Yorker-ness and an early childhood spent visiting my grandparents there made a deep impression, leaving its imprint on my heart. Put simply, I care about what happens to New York City and the people who live there. This seems obvious with hindsight, but at the time it was an eye-opening first lesson that you can care about research in a wholly different way. In fact, caring in this way is what will propel you through the inevitable practical and analytical obstacles any researcher faces when conducting long-term research.

I knew early on that my particular interests and questions demanded qualitative research methods. I wanted to understand the NFIP as an institution and an experience. I wanted to understand how its seemingly straightforward logic of information and incentives worked on the ground, or didn't, or sometimes worked to do things people didn't expect, want, or know how to manage. Much of the available scholarship on the NFIP, by contrast, took the view from 20,000 feet, using quantitative data or legislative histories to give a sense of the overall scope of the program, how it had changed from an official regulatory perspective, and its aggregate effects. My orientation toward experience, perception, belief, and relations (between people, as well as between people and things, like floods and maps and premiums) implied that I needed to conduct some qualitative fieldwork: to both talk to people and observe changes as they unfolded.[1]

I began with this general set of interests rather than a clear set of hypotheses or variables, guided very much by what Kristin Luker calls a "logic of discovery."[2] Practically speaking, this meant that the research developed in a kind of iterative fashion. As I learned more about the NFIP, I figured out which key actors were implicated—and thus were people I ought to interview; what and where the relevant sites were for seeing the NFIP in action; and which documents I might consult to fill in the picture of both how this system was designed and deployed, and how people justified or contested it. As I got to know people, they invited me to come along to important events. My research methods training at Berkeley had taught me to strive for an abundance of data, which meant following the story and thinking carefully about what different kinds of evidence could tell me about my phenomenon of interest, both its character and its effects.

This logic of discovery also allowed me to learn from my mistakes in the field. For instance, when I began the project, it was to me self-evidently a story about climate change and how it was hitting ordinary people in the pocketbook. The title of the project had the words "climate change" in it and my informed consent documents, which I handed to interviewees at the start of our conversations, therefore had "climate change" in big letters across the top. But I learned quickly that this had the undesirable effect of driving the conversation in a particular direction. For some people, in particular residents who were hearing distressing suggestions from many experts and commentators that they did not have a viable future in a climate-changed New York, it was off-putting and undermined their trust in me as someone who could really hear and understand the problems they were facing, as they saw them. They saw me as just another person who was going to tell them they needed to move on. I filed an amendment to Berkeley's research ethics Institutional Review Board to change the title of the project (to "Insurance for New and Changing Catastrophe Risks") so that what appeared on the consent form didn't set in motion these kinds of unanticipated reactions. I still did, and do, see the project as one about climate change, but this pivot allowed me to see much more clearly precisely *how* that was the case. It allowed me access to what my research participants themselves understood climate change to mean and how they saw it connected to their own work, lives, and futures. If research participants didn't bring it up themselves, I would wait until the very end of our conversation to raise the topic, and in that way uncovered the ambiguity and ambivalence described in the chapters of this book.

By the time I sat down to write this book, I had been collecting and analyzing data on the NFIP for about five years, including and beyond the dissertation. The bulk of the interviews and ethnographic observation took place on research trips over the course of October 2013 to November 2015. I would head to New York City (and sometimes other East Coast locations, as indicated in the next section) for a few months to collect data, then return to my desk in Berkeley to transcribe, analyze, and do some drafting and workshopping of the material. These periods of reflection between trips would help to inform my objectives and strategies for subsequent trips. While at Berkeley and as the project continued beyond the dissertation and my time there as a PhD student, I continued to collect and analyze interview and textual data.

QUALITATIVE METHODS FOR STUDYING FLOOD INSURANCE

Early on, I decided to organize the project around key processes of risk classification, calculation, and distribution. Through tracking how these processes worked on the ground, I hoped to gain an understanding of how the actors involved encountered, framed, and resolved any problems as they came up. My orientation toward processes and problem-solving, rather than predetermined key actors or organizations, predefined fields, or pre-delineated boundaries, allowed an empirical openness that captured these issues as they developed and as actors attempted to navigate them in context and through interaction with each other.[3] I derived inspiration from "trouble-case" methodology, originated by Karl N. Llewellyn and E. Adamson Hoebel in the study of law, as well as relational approaches to ethnography and qualitative fieldwork more generally, both of which emphasize the "points of contact and conflict" between differently positioned actors.[4] These points are where interpretations of official processes are articulated, contested, and defended. Relational approaches, particularly in economic sociology and in science and technology studies, focus on how sites, agents, and material objects work together to enact social relations and formations.[5] My approach to fieldwork similarly followed the relational turn in urban studies, which stays "close to practice" in order to draw attention to the work that goes into constituting coherent "things"—be they policies, buildings, or flood zones.[6] I also saw relational approaches in sociological fieldwork as epistemologically coherent with policy-focused analysis in political science, which shaped my approach to analyzing the development of legislation around flood insurance over the years. In outlining this approach, Jacob Hacker and Paul Pierson observe that "politics is centrally about the exercise of government authority for particular substantive purposes"; in other words, it's about changing public policy rather than gaining office. Policy is therefore a terrain of struggle as well as the prize of political action, and appreciating this helps us to see how, and with what effects, actors organize and array around various proposals to change it.[7]

The practical implication of a relational orientation for my interview strategy was that rather than sample for a representative set of homeowners or set of experts or any other predefined category, I sought out respondents who could provide different angles of view on these central flood insurance processes of classification, calculation, and distribution—a kind of sampling for range.[8] Part of the reason for doing so was that any given research participant might inhabit multiple categories, as in the case, for instance, of the Army Corps of Engineer employee working on flood mitigation ("expert") who was also a flood zone resident with an NFIP policy ("homeowner"). As Brian Wynne has observed in his own sociocultural studies of risk, people inhabit multifaceted and plural social networks and identities, which can give rise to an ambivalence of belief and trust—which was also the case here, for experts and professionals who got involved in the conflicted calculations of flood zone residents.[9] Furthermore, as Mario Small has argued, "representativeness," in a statistical sense that would allow one to generalize to unobserved empirical cases, is more generally an inappropriate objective for qualitative research. Instead, he suggests that each interview is best understood as a case, one piece of knowledge that can inform future cases—both in terms of who the researcher approaches next, and what they ask them about.[10] To identify and recruit initial interviewees, I would source names from local media, local and federal government websites, and the websites and social media of local advocacy organizations.

At later stages, to recruit respondents, I used the well-worn technique of snowball sampling, where respondents give you the names of or introduce you to your next respondents.[11] This is what I did to meet people in Rockaway, for instance. One morning, I finished an interview near the Beach 90th Street subway stop, asked whom I might talk to next, and my interviewee called a friend in Belle Harbor and told him he was sending me that way. His friend wouldn't be ready for another few hours, though, so he dropped me at a local surf shop so that I could interview the owner (another friend), who then agreed to drive me down the peninsula to Belle Harbor at the appointed time. In Broad Channel, I interviewed the webmaster of a popular local blog, who posted a notice about my research project and how to contact me, which helped to recruit more participants there. People would tell me about the situations their neighbors were in, and then walk me next door to meet them. Snowballing also worked when I was trying to reach professionals and politicians working on flood insurance. A housing counselor put me in touch with a legal aid attorney she had sought out for guidance. A local city official pointed me toward the risk and insurance experts she had been consulting on the city's flood mapping challenges. My aunt got her local state senator to take my call. Ultimately, the project draws on interviews with seventy people: homeowners, housing counselors and activists, disaster case managers, lawyers, insurance brokers and consumer advocates, meteorologists and other natural hazards/risk experts, engineers, representatives of think tanks and policy organizations, environmentalists, insurance industry representatives, city and state elected officials, and local and federal officials with public agencies. Most of these interviews took place in New York City, but as Biggert-Waters and Stop FEMA Now came more centrally into view, I traveled also to Long Island, New York; New Jersey; and Washington, DC, to sit down with people who could tell me about what was at stake and what they were doing about it. Fifteen interviews took place by phone, either because respondents were too busy to meet in person (as in the case of the state senator) or because I was back at my desk in Berkeley, between research trips.

When I did interviews, as part of the informed consent procedure, I would give respondents options for how they wanted to be identified in any subsequent publications. Many people were comfortable being identified by name; others preferred a pseudonym or only to be identified by job title or area of residence. I have followed those wishes here.

I knew there were also elements of this story that I could and should observe first-hand, as I was conducting the research at a time of significant contestation over the NFIP in the wake of Biggert-Waters. My strategy for ethnographic observation was to follow the trouble over how the NFIP classifies, calculates, and distributes risk as it manifested in different sites. My efforts to do so were helped considerably by local organizations and agencies that I spent a lot of time with. The Center for New York City Neighborhoods brought me along to its flood insurance help desks in several different outer-borough neighborhoods. At these help desks, residents could come in with questions about flood maps and insurance and seek professional assistance at a number of different stations. There were typically architects, insurance and housing counselors, disaster case managers, and representatives from the city's Sandy recovery program, Build It Back, present at each help desk. I was allowed to sit and observe these encounters between residents and professionals and to conduct additional informal ethnographic interviews with those professionals in the time between consultations. A contact at the city's Office of Recovery and Resiliency brought me to meetings where city officials brainstormed about how to communicate with residents about the changes to flood insurance premiums. I spent the most time with Zone A New York, started by two Staten Island residents after Sandy, which was working to organize residents around Sandy recovery and climate change resilience. I canvassed door-to-door with one of their leaders as well as a volunteer liaison for FEMA, talking to Staten Islanders about flood insurance and the possibility of pursuing a buyout. I eventually engaged in a bit of public sociology with Zone A, as they asked me to author a series of blog posts on flood insurance.[12] These flood insurance blogs were meant to communicate, in plain English, some of the complicated requirements of and changes to the NFIP for New York City homeowners. They called me their "flood insurance expert" on their website. In New York City, other sites of ethnographic data collection included town halls and public hearings; Sandy anniversary vigils and recovery meetings; professional meetings of architects, planners, designers, and construction managers; and meetings of legal clinics and housing organizations providing services to homeowners dealing with insurance policy changes. I also sought out opportunities for ethnographic observation of some of the national-level reform discussion. I attended open meetings of the National Academy of Sciences committee working on flood insurance affordability reports in Washington, DC, and also joined virtual meetings that took place via webinar. I also joined webinars of the Technical Mapping Advisory Council. In New Jersey, George Kasimos took me along with a group of Stop FEMA Now members to a listening session of the state senate, where they attempted to enlist state politicians in their cause.

The data collection for the historical piece of the project took place at the U.S. National Archives in Washington, DC, and College Park, Maryland, in July and August 2014. I collected archival data of congressional reports and floor debates surrounding the passage of the National Flood Insurance Act of 1968, the authorizing legislation for the NFIP, as well as its reauthorization in 1973. I also collected federal agency documents from HUD and FEMA, including the initial reports that outlined the promises and limitations of different structures for the NFIP. With the archival data I sought to document not only the sequence of events, but also the rationales and objectives of officials and policymakers for creating the NFIP. The archival data came from Record Groups 207, 233, and 311 at the National Archives.

Buttressing this original data collection was a wealth of textual sources on the NFIP by actors inside and outside government. These included scholarship and policy briefs published by the Wharton Risk Management Center at the University of Pennsylvania, which has been home to some of the nation's foremost experts on the NFIP, such as Howard Kunreuther, Erwann Michel-Kerjan, and Carolyn Kousky. I also consulted reports by federal government agencies and organizations, including the Government Accountability Office, the Congressional Budget Office, the Congressional Research Service, FEMA, and the National Academy of Sciences. For New York City, I collected materials from the New York City Office of the Mayor and its various departments. I also drew upon materials from the Union of Concerned Scientists, the Natural Resources Defense Council, the Insurance Information Institute, the Association of State Floodplain

Managers, and other stakeholder groups. Media accounts, official and technical documents related to flood insurance rate maps and insurance rating, produced by FEMA and its contractors; congressional transcripts; and political materials (emails, tweets, fliers, websites, etc.) created by supporters and opponents of Biggert-Waters also inform the analysis here. I treated these texts not only as valuable sources of information on the NFIP, but also as artefacts that expressed the claims, visions, and commitments of their respective authors.

WRITING THIS BOOK

It's tempting to think of a completed dissertation as a first draft of a book. But for me, the transformation involved a near-complete rewrite. Dissertations are necessarily a different genre of writing. There, you try to prove your mettle against other sociologists working on the big conceptual topics you're taking on. You spend a lot of time and words on building the theoretical scaffolding of your arguments. As a result, a relatively small slice of data actually appears, when you consider the sum total of what you've collected and analyzed. Books get to tell more of the actual story. So while the task was at times overwhelming, I welcomed the opportunity to feature more quotations from the interviews and more ethnographic details than could appear in the dissertation. I also was able to collect and include more data, and address new facets of the story, after the dissertation was filed. The work on New York City's flood map appeal, for instance, took place after I had moved to the United Kingdom to take a job in the Department of Sociology at the London School of Economics. This data collection actually started in the service of a short feature for *Harpers Monthly* magazine, which I cowrote with an environmental journalist, Elizabeth Rush.[13]

The analytical through-line of the book also emerged later. The dissertation had been organized around three related processes, but ones that I examined and discussed in relation to distinct research questions and literatures. The thematic of loss and the unifying framework of moral economies were things that came into view only once I was able to take another step back and view the story as a whole. This came from mulling over this project, from the hard work of trying to get some distance from the nitty-gritty of a case I knew so well, but also from thinking about a lot of things that were not this project. My years of work on the NFIP coincided with the release of increasingly detailed, scary, and urgent warnings from climate scientists about how our world has already changed and what may be in store. Reading these reports led me to reckon, intellectually and emotionally, with the question of how societies face destabilizing losses. Insurance provides a way to engage productively with that question.

NOTES

INTRODUCTION: INSURANCE AND THE PROBLEM OF LOSS IN A CLIMATE-CHANGED UNITED STATES

1. Interview, October 18, 2013.
2. Kasimos later posted a short video of this first meeting of Stop FEMA Now to You-Tube (though he mistyped the date; the meeting actually took place in February 2013). George Kasimos, "Raw Video of Our First Meeting in February 2012," YouTube video, February 10, 2013, https://www.youtube.com/watch?v=4n0Kz Z11BJk.
3. This by now robust tradition within economic sociology is most closely associated with the work of Michel Callon and his coauthors. See Koray Caliskan and Michel Callon, "Economization Part 1: Shifting Attention from the Economy Towards Processes of Economization," *Economy and Society* 38 (2009): 369–398; Koray Caliskan and Michel Callon, "Economization Part 2: A Research Programme for the Study of Markets," *Economy and Society* 39 (2010): 1–32; Michel Callon, Yuval Millo, and Fabien Muniesa, eds., *Market Devices* (Malden, MA: Blackwell, 2007).
4. Michel Callon, "An Essay on the Growing Contribution of Economic Markets to the Proliferation of the Social," *Theory, Culture & Society* 24, nos. 7–8 (2007): 139–163.
5. Wendy Espeland, *The Struggle for Water: Politics, Rationality, and Identity in the American Southwest* (Chicago: University of Chicago Press, 1998); Wendy Espeland and Mitchell Stevens, "Commensuration as a Social Process," *Annual Review of Sociology* 24 (1998): 313–343.
6. John Urry, *Climate Change and Society* (Cambridge: Polity Press, 2011).
7. This book pursues a broader vision for the sociology of climate change as a sociology of loss, which I first outlined in Rebecca Elliott, "The Sociology of Climate

Change as a Sociology of Loss," *European Journal of Sociology* 59, no. 3 (December 2018): 301–337.

8. Peter Marris, *Loss and Change* (London: Routledge, 1986).

9. Jon Barnett, Petra Tschakert, Lesley Head, and W. Neil Adger, "A Science of Loss," *Nature Climate Change* 6 (November 2016): 976–978; W. Neil Adger, Jon Barnett, F. S. Chapin III, and Heidi Ellemor, "This Must Be the Place: Underrepresentation of Identity and Meaning in Climate Change Decision-Making," *Global Environmental Politics* 1, no. 2 (2011): 1–25; Espeland, *The Struggle for Water*.

10. Kasia Paprocki, "All That Is Solid Melts into the Bay: Anticipatory Ruination and Climate Change Adaptation," *Antipode* 51, no. 1 (2019): 295–315. Regarding the simultaneously real and symbolic power of climate change, see Mike Hulme, "Cosmopolitan Climates: Hybridity, Foresight and Meaning," *Theory, Culture & Society* 27, nos. 2–3 (2010): 267–276.

11. For more on plural understandings of and mobilizations around investments in homes, see Debbie Becher, *Private Property and Public Power* (New York: Oxford University Press, 2014).

12. Tom Baker, "Risk, Insurance, and the Social Construction of Responsibility," in *Embracing Risk: The Changing Culture of Insurance and Responsibility*, ed. Tom Baker and Jonathan Simon (Chicago: University of Chicago Press, 2002), 33–51. Baker notes that insurance can participate in the social construction of responsibility in many senses of the word: not only accountability and causality, but also trustworthiness, freedom, and solidarity.

13. Daniel Aldana Cohen, "The Other Low-Carbon Protagonists: Poor People's Movements and Climate Politics in Sao Paulo," in *The City is the Factory: New Solidarities and Spatial Strategies in an Urban Age*, ed. Miriam Greenberg and Penny Lewis (Ithaca, NY: Cornell University Press, 2017), 140–157, 143.

14. Carolyn Kousky, "Financing Flood Losses: A Discussion of the National Flood Insurance Program," *Risk Management and Insurance Review* 21, no. 1 (2018): 11–32.

15. For instance, Joe Flood writes about New York City at the vanguard of urban governance techniques in relation to fire prevention and response; Joe Flood, *The Fires: How a Computer Formula, Big Ideas, and the Best of Intentions Burned Down New York City-And Determined the Future of Cities* (New York: Riverhead Books, 2010).

16. C. Wright Mills, *The Sociological Imagination* (New York: Oxford University Press, 1959).

17. On the laypeople versus expert and emotional versus rational tension in risk research, see Deborah Lupton, "Risk and Emotion: Towards an Alternative Theoretical Perspective," *Health, Risk & Society* 15, no. 8 (2013): 634–647; Brian Wynne, "May the Sheep Safely Graze? A Reflexive View of the Expert-Lay Knowledge Divide," in *Risk, Environment and Modernity*, ed. Scott Lash, Bronislaw Szerszynski, and Brian Wynne (London: SAGE Publications, 1996), 44–83; Didier Fassin, ed., *At the Heart of the State: The Moral World of Institutions* (London: Pluto Press, 2015).

18. Sarah Quinn, *American Bonds: How Credit Markets Shaped a Nation* (Princeton, NJ: Princeton University Press, 2019); Elisabeth Clemens, "Lineages of the Rube Goldberg State: Building and Blurring Public Programs, 1900–1940," in *Rethinking*

Political Institutions: the Art of the State, ed. Ian Shapiro, Stephen Skowronek, and Daniel Galvin (New York: New York University Press, 2007), 187–215; William J. Novak, "The Myth of the 'Weak' American State," *American Historical Review* 113, no. 3 (2008): 752–772; Christopher Howard, *The Welfare State Nobody Knows: Debunking Myths about U.S. Social Policy* (Princeton, NJ: Princeton University Press, 2006); David Moss, *When All Else Fails: Government as the Ultimate Risk Manager* (Cambridge, MA: Harvard University Press, 2004).

19. Max Weber, "Science as a Vocation," in *From Max Weber: Essays in Sociology*, ed. H. H. Gerth and C. Wright Mills (New York: Oxford University Press, 1946 [1919]), 129–156, 139.

20. Ian Hacking, *The Taming of Chance* (Cambridge: Cambridge University Press, 1990); see also Theodore M. Porter, *The Rise of Statistical Thinking, 1820–1900* (Princeton, NJ: Princeton University Press, 1986); Theodore M. Porter, *Trust in Numbers: The Pursuit of Objectivity in Science and Public Life* (Princeton, NJ: Princeton University Press, 1995); Peter L. Bernstein, *Against the Gods: The Remarkable Story of Risk* (New York: Wiley, 1998); Dan Bouk, *How Our Days Became Numbered: Risk and the Rise of the Statistical Individual* (Chicago: University of Chicago Press, 2015); Michael Power, *Organized Uncertainty* (Oxford: Oxford University Press, 2007).

21. Stephen Collier, "Neoliberalism and Natural Disaster: Insurance as a Political Technology of Catastrophe," *Journal of Cultural Economy* 7, no. 3 (2014): 273–290.

22. James C. Scott, *Seeing Like a State: How Certain Schemes to Improve the Human Condition Have Failed* (New Haven, CT: Yale University Press, 1999), 43. See also J. B. Harley, "Deconstructing the Map," *Cartographica* 26, no. 2 (1989): 1–20; Jeremy W. Crampton and John Krygier, "An Introduction to Critical Cartography," *ACME: An International E-Journal for Critical Cartographies* 4, no. 1 (2006): 11–33; Timothy Mitchell, *Rule of Experts* (Berkeley: University of California Press, 2002); Denis Wood, *Rethinking the Power of Maps* (London: Guilford, 2010); Pat O'Malley and Alex Roberts, "Governmental Conditions for the Economization of Uncertainty," *Journal of Cultural Economy* 7, no. 3 (2014): 253–272; Michel Foucault, *Security, Territory, Population: Lectures at the Collège de France 1977-78* (New York: Palgrave Macmillan, 2007).

23. 119 *Congressional Record*, House, Part 2. 93rd Congress, 1st sess. (1973), H557.

24. Scott Gabriel Knowles and Howard C. Kunreuther, "Troubled Waters: The National Flood Insurance Program in Historical Perspective," *Journal of Policy History* 26, no. 3 (2014): 327–353.

25. Duff Wilson, Ryan McNeill, and Deborah J. Nelson, "Water's Edge: The Crisis of Rising Sea Levels, Part 3," *Reuters*, November 24, 2014, https://www.reuters.com/investigates/special-report/waters-edge-the-crisis-of-rising-sea-levels/. Reuters' analysis used data from the National Oceanic Atmospheric Administration's Coastal Change Analysis Program, which shows dominant land use in thirty-square-meter areas. Reuters examined areas only within about one-eighth of a mile of the mean higher high-water coastline as mapped by NOAA for the contiguous United States. Louisiana was excluded because of insufficient data.

26. Author's analysis of national dataset from floodzonedata.us, a project of the New York University Furman Center. Estimates of these figures vary, depending on the data used. For instance, a 2018 study settled on a floodplain population of

41 million, arguing that FEMA had seriously underestimated its figures; see Oliver E. J. Wing, Paul D. Bates, Andrew M. Smith, Christopher C. Sampson, Kris A. Johnson, Joseph Fargione, and Philip Morefield, "Estimates of Present and Future Flood Risk in the Conterminous United States," *Environmental Research Letters* 13, no. 3 (2018): 1–7.

27. "Policy & Claims Statistics for Flood Insurance," Federal Emergency Management Agency, accessed February 13, 2020, https://www.fema.gov/policy-claim-statistics -flood-insurance.

28. FEMA defines "severe repetitive loss" properties as those that have filed four or more claims of more than $5,000, or two to three claims that cumulatively exceed the building's value.

29. Natural Resources Defense Council, "Seeking Higher Ground," Issue Brief, July 2017, https://www.nrdc.org/sites/default/files/climate-smart-flood-insurance -ib.pdf.

30. "Fast Facts: Economics and Demographics," National Oceanic and Atmospheric Administration, Office for Coastal Management, accessed March 8, 2019, https:// coast.noaa.gov/states/fast-facts/economics-and-demographics.html.

31. AIR Worldwide, *The Coastline at Risk: 2016 Update to the Estimated Insured Value of U.S. Coastal Properties* (Boston: AIR Worldwide, 2016).

32. Congressional Budget Office, *Potential Increases in Hurricane Damage in the United States: Implications for the Federal Budget* (Washington, DC: Government Printing Office, June 2016), https://www.cbo.gov/publication/51518.

33. AECOM, *The Impact of Climate Change and Population Growth on the National Flood Insurance Program Through 2100* (Washington, DC: Federal Emergency Management Agency, June 2013).

34. National Oceanic and Atmospheric Administration, *Patterns and Projections of High Tide Flooding Along the U.S. Coastline Using a Common Impact Threshold* (Washington, DC: National Oceanic and Atmospheric Administration, February 2018), https:// tidesandcurrents.noaa.gov/publications/techrpt86_PaP_of_HTFlooding.pdf.

35. Federal Emergency Management Agency, *An Affordability Framework for the National Flood Insurance Program* (Washington, DC: Federal Emergency Management Agency, April 17, 2018), 11. The Furman Center analysis groups census tracts into several categories based on the census tract's poverty rate in 2011–2015. Low-poverty census tracts are defined as those where the share of the population in poverty was less than 10 percent; moderate-poverty tracts are defined as those where the share of the population in poverty was between 10 percent and 30 percent; and high-poverty tracts are defined as those where the share of the population in poverty was greater than 30 percent. NYU Furman Center, *Population in the U.S. Floodplains* (New York: New York University, December 2017), https:// furmancenter.org/files/Floodplain_PopulationBrief_12DEC2017.pdf.

36. Union of Concerned Scientists, *Underwater: Rising Seas, Chronic Floods, and the Implications for US Coastal Real Estate* (Washington, DC: Union of Concerned Scientists, 2018), https://www.ucsusa.org/global-warming/global-warming-impacts /sea-level-rise-chronic-floods-and-us-coastal-real-estate-implications.

37. Rawle O. King, *The National Flood Insurance Program: Status and Remaining Issues for Congress* (Washington, DC: Congressional Research Service, 2013).

38. In 2018, the NFIP had about $16 billion of its debt forgiven.

39. Government Accountability Office, *GAO-19-157SP: High-Risk Series, Substantial Efforts Needed to Achieve Greater Progress on High-Risk Areas* (Washington, DC: Government Accountability Office, 2019), https://www.gao.gov/highrisk/national _flood_insurance/why_did_study.

40. Logan Strother, "The National Flood Insurance Program: A Case Study in Policy Failure, Reform, and Retrenchment," *Policy Studies Journal* 46, no. 2 (2016): 452–480, 452.

41. Jeff Goodell, *The Water Will Come: Rising Seas, Sinking Cities, and the Remaking of the Civilized World* (New York: Little, Brown, 2017), 108; see also Gilbert M. Gaul, *The Geography of Risk: Epic Storms, Rising Seas, and the Cost of America's Coasts* (New York: Sarah Crichton Books, 2019.

42. Economists, in dialogue with cognitive psychologists, have recognized that the "signal" provided by the calculation and pricing of risk often fails to convince individuals to take any steps at all. The promises of risk information run aground on various peculiarities related to how individuals make decisions about the future. Some interpret this as "irrationality"; others describe this a kind of systematic bias that derives from the use of heuristics to process information. In either case, action is intelligible as a function of individual cognition. See Daniel Ellsberg, "Risk, Ambiguity, and the Savage Axioms," *Quarterly Journal of Economics* 75, no. 4 (1961): 643–669; Daniel Kahneman, Paul Slovic, and Amos Tversky, eds., *Judgment Under Uncertainty: Heuristics and Biases* (New York: Cambridge University Press, 1982); Justin Gallagher, "Learning About an Infrequent Event: Evidence from Flood Insurance Take-Up in the United States," *American Economic Journal: Applied Economics* 6, no. 3 (2014): 206–233; Howard Kunreuther, Nathan Novemsky, and Daniel Kahneman, "Making Low Probabilities Useful," *Journal of Risk and Uncertainty* 23 (September 2001): 103–120; Paul Slovic, "Perception of Risk," *Science* 236, no. 4799 (1987): 280–285.

43. Tom Baker, "On the Genealogy of Moral Hazard," *Texas Law Review* 75, no. 2 (1996): 237–292; Carol Heimer, *Reactive Risk and Rational Action: Managing Moral Hazard in Insurance Contracts* (Berkeley: University of California Press, 1985).

44. On the growth machine generally, see John R. Logan and Harvey Molotch, *Urban Fortunes: The Political Economy of Place* (Berkeley: University of California Press, 1987); Harvey Molotch and John R. Logan, "Tensions in the Growth Machine: Overcoming Resistance to Value-Free Development," *Social Problems* 3, no. 5 (1984): 483–499. On the political economy of natural hazards, risk, and disaster, see Kathleen J. Tierney, *The Social Roots of Risk* (Palo Alto, CA: Stanford University Press, 2014); Raymond J. Burby, "Hurricane Katrina and the Paradoxes of Government Disaster Policy: Bringing About Wise Governmental Decisions for Hazardous Areas," *Annals of the American Academy of Political and Social Science* 604 (2006): 171–191; Karen M. O'Neill, *Rivers by Design: State Power and the Origins of U.S. Flood Control* (Durham, NC: Duke University Press, 2006); Kevin Fox Gotham, "Coastal Restoration as Contested Terrain: Climate Change and the Political Economy of Risk Reduction in Louisiana," *Sociological Forum* 31, no. S1 (2016): 787–806; Kevin Fox Gotham, "Antinomies of Risk Reduction: Climate Change and the Contradictions of Coastal Restoration," *Environmental Sociology* 2, no. 2 (2016): 208–219. On the political economy of the NFIP, see Ted Steinberg, *Acts of God: The Unnatural History of Natural Disaster in America* (Oxford: Oxford

University Press, 2006), chap. 5; William R. Freudenberg, Robert B. Gramling, Shirley Laska, and Kai Erikson *Catastrophe in the Making: The Engineering of Katrina and the Disasters of Tomorrow* (Washington, DC: Island Press, 2009).

45. Henry Rothstein, Michael Huber, and George Gaskell, "A Theory of Risk Colonization: The Spiraling Regulatory Logics of Societal and Institutional Risk," *Economy & Society* 35, no. 1 (2006): 91–112; Henry Rothstein, "The Institutional Origins of Risk: A New Agenda for Risk Research," *Health, Risk & Society* 8, no. 3: 215–221; Charles Perrow, *Normal Accidents* (Princeton, NJ: Princeton University Press, 1999); Michael Power, *Organized Uncertainty* (Oxford: Oxford University Press, 2007); Bridget M. Hutter and Sally Lloyd-Bostock, *Regulatory Crisis: Negotiating the Consequences of Risk, Disasters and Crisis* (Cambridge: Cambridge University Press, 2017).

46. Ulrich Beck, *Risk Society* (New York: SAGE Publications, 1992); Ulrich Beck, *World Risk Society* (London: Polity Press, 1999); Ulrich Beck, "Living in the World Risk Society," *Economy and Society* 35, no. 3 (2006): 329–345; Ulrich Beck, *World at Risk* (London: Polity Press, 2009); see also Anthony Giddens, "Risk and Responsibility," *Modern Law Review* 62, no. 1 (1999): 1–10; Zygmunt Bauman, *Modernity and Ambivalence* (Cambridge: Polity Press, 1991).

47. This thesis has generated vigorous debate among insurance scholars, who have argued, on the basis of empirical data on the activity of insurers, that insurance has in fact shown a great deal of scientific, technical, and financial creativity in grappling with catastrophic risks. The concluding chapter describes these activities in greater detail as they pertain to climate change.

48. James C. Scott, *The Moral Economy of the Peasant: Rebellion and Subsistence in Southeast Asia* (New Haven, CT: Yale University Press, 1977), 4.

49. E. P. Thompson, "The Moral Economy of the English Crowd in the Eighteenth Century," *Past & Present* 50, no. 1 (1971): 76–136; Tim Rogan, *The Moral Economists: R. H. Tawney, Karl Polanyi, E. P. Thompson, and the Critique of Capitalism* (Princeton, NJ: Princeton University Press, 2018).

50. Fassin, ed., *At the Heart of the State*; Wendy Wolford, "Agrarian Moral Economies and Neoliberalism in Brazil: Competing Worldviews and the State in the Struggle for Land," *Environment and Planning A* 37, no. 2 (2005): 241–261.

51. Émile Durkheim, *The Elementary Forms of Religious Life* (New York: The Free Press, 1995 [1912]); Marion Fourcade and Kieran Healy, "Moral Views of Market Society," *Annual Review of Sociology* 33 (2007): 285–311; Marion Fourcade, "The Fly and the Cookie: Alignment and Unhingement in 21st-Century Capitalism," *Socio-Economic Review* 15, no. 3 (2017): 661–678; Viviana Zelizer, *Economic Lives: How Culture Shapes the Economy* (Princeton, NJ: Princeton University Press, 2010); Roi Livne, "Economies of Dying: The Moralization of Economic Scarcity in U.S. Hospice Care," *American Sociological Review* 79, no. 5 (2014): 888–911; Didier Fassin, "Compassion and Repression: The Moral Economy of Immigration Policies in France," *Cultural Anthropology* 20, no. 3 (2005): 362–387; Adam Reich, *Selling Our Souls: The Commodification of Hospital Care in the United States* (Princeton, NJ: Princeton University Press, 2014).

52. Cf. Scott, *The Moral Economy of the Peasant*.

53. James McCarthy, "First World Political Ecology: Lessons from the Wise Use Movement," *Environment and Planning A* 34, no. 7 (2002): 1281–1302.

54. Fourcade, "The Fly and the Cookie," 662; Fourcade and Healy, "Moral Views of Market Society."

55. Espeland, *The Struggle for Water.*

56. Pat O'Malley, "Risk and Responsibility," in *Foucault and Political Reason: Liberalism, Neo-liberalism and Rationalities of Government,* ed. Andrew Barry, Thomas Osborne, and Nikolas Rose (London: University College London Press, 1996), 197–198.

57. Tom Baker, "Containing the Promise of Insurance: Adverse Selection and Risk Classification," *Connecticut Insurance Law Journal* 9, no. 2 (2002): 371–396; see also Porter, *Trust in Numbers.* Such conceptions of fairness obtain beyond the case of insurance, as Marion Fourcade and Kieran Healy show in their study of how corporations use personal data to classify and rank consumers. In markets, calculative methods that sort people in various ways are often viewed as dispassionate and therefore fair. See Marion Fourcade and Kieran Healy, "Seeing Like a Market," *Socio-Economic Review* 15, no. 1 (2017): 9–29.

58. Barbara Kiviat, "The Moral Limits of Predictive Practices: The Case of Credit-Based Insurance Scores," *American Sociological Review* 84, no. 6 (2019): 1134–1158.

59. Tom Baker and Jonathan Simon, eds., *Embracing Risk: The Changing Culture of Insurance and Responsibility* (Chicago: University of Chicago Press, 2002).

60. Viviana Zelizer, *Morals and Markets: The Development of Life Insurance in the United States* (New York: Columbia University Press, 1979). See also Sarah Quinn, "The Transformation of Morals in Markets: Death, Benefits, and the Exchange of Life Insurance Policies," *American Journal of Sociology* 114, no. 3: 738–780; Bouk, *How Our Days Became Numbered.*

61. Stephen Hilgartner, "The Social Construction of Risk Objects," in *Organizations, Uncertainty and Risk,* ed. James F. Short and Lee Clarke (Oxford: Westview Press, 1992), 39–53; Heimer, *Reactive Risk and Rational Action.*

62. Carol Heimer, "Insurers as Moral Actors," in *Risk and Morality,* ed. Richard V. Ericson and Aaron Doyle (Toronto: University of Toronto Press, 2003), 284–316.

63. Francois Ewald, *The Birth of Solidarity: The History of the French Welfare State* (Durham, NC: Duke University Press, 2020); Francois Ewald, "Insurance and Risk," in *The Foucault Effect: Studies in Governmentality,* ed. Graham Burchell, Colin Gordon, and Peter Miller (Chicago: University of Chicago Press, 1991), 197–210.

64. Turo-Kimmo Lehtonen and Jyri Liukko, "The Forms and Limits of Insurance Solidarity," *Journal of Business Ethics* 103, no. 1 (2011): 33–44; Mitchell Dean, "Risk, Calculable and Incalculable," in *Risk and Sociocultural Theory: New Directions and Perspectives,* ed. Deborah Lupton (Cambridge: Cambridge University Press, 1999), 131–159; Luis Lobo-Guerrero, *Insuring Security: Biopolitics, Security, and Risk* (Abingdon, UK: Routledge, 2011).

65. Baker, "On the Genealogy of Moral Hazard," 291.

66. Fourcade and Healy describe such market-based actuarial practices as an example of "boundary classifications," whereby market institutions establish individual or collective designations of being "in" or "out," i.e., of having access to goods and services or not. See Marion Fourcade and Kieran Healy, "Classification

Situations: Life-Chances in the Neoliberal Era," *Accounting, Organizations and Society* 38, no. 8 (2013): 559–572; Gregory D. Squires, ed., *Insurance Redlining: Disinvestment, Reinvestment, and the Evolving Role of Financial Institutions* (Washington, DC: Urban Institute Press, 1997); Manuel B. Aalbers, *Place, Exclusion, and Mortgage Markets* (Oxford: Wiley-Blackwell).

67. Turo-Kimmo Lehtonen and Jyri Liukko, "Producing Solidarity, Inequality, and Exclusion Through Insurance," *Res Publica* (May 2015): 1–15; Deborah Stone, "Beyond Moral Hazard: Insurance as Moral Opportunity," in *Embracing Risk: The Changing Culture of Insurance and Responsibility*, ed. Tom Baker and Jonathan Simon (Chicago: University of Chicago Press, 2002), 52–79; Pat O'Malley, *Risk, Uncertainty and Government* (London: The Glass House Press, 2004).

68. Ewald, *The Birth of Solidarity*; Ewald, "Insurance and Risk."

69. Dean, "Risk, Calculable and Incalculable," 139.

70. David Garland, "The Rise of Risk," in *Risk and Morality*, ed. Richard V. Ericson and Aaron Doyle (Toronto: University of Toronto Press, 2003), 48–86; David Garland, "The Welfare State: A Fundamental Dimension of Modern Government," *European Journal of Sociology* 55, no. 3 (2014): 327–364. See also Moss, *When All Else Fails*; Stone, "Beyond Moral Hazard."

71. See, for instance, Brian Steensland, "Cultural Categories and the American Welfare State: The Case of Guaranteed Income Policy," *American Journal of Sociology* 111, no. 5 (2006): 1273–1326; Michael B. Katz, *The Undeserving Poor: From the War on Poverty to the War on Welfare* (New York: Pantheon Books, 1989); Joel F. Handler and Yeheskel Hasenfeld, *The Moral Construction of Poverty: Welfare Reform in America* (Newbury Park, CA: Sage Publications, 1991).

72. Michele Landis Dauber, *The Sympathetic State: Disaster Relief and the Origins of the American Welfare State* (Chicago: University of Chicago Press, 2013); Garland, "The Rise of Risk."

73. Anne Schneider and Helen Ingram, *Deserving and Entitled: Social Constructions and Public Policy* (Albany: State University of New York Press, 2005); Martin Gilens, *Why Americans Hate Welfare: Race, Media and the Politics of Antipoverty Policy* (Chicago: University of Chicago Press, 1999).

74. Dauber, *The Sympathetic State*.

75. See also Michele L. Landis, "Fate, Responsibility, and 'Natural' Disaster Relief: Narrating the American Welfare State," *Law & Society Review* 33, no. 2 (1999): 257–318.

76. Moss, *When All Else Fails*.

77. Suzanne Mettler, *The Submerged State: How Invisible Government Policies Undermine American Democracy* (Chicago: University of Chicago Press, 2011); see also Isaac Martin, *The Permanent Tax Revolt: How the Property Tax Transformed American Politics* (Stanford, CA: Stanford University Press, 2008); Christopher Howard, *The Welfare State Nobody Knows*; James R. Dunn, "Security, Meaning, and the Home," in *Social Resilience in the Neoliberal Era*, ed. Peter A. Hall and Michèle Lamont (Cambridge: Cambridge University Press, 2013), 183–205; Keeanga-Yamahtta Taylor, *Race for Profit: How Banks and the Real Estate Industry Undermined Black Homeownership* (Chapel Hill: University of North Carolina Press, 2019); Brian McCabe, *No Place Like Home: Wealth, Community, and the Politics of Homeownership* (New York: Oxford University Press, 2016); Nancy H. Kwak,

A World of Homeowners: American Power and the Politics of Housing Aid (Chicago: University of Chicago Press, 2015); Kenneth T. Jackson, *Crabgrass Frontier: The Suburbanization of the United States* (Oxford: Oxford University Press, 1985).

78. This work has been helpfully summarized in a recent publication by the American Sociological Association Climate Change Task Force; Riley E. Dunlap and Robert J. Brulle, eds., *Climate Change and Society: Sociological Perspectives* (Oxford: Oxford University Press, 2015).

79. The disaster studies literature is vast and includes work by sociologists, historians, anthropologists, and political scientists. Studies in this field include (among numerous others), Michael Eric Dyson, *Come Hell or High Water: Hurricane Katrina and the Color of Disaster* (New York: Basic Civitas Books, 2006); Kai Erikson, *Everything in Its Path: Destruction of Community in the Buffalo Creek Flood* (New York: Simon and Schuster, 1976); Alice Fothergill, *Heads Above Water: Gender, Class, and Family in the Grand Forks Flood* (Albany: State University of New York Press, 2004); Alice Fothergill and Lori Peek, *Children of Katrina* (Austin: University of Texas Press, 2015); Freudenberg et al., *Catastrophe in the Making*; Kevin Fox Gotham and Miriam Greenberg, *Crisis Cities: Disaster and Redevelopment in New York and New Orleans* (New York: Oxford University Press, 2014); Andy Horowitz, *Katrina: A History, 1915–2015* (Cambridge, MA: Harvard University Press, 2020); Eric Klinenberg, *Heat Wave: A Social Autopsy of Disaster in Chicago* (Chicago: University of Chicago Press, 2002); Scott Gabriel Knowles, *The Disaster Experts: Mastering Risk in Modern America* (Philadelphia: University of Pennsylvania Press, 2011); Steve Kroll-Smith, *Recovering Inequality: Hurricane Katrina, the San Francisco Earthquake of 1906, and the Aftermath of Disaster* (Austin: University of Texas Press, 2018); Andrew Lakoff, ed., *Disaster and the Politics of Intervention* (New York, Columbia University Press, 2010); Charles Perrow, *Normal Accidents: Living with High-Risk Technologies* (Princeton, NJ: Princeton University Press, 1999); Jacob Remes, *Disaster Citizenship: Survivors, Solidarity, and Power in the Progressive Era* (Urbana: University of Illinois Press, 2016); Gregory L. Simon, *Flame and Fortune in the American West: Urban Development, Environmental Change, and the Great Oakland Hills Fire* (Berkeley: University of California Press, 2016); Ben Wisner, Piers Blaikie, Terry Cannon, and Ian Davis, *At Risk: Natural Hazards, People's Vulnerability, and Disasters*, 2nd ed. (New York: Routledge, 2003).

80. On how and why these styles of reasoning are consequential more broadly, see Daniel Hirschman and Elizabeth Popp Berman, "Do Economists Make Policies? On the Political Effects of Economics," *Socio-Economic Review* 12, no. 4 (2014): 779–811.

1. TRANSFORMING THE MANAGEMENT OF LOSS: THE ORIGINS OF THE NATIONAL FLOOD INSURANCE PROGRAM

1. Richard Eder, "Johnson Directs Relief," *New York Times*, September 12, 1965.

2. Andy Horowitz, "Hurricane Betsy and the Politics of Disaster in New Orleans's Lower Ninth Ward, 1965–1967," *Journal of Southern History* 80, no. 4 (2014): 893–934.

3. "LBJ and Senator Russell Long on Hurricane Betsy," White House Tapes, UVA Miller Center, September 10, 1965, Conversation Number, WH6509.03–8847, https://millercenter.org/the-presidency/educational-resources/lbj-and-senator -russell-long-on-hurricane-betsy.

4. Erwann O. Michel-Kerjan, "Catastrophe Economics: The National Flood Insurance Program," *Journal of Economic Perspectives* 24, no. 4 (Fall 2010): 165–186; David Remnick, "High Water," *New Yorker*, October 3, 2005, https://www .newyorker.com/magazine/2005/10/03/high-water.

5. Eder, "Johnson Directs Relief."

6. Rawle O. King, *The National Flood Insurance Program: Status and Remaining Issues for Congress* (Washington, DC: Congressional Research Service, 2013).

7. Lyndon B. Johnson, "Statement by the President Upon Signing the Southeast Hurricane Disaster Relief Act of 1965," November 8, 1965, Presidency Project, http:// www.presidency.ucsb.edu/ws/?pid=27358.

8. Michel-Kerjan, "Catastrophe Economics."

9. J. Robert Hunter, "Testimony of J. Robert Hunter, Director Of Insurance, Consumer Federation of America Before the Committee on Banking, Housing, and Urban Affairs of the United States Senate Regarding Oversight of the National Flood Insurance Program," October 18, 2005.

10. David Moss, *When All Else Fails: Government as the Ultimate Risk Manager* (Cambridge, MA: Harvard University Press, 2004), 21.

11. Wendy Espeland, *The Struggle for Water: Politics, Rationality, and Identity in the American Southwest* (Chicago: University of Chicago Press, 1998).

12. Robert Hinshaw, *Living with Nature's Extremes: The Life of Gilbert Fowler White* (Boulder, CO: University of Colorado Press, 2006), 140.

13. Michele Landis Dauber, *The Sympathetic State: Disaster Relief and the Origins of the American Welfare State* (Chicago: University of Chicago Press, 2013); Gareth Davies, "The Emergence of a National Politics of Disaster, 1865–1900," *Journal of Policy History* 26, no. 3 (2014): 305–326, 321; Wesley Shrum, "What Caused the Flood? Controversy and Closure in the Hurricane Katrina Disaster," *Social Studies of Science* 44, no. 1 (2014): 3–33.

14. Gareth Davies, "Dealing with Disaster: The Politics of Catastrophe in the United States, 1789–1861," *American Nineteenth Century History* 14, no. 1 (2013): 53–72; Kathleen J. Tierney, "From the Margins to the Mainstream? Disaster Research at the Crossroads," *Annual Review of Sociology* 33 (2007): 503–525; Ted Steinberg, *Acts of God: The Unnatural History of Natural Disaster in America* (Oxford: Oxford University Press, 2006); Michele L. Landis, "Let Me Next Time Be Tried by Fire: Disaster Relief and the Origins of the American Welfare State 1789–1874," *Northwestern University Law Review* 92, no. 3 (1998): 967–1034. In *The Sympathetic State*, Dauber shows that the federal government was making its first direct payments for disaster relief in 1790.

15. Patrick S. Roberts, "Private Choices, Public Harms: The Evolution of National Disaster Organizations in the United States," in *Disaster and the Politics of Intervention*, ed. Andrew Lakoff (New York, Columbia University Press, 2010), 42–69, 45.

16. Steinberg, *Acts of God*, 5.

17. Karen M. O'Neill, *Rivers by Design: State Power and the Origins of U.S. Flood Control* (Durham, NC: Duke University Press, 2006); Rutherford H. Platt, *Disasters*

and Democracy: The Politics of Extreme National Events (Washington, DC: Island Press, 1999).

18. Platt, Disasters and Democracy; Theodore M. Porter, Trust in Numbers: The Pursuit of Objectivity in Science and Public Life (Princeton, NJ: Princeton University Press, 1995); Hinshaw, Living with Nature's Extremes.

19. Quoted in Hinshaw, Living with Nature's Extremes, 18.

20. Andrew Morris, "Hurricane Camille and the New Politics of Federal Disaster Relief, 1965–1970," Journal of Policy History 26, no. 3 (2014): 406–426; Patrick S. Roberts, Disasters and the American State (Cambridge: Cambridge University Press, 2013).

21. Roberts, Disasters and the American State.

22. Stephen Collier, "Neoliberalism and Natural Disaster: Insurance as a Political Technology of Catastrophe," Journal of Cultural Economy 7, no. 3 (2014): 273–290.

23. Roberts, Disasters and the American State, 52.

24. David Moss, "Courting Disaster? The Transformation of Federal Disaster Policy Since 1803," in The Financing of Catastrophe Risk, ed. Kenneth A. Froot (Chicago: University of Chicago Press, 1999), 307–362; Moss, When All Else Fails, 262; Scott Gabriel Knowles and Howard C. Kunreuther, "Troubled Waters: The National Flood Insurance Program in Historical Perspective," Journal of Policy History 26, no. 3 (2014): 327–353; Diane P. Horn and Baird Webel, Private Flood Insurance and the National Flood Insurance Program (Washington, DC: Congressional Research Service, 2019).

25. U.S. House, 113 Congressional Record 1967, 90th Congress, 1st session, Nov. 1, 1967, p. 30784.

26. Hinshaw, Living with Nature's Extremes. White's ideas developed in dialogue with his mentor at the University of Chicago, Harlan H. Barrows, a professor of geography. In a 1936 report to Congress, Barrows argued for spatial planning as a way to guide habitation away from high-risk areas, a cost-effective strategy that would reduce the need for flood protection and disaster relief; see Martin Reuss, "Coping with Uncertainty: Social Scientists, Engineers, and Federal Water Resources Planning," Natural Resources Journal 32, no. 1 (1992): 101–135.

27. Kenneth T. Jackson, Crabgrass Frontier: The Suburbanization of the United States (Oxford: Oxford University Press, 1985); Collier, "Neoliberalism and Natural Disaster."

28. Hinshaw, Living with Nature's Extremes; James Porter and David Demeritt, "Flood-Risk Management, Mapping, and Planning: The Institutional Politics of Decision Support in England," Environment and Planning A 44, no. 10 (2012): 2359–2378.

29. Collier, "Neoliberalism and Natural Disaster"; William R. Freudenberg, Robert B. Gramling, Shirley Laska, and Kai Erikson, Catastrophe in the Making: The Engineering of Katrina and the Disasters of Tomorrow (Washington, DC: Island Press, 2009); O'Neill, Rivers by Design; Steinberg, Acts of God.

30. Moss, "Courting Disaster?"

31. Quoted in Collier, "Neoliberalism and Natural Disaster," 274.

32. As Bergsma notes in the context of the NFIP's history, drawing on the work of Paul A. Sabatier, public policies are based on often implicit causal theories of how the world operates. See Emmy Bergsma, "Geographers Versus Managers: Expert Influence on the Construction of Values Underlying Flood Insurance in the United

States," *Environmental Values* 25, no. 6 (2016): 687–705; Paul A. Sabatier, "An Advocacy Coalition Framework of Policy Change and the Role of Policy-Oriented Learning Therein," *Policy Sciences* 21, nos. 2–3 (1988): 129–168.

33. Collier, "Neoliberalism and Natural Disaster."

34. Hinshaw, *Living with Nature's Extremes*, 36.

35. Hinshaw, *Living with Nature's Extremes*, 137–138.

36. Federal Emergency Management Agency (FEMA), *A Chronology of Major Events Affecting the National Flood Insurance Program* (Washington, DC: FEMA, 2005), 4.

37. This legislative history appears in the 1967 *Congressional Record*, where Senator Thomas J. Dodd (D-CT) added an excerpt of the original 1956 hearings to the record during that session; see 113 *Congressional Record* 1967 Senate, S13027–13036.

38. 113 *Cong. Rec.* 1967 Senate, S8727.

39. Dan R. Anderson, "The National Flood Insurance Program: Problems and Potential," *Journal of Risk and Insurance* 41, no. 4 (1974): 579–599.

40. 113 *Cong. Rec.* 1967 House: H14333.

41. Collier, "Neoliberalism and Natural Disaster."

42. Department of Housing and Urban Development (HUD), *Insurance and Other Programs for Financial Assistance to Flood Victims* (Washington, DC: HUD, 1966).

43. U.S. House, "Final Report on the Federal Flood Indemnity Administration," by the Housing and Home Finance Agency. House Doc. 426, 85th Congress, 2nd sess., 1958.

44. Moss, *When All Else Fails*; Saul J. Singer, "Flooding the Fifth Amendment: The National Flood Insurance Program and the 'Takings' Clause," *Boston College Environmental Affairs Law Review* 17, no. 2 (1990): 323–370; Michel-Kerjan, "Catastrophe Economics."

45. Quoted in W. B. Langbein, "Flood Insurance," *Land Economics* 29, no. 4 (1953): 323–330, 329.

46. Hinshaw, *Living With Nature's Extremes*, 139, 141.

47. For more on the role social scientists played during this period of American water management, see Reuss, "Coping with Uncertainty."

48. Collier, "Neoliberalism and Natural Disaster," 275.

49. These low-interest loans exploded in volume after World War II, due to a combination of rising losses and liberalized provisions. However, the loan program was faulted for being poorly administered and for failing to compensate individuals fully; see Collier, "Neoliberalism and Natural Disaster, 280.

50. Pat O'Malley, "Governable Catastrophes: A Comment on Bougen," *Economy and Society* 32, no. 2 (2003): 275–279, 278; Mitchell Dean, "Risk, Calculable and Incalculable," in *Risk and Sociocultural Theory: New Directions and Perspectives,* ed. Deborah Lupton, (Cambridge: Cambridge University Press, 1999), 131–159.

51. Kevin Fox Gotham, *Race, Real Estate, and Uneven Development* (Albany: State University of New York Press, 2002); Douglas S. Massey and Nancy A. Denton, *American Apartheid: Segregation and the Making of the Underclass* (Cambridge, MA: Harvard University Press, 1998; Richard Rothstein, *The Color of Law: A Forgotten History of How Our Government Segregated America* (New York: Liveright, 2017); Keeanga-Yamahtta Taylor, *Race for Profit: How Banks and the Real Estate Industry Undermined Black Homeownership* (Chapel Hill: University of North Carolina

Press, 2019); David M. P. Freund, *Colored Property: State Policy and White Racial Politics in Suburban America* (Chicago: University of Chicago Press, 2007).

52. Porter, *Trust in Numbers;* Scott Gabriel Knowles, *The Disaster Experts: Mastering Risk in Modern America* (Philadelphia: University of Pennsylvania Press, 2011); Joe Flood, *The Fires: How a Computer Formula, Big Ideas, and the Best of Intentions Burned Down New York City-And Determined the Future of Cities* (New York: Riverhead Books, 2010); Daniel Hirschman and Elizabeth Popp Berman, "Do Economists Make Policies? On the Political Effects of Economics," *Socio-Economic Review* 12, no. 4 (2014): 779–811.

53. Resources for the Future was founded in 1952 by the Ford Foundation to conduct research primarily on U.S. public policy concerning natural resources. RFF supported research projects of Gilbert White, who joined the RFF Board of Trustees beginning in the late 1960s and served as board chairman for five years beginning in 1974.

54. HUD, *Insurance and Other Programs,* 51.

55. HUD, *Insurance and Other Programs,* 48.

56. HUD, *Insurance and Other Programs,* 69.

57. HUD, *Insurance and Other Programs,* 76.

58. Collier, "Neoliberalism and Natural Disaster."

59. HUD, *Insurance and Other Programs,* 60.

60. Collier, "Neoliberalism and Natural Disaster," 287. For this reason, Collier concludes, we cannot "reliably locate neoliberalism at a single point on the political map": "Instead, we find a more complex layering of problems, events, styles of thinking, and political positions that scrambles many familiar categories and distinctions."

61. HUD, *Insurance and Other Programs,* 68, 116–117.

62. HUD, *Insurance and Other Programs,* 129.

63. HUD, *Insurance and Other Programs,* 129–130.

64. Taylor, *Race for Profit,* 19; Jackson, *Crabgrass Frontier;* Constance Perin, *Everything in Its Place: Social Order and Land Use in America* (Princeton, NJ: Princeton University Press, 1977); Sarah Quinn, *American Bonds: How Credit Markets Shaped a Nation* (Princeton, NJ: Princeton University Press, 2019); Nancy H. Kwak, *A World of Homeowners: American Power and the Politics of Housing Aid* (Chicago: University of Chicago Press, 2015).

65. HUD, *Insurance and Other Programs,* 132.

66. For a more detailed account of Krutilla's contributions to the task force, see Collier, "Neoliberalism and Natural Disaster."

67. Another important outcome of the report was Executive Order 11296, which mandated for the first time that federal agencies formally incorporate flood planning into their programs, including construction of new federal buildings, structures, roads, or other facilities, as well as flood-proofing where practical and economical. Agencies responsible for extending federal grants, loans, or mortgage insurance were also to evaluate flood hazards to minimize potential losses. The Corps and the TVA would be responsible for preparing all flood hazard information reports. See Hinshaw, *Living with Nature's Extremes,* 150.

68. Task Force on Federal Flood Control Policy, *Unified National Program for Managing Flood Losses* (Washington, DC: Government Printing Office, 1966), 12.

69. Task Force on Federal Flood Control Policy, *Unified National Program*, 25, 14, 15.
70. Task Force on Federal Flood Control Policy, *Unified National Program*, 16.
71. Task Force on Federal Flood Control Policy, *Unified National Program*, 38.
72. Task Force on Federal Flood Control Policy, *Unified National Program*, 38, 17, 39.
73. Such ideas bear a resemblance to what Albert Hirschman characterizes as the "perversity thesis," mobilized since the French Revolution to criticize progressive reforms in particular. This is the idea that "the attempt to push society in a certain direction will result in its moving all right, but in the opposite direction." See Albert O. Hirschman, The *Rhetoric of Reaction: Perversity, Futility, Jeopardy* (Cambridge, MA: Harvard University Press, 1991). See also Margaret R. Somers and Fred Block, "From Poverty to Perversity: Ideas, Markets, and Institutions over 200 Years of Welfare Debate," *American Sociological Review* 70, no. 2 (2005): 260–287.
74. Tom Baker, "On the Genealogy of Moral Hazard," *Texas Law Review* 75, no. 2 (1996): 237–292, 290. On moral hazard, see also Carol Heimer, *Reactive Risk and Rational Action: Managing Moral Hazard in Insurance Contracts* (Berkeley: University of California Press, 1985).
75. 113 *Cong. Rec.* 1967, H14330.
76. 113 *Cong. Rec.* 1967, S8728.
77. U.S. House, Subcommittee on Housing 1967, 3.
78. 113 *Cong. Rec.* 1967, 30783.
79. 113 *Cong. Rec.* 1967, S30807–30808.
80. Horowitz, "Hurricane Betsy," 895.
81. 113 *Cong. Rec.* 1967, 30782.
82. 113 *Cong. Rec.* 1967, 30796.
83. 113 *Cong. Rec.* 1967, 30798.
84. HUD, *Insurance and Other Programs*, 131.
85. FEMA, *A Chronology of Major Events*.
86. Hinshaw, *Living with Nature's Extremes*, 155.
87. Gilbert White was highly critical of having one national standard for evaluating flood risk, believing this discouraged communities from looking at their particular flood problems and coming up with solutions that were suited to them. See Hinshaw, *Living with Nature's Extremes*, 156.
88. Platt, *Disasters and Democracy*.
89. Knowles and Kunreuther, "Troubled Waters," 339.
90. Adelle Thomas and Robin Leichenko, "Adaptation Through Insurance: Lessons from the NFIP," *International Journal of Climate Change Strategies and Management* 3, no. 3 (2011): 250–263.
91. Government Accountability Office, *CED-78-122: HUD's Determination to Convert from Industry to Government Operation of the National Flood Insurance Program* (Washington, DC: Government Accountability Office, 1978).
92. Anderson, "The National Flood Insurance Program"; Associated Press, "Flood Insurance Premiums to be Cut Tomorrow," *New York Times*, July 9, 1972.
93. FEMA, *A Chronology of Major Events*.
94. Hinshaw, *Living with Nature's Extremes*, 156.
95. 119 *Cong. Rec.* 1973 House, H557.
96. 119 *Cong. Rec.* 1973, H556–557.

97. 119 *Cong. Rec.* 1973, H7539.

98. Steinberg, *Acts of God.*

99. Hinshaw, *Living with Nature's Extremes,* 174.

100. FEMA, *A Chronology of Major Events*; R. W. Apple Jr., "Nixon Signs Bill on Flood Policies," *New York Times,* January 1, 1974. The mandatory purchase requirement was strengthened two decades later with the National Flood Insurance Reform Act of 1994, which aimed to increase enforcement through provisions (still in force today) such as: coverage now is required over the life of a loan; lenders must escrow flood insurance payments when already requiring escrows; lenders need to obtain a flood policy if a borrower does not; and, failure to comply with the mandatory purchase requirement can result in lenders being fined; see Committee on the Affordability of National Flood Insurance Program Premiums, *Affordability of National Flood Insurance Program Premium: Report 1* (Washington, DC: National Academies Press, 2015).

101. Leonard Sloane, "Personal Finance: Flood Insurance," *New York Times,* December 2, 1974.

102. B. Drummond Ayers, "Flood Experts Call for Curbs on Development in Low-Lying Areas," *New York Times,* May 27, 1973.

103. FEMA, *A Chronology of Major Events.*

104. Ernest B. Abbott, "Floods, Flood Insurance, Litigation, Politics—and Catastrophe: The National Flood Insurance Program," *Sea Grant Law and Policy Journal* 1, no. 1 (2008): 129–155; Committee on the Affordability of National Flood Insurance Program Premiums, Report 1.

105. FEMA, *A Chronology of Major Events,* 18–19.

106. Platt, *Disasters and Democracy,* 12.

107. Platt, *Disasters and Democracy*; Tierney, "From the Margins to the Mainstream?"

108. Morris, "Hurricane Camille," 420.

109. Junia Howell and James R. Elliott, "Damages Done: The Longitudinal Impacts of Natural Hazards on Wealth Inequality in the United States," *Social Problems* 66, no. 3 (2019): 448–467.

110. Paul Pierson, "The New Politics of the Welfare State," *World Politics* 48, no. 2 (1996): 143–179.

111. Hunter, "Testimony of J. Robert Hunter," 2.

112. Taylor, *Race for Profit.*

113. Knowles and Kunreuther, "Troubled Waters," 342.

114. Hunter, "Testimony of J. Robert Hunter," 2.

115. General Accounting Office, *RED-76-94: Formidable Administrative Problems Challenge Achieving National Flood Insurance Program Objectives* (Washington, DC: The General Accounting Office, 1976); Steinberg, *Acts of God.*

116. Steinberg, *Acts of God,* 104.

117. In 1985, FEMA actually sued St. Bernard and Jefferson Parishes in Louisiana, along with various home builders, engineers, and surveyors, for issuing building permits and constructing entire neighborhoods in flood-prone areas. The government claimed effectively breach of contract: the NFIP had made insurance available on the condition that the communities enforce floodplain ordinances and they had not done so. It sought to recover the costs of paying for flood damage in these areas. In *United States vs. St. Bernard Parish,* the Fifth Circuit ruled against the federal

government; the only federal enforcement option was suspension from the program. See Abbott, "Floods, Flood Insurance, Litigation, Politics—and Catastrophe."

118. Ben Wisner, Piers Blaikie, Terry Cannon, and Ian Davis, *At Risk: Natural Hazards, People's Vulnerability and Disasters* (New York: Routledge, 1994); Alice Fothergill, Enrique G. M. Maestas, and JoAnne DeRouen Darlington, "Race, Ethnicity, and Disasters in the United States: A Review of the Literature," *Disasters* 23, no. 2 (1999): 156–173; James R. Elliott, Timothy J. Haney, and Petrice Sams-Abiodun, "Limits to Social Capital: Comparing Network Assistance in Two New Orleans Neighborhoods Devastated by Hurricane Katrina," *Sociological Quarterly* 51, no. 4 (2010): 624–648.

119. Steinberg, *Acts of God*, 105.

120. Hinshaw, *Living with Nature's Extremes*; Steinberg, *Acts of God*, 203.

121. Steinberg, *Acts of God*, 111; Platt, *Disasters and Democracy*.

122. Bergsma, "Geographers Versus Managers."

123. Abbott, "Floods, Flood Insurance, Litigation, Politics—and Catastrophe." The "average loss year" is calculated by averaging the losses experienced over the life of the program since its establishment in 1968. The new requirement meant that in any given year, the NFIP was collecting enough in total premiums to cover this average figure; see Bergsma, "Geographers Versus Managers."

124 Abbott, "Floods, Flood Insurance, Litigation, Politics—and Catastrophe."

125. U.S. Senate Committee on Banking and Currency. 1967. *Report of the Committee on Banking and Currency, United States Senate, To Accompany S. 1985. Operation of the Flood Insurance Program*. Washington, DC: Government Printing Office.

126. Hunter, "Testimony of J. Robert Hunter"; Abbott, "Floods, Flood Insurance, Litigation, Politics—and Catastrophe."

127. U.S. House 1967, 2–4; 113 *Cong. Rec.* 1967 Senate.

128. Hunter, "Testimony of J. Robert Hunter."

129. FEMA, *A Chronology of Major Events*; Government Accountability Office, *GAO-0455. Flood Insurance: Opportunities Exist to Improve Oversight of the WYO Program* (Washington, DC: Government Accountability Office, 2009).

130. Suzanne Mettler, *The Submerged State: How Invisible Government Policies Undermine American Democracy* (Chicago: University of Chicago Press, 2011).

131. Abbott, "Floods, Flood Insurance, Litigation, Politics—and Catastrophe," 144; Michel-Kerjan, "Catastrophe Economics."

132. Quoted in Hinshaw, *Living with Nature's Extremes*, 175.

133. Hinshaw, *Living with Nature's Extremes*, 183.

134. Quoted in Hinshaw, *Living with Nature's Extremes*, 175.

135. Allison Plyer, "Facts for Features: Katrina Impact," The Data Center, last modified August 26, 2016, https://www.datacenterresearch.org/data-resources/katrina/facts-for-impact/.

136. Congressional Budget Office, *The National Flood Insurance Program: Financial Soundness and Affordability* (Washington, DC: Government Printing Office, September 2017).

137. Diane P. Horn and Baird Webel, *Introduction to the National Flood Insurance Program (NFIP)* (Washington, DC: Congressional Research Service, 2019).

138. Abbott, "Floods, Flood Insurance, Litigation, Politics—and Catastrophe."

139. On the growth machine, see John R. Logan and Harvey Molotch, *Urban Fortunes: The Political Economy of Place* (Berkeley: University of California Press, 1987); Harvey Molotch and John R. Logan, "Tensions in the Growth Machine: Overcoming Resistance to Value-Free Development," *Social Problems* 3, no. 5 (1984): 483–499.

140. Freudenberg, Gramling, Laska, and Erikson, Catastrophe in the Making; Kevin Fox Gotham, "Antinomies of Risk Reduction: Climate Change and the Contradictions of Coastal Restoration," *Environmental Sociology* 2, no. 2 (2016): 208–219.

141. Collier, "Neoliberalism and Natural Disaster," 281.

142. Taylor, *Race for Profit*, 88. These measures nevertheless compounded discrimination in housing markets through practices of what Taylor calls "predatory inclusion."

2. LOSING GROUND: VALUES AT RISK
IN AN AMERICAN FLOODPLAIN

1. Interview, October 18, 2013.

2. Field notes, October 29, 2014.

3. Scott Stringer, *On the Frontlines: $129 Billion in Property at Risk from Flood Waters* (New York: Office of the New York City Comptroller, Bureau of Policy and Research, 2014).

4. In its *Retrofitting Guide for Homeowners* of June 2014, FEMA outlined several flood mitigating options for properties in the floodplain. At that time, and when New Yorkers were contending with the changes to flood maps and insurance, elevating was the only option that lowered flood insurance premiums in the flood zones. FEMA hired a contractor to study "partial mitigation" options and how they might be included in insurance rating. Federal Emergency Management Agency (FEMA), *Homeowner's Guide to Retrofitting: Six Ways to Protect Your Home from Flooding* (Washington, DC: Federal Emergency Management Agency, 2014). NFIP policyholders may also benefit from lower premiums if their communities participate in the Community Rating System (CRS).

5. Diane P. Horn and Baird Webel, *Introduction to the National Flood Insurance Program (NFIP)* (Washington, DC: Congressional Research Service, 2019).

6. Brett Christophers, "The Allusive Market: Insurance of Flood Risk in Neoliberal Britain," *Economy and Society* 48, no. 1 (2019): 1–29, 17.

7. Author's analysis of data from Floodzonedata.us and Measure of America's data2go.nyc.

8. Urban Institute, "Reducing the Racial Homeownership Gap," accessed June 11, 2020, https://www.urban.org/policy-centers/housing-finance-policy-center/projects/reducing-racial-homeownership-gap.

9. Al Shaw, "How Well Did FEMA's Maps Predict Sandy's Flooding," *ProPublica*, December 6, 2013.

10. Kim Knowlton, "Make Health a Priority Post-Sandy, Put Climate Change on the Map," *Natural Resources Defense Council: Switchboard*, October 22, 2013.

11. David W. Chen, "In New York, Drawing Flood Maps Is a 'Game of Inches,'" *New York Times*, January 7, 2018.

12. From the start of the NFIP in 1968 until the 1990s, flood maps were created and stored in paper format. In 1997, FEMA developed its first flood Map Moderniza-tion plan that specified the steps necessary to convert the nation's flood maps into digital format. These efforts extended through 2008, at which point 92 percent of FIRMs were digitized.

13. William S. Nechamen, Letter to David I. Maurstad, January 24, 2005.

14. City of New York, *PlaNYC: A Stronger, More Resilient New York* (New York: Office of the Mayor, 2013).

15. City of New York, *PlaNYC Progress Report 2008: A Greener, Greater New York* (New York: Office of the Mayor, 2008); City of New York, *PlaNYC Progress Report 2009: A Greener, Greater New York* (New York: Office of the Mayor, 2009); City of New York, *PlaNYC Progress Report 2010: A Greener, Greater New York* (New York: Office of the Mayor, 2010); City of New York, *PlaNYC: A Greener, Greater New York* (New York: Office of the Mayor, 2011).

16. Interview, March 6, 2014; Interview, March 20, 2014. With FEMA's funding as a persistent obstacle, New York City actually offered to provide some topographi-cal data for the update process, which had initially been collected for a study about putting solar panels on city rooftops. In its Procedural Memorandum 61, published in September 2010, FEMA stated that it would only be starting new studies in areas where there were already existing updated and accurate topographic data or in areas that had sufficient need and risk to necessitate FEMA funding data acquisi-tion. New York City's ability to provide the topographical data therefore put it at an advantage for getting updated risk maps.

17. Lloyd Dixon, Noreen Clancy, Benjamin M. Miller, Sue Hoegberg, Michael M. Lewis, Bruce Bender, Samara Ebinger, Mel Hodges, Gayle M. Syck, Caroline Nagy, and Scott R. Choquette, *The Cost and Affordability of Flood Insurance in New York City* (Santa Monica, CA: RAND Corporation, 2017).

18. City of New York, *PlaNYC: A Stronger, More Resilient New York*.

19. Interview, March 20, 2014.

20. FEMA released the city-revised ABFEs to the public in two phases, in January (for open shoreline areas) and February 2013 (for sheltered areas). The open shoreline areas are: South Queens, southern Brooklyn, the southeast shore of Staten Island, and the portion of the Bronx adjacent to Long Island Sound. The sheltered areas are: the west and north shores of Staten Island, the rest of Brooklyn on New York Harbor and along the East River, the portions of the Bronx and Queens on the upper East River, and all of Manhattan.

21. Department of City Planning, *Coastal Climate Resiliency: Retrofitting Buildings for Flood Risk* (New York: Department of City Planning, 2014). "Substantially improved" (any repair, reconstruction, rehabilitation, addition or improvement of a building with cost equaling or exceeding 50 percent of the current market value of the building) buildings are required to comply with flood-resistant construc-tion requirements.

22. Clare Trapasso, "Sandy-Ravaged Homeowners to Rally Against High Flood Insur-ance Premiums," *New York Daily News*, August 30, 2013.

23. Dixon et al., *The Cost and Affordability of Flood Insurance*.

24. Field notes, October 16, 2014; Dixon et al., *The Cost and Affordability of Flood Insur-ance*; Zachary Paganini, "Underwater: Resilience, Racialized Housing, and the

National Flood Insurance Program in Canarsie," *Geoforum* 104 (August 2019): 25–35.

25. Furman Center and the Moelis Institute for Affordable Housing Policy, *Sandy's Effects on Housing in New York City* (New York: Furman Center, 2013), http://furmancenter.org/files/publications/SandysEffectsOnHousingInNYC.pdf.

26. Lloyd Dixon, Noreen Clancy, Bruce Bender, Aaron Kofner, David Manheim, and Laura Zakaras, *Flood Insurance in New York City Following Hurricane Sandy* (Santa Monica, CA: RAND Corporation, 2013), 2–3.

27. James Porter and David Demeritt, "Flood-Risk Management, Mapping, and Planning: The Institutional Politics of Decision Support in England," *Environment and Planning A* 44, no. 10 (2012): 2359–2378.

28. Stuart N. Lane, Catharina Landström, and Sarah J. Whatmore, "Imagining Flood Futures: Risk Assessment and Management in Practice," *Philosophical Transactions of the Royal Society A* 369 (2011): 1784–1806.

29. Wouter Botzen, Howard Kunreuther, and Erwann O. Michel-Kerjan, *Understanding Individual Flood Risk Perceptions and Flood Insurance Choices to Build More Resilient Communities: A Survey of New York City Residents* (Philadelphia: Wharton Risk Management Center, 2014).

30. See John Tulloch and Deborah Lupton, *Risk and Everyday Life* (London: SAGE Publications, 2003), 108; Deborah Lupton, "Risk and Emotion: Towards an Alternative Theoretical Perspective," *Health, Risk & Society* 15, no. 8 (2013): 634–647; Charles Perrow, *Normal Accidents* (Princeton, NJ: Princeton University Press, 1999), chap. 9; Nick F. Pidgeon, Peter Simmons, and Karen L. Henwood, "Risk, Environment and Technology," in *Risk in Social Science*, ed. Peter Taylor-Gooby and Jens Zinn (Oxford: Oxford University Press, 2006), 94–116; Brian Wynne, "Risk and Social Learning: Reification to Engagement," in *Social Theories of Risk*, ed. Sheldon Krimsky and Dominic Golding (London: Praeger, 1992), 275–297; Jamie Baxter and Daniel Lee, "Explaining the Maintenance of Low Concern Near a Hazardous Waste Treatment Facility," *Journal of Risk Research* 7, nos. 7–8 (2004): 705–729; Alan Irwin, Peter Simmons, and G. Walker, "Faulty Environments and Risk Reasoning: The Local Understanding of Industrial Hazards," *Environment and Planning A* 31, no. 7 (1999): 1311–1326; Karen A. Parkhill, Nick F. Pidgeon, Karen L. Henwood, Peter Simmons, and Dan Venables, "From the Familiar to the Extraordinary: Local Residents' Perceptions of Risk When Living with Nuclear Power in the UK," *Transactions of the Institute of British Geographers* 35, no. 1 (2010): 39–58; Iain Wilkinson, "Social Theories of Risk Perception: At Once Indispensable and Insufficient," *Current Sociology* 49, no. 1 (2001): 1–22; Alan Irwin and Brian Wynne, eds., *Misunderstanding Science? The Public Reconstruction of Science and Technology* (Cambridge,: Cambridge University Press, 1996); among others.

31. Gerda Reith, "Uncertain Times: The Notion of 'Risk' and the Development of Modernity," *Time & Society* 13, nos. 2–3 (2004): 383–402.

32. Interview, February 26, 2014.

33. Tulloch and Lupton, *Risk in Everyday Life*, 107.

34. Interview, October 21, 2014.

35. For more on the contradictory character of many risk-reducing measures, see Kevin Fox Gotham, "Coastal Restoration as Contested Terrain: Climate Change

and the Political Economy of Risk Reduction in Louisiana," *Sociological Forum* 31, no. S1 (2016): 787–806.

36. Arlie Russell Hochschild shows this kind of moral reasoning at work in her study of conservative Louisianans who, though they live in some of the most degraded, dangerous, and polluted environments in the country, vociferously object to the kind of government regulation that would curtail the activities of the worst polluters. Arlie Russell Hochschild, *Strangers in the Their Own Land: Anger and Mourning on the American Right* (New York: The New Press, 2016).

37. Interview, October 23, 2014.

38. Interview, March 18, 2014.

39. Federal Emergency Management Agency (FEMA), *Homeowner's Guide to Retrofitting.*

40. Department of City Planning, *Coastal Climate Resiliency*, 16.

41. Field notes, October 18, 2014.

42. Superstorm Research Lab, *A Tale of Two Sandys* (New York: Superstorm Research Lab, 2013, 13).

43. Field notes, October 24, 2014.

44. Wynne, "Risk and Social Learning."

45. Interview, February 26, 2014.

46. Field notes, March 21, 2014.

47. Karen M. O'Neill and Daniel J. Van Abs, eds., *Taking Chances: The Coast after Hurricane Sandy* (New Brunswick, NJ: Rutgers University Press, 2016), 213.

48. Interview, October 31, 2014.

49. Karen Henwood, Nick Pidgeon, Sophie Sarre, Peter Simmons, and Noel Smith, "Risk, Framing and Everyday Life: Epistemological and Methodological Reflections from Three Socio-Cultural Projects," *Health, Risk & Society* 10, no. 5 (2008): 421–438, 433.

50. Eventually, more than 1600 homeowners actually filed suit claiming that they were underpaid by the Write-Your-Own (WYO) private insurance companies that administer flood insurance claims on behalf of the NFIP. Evidence was uncovered that engineering reports commissioned by the WYOs had been doctored in order to reduce payments to homeowners. The lawsuits led FEMA to reopen the claims process, giving 144,000 homeowners the chance to refile their claims. See Emma Schwartz, "Millions More Paid To Superstorm Sandy Victims After Fraud Claims," *PBS Frontline*, November 8, 2017, https://www.pbs.org/wgbh/frontline/article /millions-more-paid-to-superstorm-sandy-victims-after-fraud-claims/.

51. Field notes, October 18, 2014.

52. Field notes, October 24, 2014.

53. Field notes, March, 25 2014.

54. For an analysis of how understandings of near and far vis-à-vis climate change are socially constructed and politically consequential, see Kari M. Norgaard, *Living in Denial: Climate Change, Emotions, and Everyday Life* (Cambridge, MA: MIT Press, 2011).

55. Interview, October 31, 2014.

56. Interview, October 23, 2014.

57. Interview, November 18, 2013.

58. Tulloch and Lupton, *Risk and Everyday Life*, 110.

59. Liz Koslov, "How Maps Make Time: The Temporal Politics of Life in the Flood Zone," *CITY* 23, nos. 4–5 (2019): 658–672.

60. John R. Logan and Harvey L. Molotch, *Urban Fortunes: The Political Economy of Place* (Berkeley: University of California Press, 1987), chap. 4.

61. Debbie Becher, *Private Property and Public Power* (New York: Oxford University Press, 2014).

62. Marion Fourcade, "Cents and Sensibility: Economic Valuation and the Nature of 'Nature,'" *American Journal of Sociology* 116, no. 6 (2011): 1721–1777; Viviana Zelizer, *Pricing the Priceless Child: The Changing Social Value of Children* (New York: Basic Books, 1985); Jens Beckert and Patrik Aspers, eds., *The Worth of Goods: Valuation and Pricing in the Economy* (Oxford: Oxford University Press, 2011); David Stark, *The Sense of Dissonance: Accounts of Worth in Economic Life* (Princeton, NJ: Princeton University Press, 2009); Luc Boltanski and Laurent Thévenot, *On Justification* (Princeton, NJ: Princeton University Press, 2006); Wendy Espeland and Mitchell Stevens, "Commensuration as a Social Process," *Annual Review of Sociology* 24 (1998): 313–343.

63. Interview, March 21, 2014.

64. Interview, October 22, 2013.

65. Harvey Molotch, William Freudenburg, and Krista Paulson, "History Repeats Itself, But How? City Character, Urban Tradition, and the Accomplishment of Place," *American Sociological Review* 65, no. 6 (2000): 791–823; Patrick Devine-Wright, "Think Global, Act Local? The Relevance of Place Attachments and Place Identities in a Climate Changed World," *Global Environmental Change* 23, no. 1 (2013): 61–69; David Burley, Pam Jenkins, Shirley Laska, and Traber Davis, "Place Attachment and Environmental Change in Coastal Louisiana," *Organization & Environment* 20, no. 3 (2007): 347–366.

66. Interview, October 31, 2014.

67. Henwood et al., "Risk, Framing and Everyday Life." See also Gotham, "Coastal Restoration."

68. Interview, October 21, 2014.

69. Kevin Fox Gotham finds similar place attachments among members of fishing communities in Louisiana, also facing threats from risk-reduction measures, whose residential propinquity and shared histories lead them to make claims for the protection of their culture and heritage; see Gotham, "Coastal Restoration." See also Henwood et al., "Risk, Framing and Everyday Life"; Debbie Becher, *Private Property and Public Power*; J. R. Dunn, "Security, Meaning, and the Home," in *Social Resilience in the Neoliberal Era*, ed. Peter A. Hall and Michèle Lamont (Cambridge: Cambridge University Press, 2013), 183–205.

70. Field notes, October 16, 2014

71. Field notes, October 28, 2014.

72. Interview, March 4, 2014.

73. Field notes, March 21, 2014.

74. David Stark, "What's Valuable?," in *The Worth of Goods: Valuation and Pricing in the Economy*, ed. Jens Beckert and Patrik Aspers (Oxford: Oxford University Press, 2011), 319–338, quote on 321.

75. Interview, October 14, 2013.

76. Interview, November 4, 2013.

77. Field notes, October 24, 2014.

78. Interview, March 18, 2014.

79. Jeremy W. Crampton and John Krygier, "An Introduction to Critical Cartography," *ACME: An International E-Journal for Critical Cartographies*, 4, no. 1 (2006): 11–33; Timothy Mitchell, *Rule of Experts* (Berkeley: University of California Press, 2002); James C. Scott, *Seeing Like a State: How Certain Schemes to Improve the Human Condition Have Failed* (New Haven, CT: Yale University Press, 1999).

80. Interview, October 23, 2014.

81. Field notes, March 1, 2014.

82. Interview, February 26, 2014.

83. Dean Curran, "Risk Society and the Distribution of Bads: Theorizing Class in the Risk Society," *British Journal of Sociology* 64, no. 1 (2013): 44–62.

84. Field notes, December 13, 2013.

85. Liz Koslov, "The Case for Retreat," *Public Culture* 28, no. 2 (2016): 359–387.

86. Though as Brian Wynne observes, the absence of dissent does not mean the presence of trust. Brian Wynne, "May the Sheep Safely Graze? A Reflexive View of the Expert-Lay Knowledge Divide," in *Risk, Environment and Modernity*, ed. Scott Lash, Bronislaw Szerszynski and Brian Wynne (London: SAGE Publications, 1996), 44–83.

87. Michel Callon, ed., *The Laws of the Markets* (London: Blackwell, 1998).

88. Henwood et al., "Risk, Framing and Everyday Life."

89. See similar findings in New Jersey in Mariana Leckner, Melanie McDermott, James K. Mitchell, and Karen M. O'Neill, "Local Responses to Hurricane Sandy: Heterogeneous Experiences and Mismatches with Federal Policy," in *Taking Chances: The Coast After Hurricane Sandy*, ed. Karen M. O'Neill and Daniel J. Van Abs (New Brunswick, NJ: Rutgers University Press, 2016), 208–221. The authors find: "These results indicate that residents weigh a wide array of factors beyond criteria such as expected flood heights and exposure to waves that are used to determine risk zones on the federal flood insurance maps … Uniform policy approaches, such as federal flood maps, also increased a sense of uncertainty and unfairness because the policies were not consistent with residents' and officials' knowledge about specific local hazards, were based on principles that they did not readily understand, and were still being worked out in the storm's aftermath. In addition, because hazard management can impinge on private property rights, residents' political ideologies as well as their trust in governments affected whether they saw management policies as beneficial or punitive."

90. Wendy Espeland, *The Struggle for Water: Politics, Rationality, and Identity in the American Southwest* (Chicago: University of Chicago Press, 1998), 37.

91. Gotham, "Coastal Restoration as Contested Terrain," 790; see also Javier Auyero and Débora Alejandra Swistun, *Flammable: Environmental Suffering in an Argentine Shantytown* (New York: Oxford University Press, 2009).

92. Tim Harries, "Feeling Secure or Being Secure? Why It Can Seem Better Not to Protect Yourself Against a Natural Hazard," *Health, Risk & Society* 10, no. 5 (2008): 479–490; Tim Harries, "The Anticipated Emotional Consequences of Adaptive Behaviour—Impacts on the Take-Up Of Household Flood-Protection Measures," *Environment and Planning A* 44, no. 3 (2012): 649–668.

93. Wynne, "Risk and Social Learning," 282.

94. This was largely the case also for residents seeking a state-funded buyout on Staten Island. In this context, talking about climate change was not seen as politically enabling or efficacious; see Liz Koslov, "Avoiding Climate Change: 'Agnostic Adaptation' and the Politics of Public Silence," *Annals of the American Association of Geographers* 109, no. 2 (2019): 568–580.

3. VISIONS OF LOSS: KNOWING AND PRICING FLOOD RISK

1. Field notes, October 27, 2014.
2. Richard Ericson, Aaron Doyle, and Dean Barry, *Insurance as Governance* (Toronto: University of Toronto Press, 2003); Richard Ericson and Aaron Doyle, *Uncertain Business: Risk, Insurance and the Limits of Knowledge* (Toronto: University of Toronto Press, 2004); Turo-Kimmo Lehtonen and Ine Van Hoyweghen, "Insurance and the Economization of Uncertainty," *Journal of Cultural Economy* 7, no. 4 (2014): 532–540.
3. Daniel Hirschman and Elizabeth Popp Berman, "Do Economists Make Policies? On the Political Effects of Economics," *Socio-Economic Review* 12, no. 4 (2014): 779–811; Pierre Lascoumes and Patrick Le Gales, "Understanding Public Policy Through Its Instruments—From the Nature of Instruments to the Sociology of Public Policy Instrumentation," *Governance* 20, no. 1 (2007): 1–21.
4. On "realist epistemology" and the sociology of disaster, see John Downer, "'737-Cabriolet': The Limits of Knowledge and the Sociology of Inevitable Failure," *American Journal of Sociology* 117, no. 3 (2011): 725–762.
5. Jill Ament, "Bureaucracy and Old Data Hobble FEMA Flood Maps," *Texas Public Radio*, March 8, 2018, http://www.tpr.org/post/bureaucracy-and-old-data-hobble-fema-flood-maps; Michael Keller, Mira Rojanasakul, David Ingold, Christopher Flavelle, and Brittany Harris, "Outdated and Unreliable: FEMA's Faulty Flood Maps Put Homeowners at Risk," *Bloomberg*, October 6, 2017, https://www.bloomberg.com/graphics/2017-fema-faulty-flood-maps/; Jen Schwartz, "National Flood Insurance Is Underwater Because of Outdated Science," *Scientific American*, March 23, 2018, https://www.scientificamerican.com/article/national-flood-insurance-is-underwater-because-of-outdated-science/; John Schwartz, James Glanz, and Andrew W. Lehren, "Builders Said Their Homes Were Out of a Flood Zone. Then Harvey Came," *New York Times*, December 2, 2017, https://www.nytimes.com/2017/12/02/us/houston-flood-zone-hurricane-harvey.html?_r=1; Chris Tomlinson, "System Rigged Against Homeowners When It Comes to Floods," *Houston Chronicle*, October 10, 2017, http://www.chron.com/business/columnists/tomlinson/article/System-rigged-against-homeowners-when-it-comes-to-12268139.php.
6. Scott Gabriel Knowles and Howard C. Kunreuther, "Troubled Waters: The National Flood Insurance Program in Historical Perspective," *Journal of Policy History* 26, no. 3 (2014): 327–353; Sarah Pralle, "Drawing Lines: FEMA and the Politics of Mapping Flood Zones," *Climatic Change* 152, no. 2 (2019): 227–237.
7. Charles Perrow, "The Disaster After 9/11: The Department of Homeland Security and the Intelligence Reorganization," *Homeland Security Affairs* 2, no. 1 (2006): 1–32; Kevin Fox Gotham, "Disaster, Inc.: Privatization and Post-Katrina Rebuilding in New Orleans," *Perspectives on Politics* 10, no. 3 (2012): 633–646.

8. Keller et al., "Outdated and Unreliable."

9. Federal Emergency Management Agency, "The National Flood Insurance Program," last updated November 15, 2018, https://www.fema.gov/national-flood -insurance-program. Based on an analysis of NFIP claims data from 1978 to 2012, Carolyn Kousky and Erwann Michel-Kerjan have also found that the frequency of flood claims outside of flood zones is often higher than that within the flood zones; see Carolyn Kousky and Erwann Michel-Kerjan, "Examining Flood Insurance Claims in the United States: Six Key Findings," *Journal of Risk and Insurance* 84, no. 3 (2015): 819–850.

10. David Hunn, Matt Dempsey, and Mihir Zaveri, "Harvey's Floods," *Houston Chronicle*, March 30, 2018, https://www.houstonchronicle.com/news/article/In-Harvey -s-deluge-most-damaged-homes-were-12794820.php.

11. Bill Dedman, "Why Taxpayers Will Bail Out the Rich When the Next Storm Hits," *NBC News*, February 18, 2014; Bill Dedman, "Meet the Flood Insurance 'Robin Hood' Who Saves Condo Owners Millions," *NBC News*, February 19, 2014.

12. Andrew Lakoff and Eric Klinenberg, "Of Risk and Pork: Urban Security and the Politics Of Objectivity," *Theory and Society* 39 (September 2010): 503–525; see also Lehtonen and Van Hoyweghen, "Insurance and the Economization of Uncertainty"; Ine Van Hoyweghen, "On the Politics of Calculative Devices," *Journal of Cultural Economy* 7, no. 3 (2014): 334–352; Kathleen J. Tierney, "Towards a Critical Sociology of Risk," *Sociological Forum* 14, no. 2 (1999): 215–242; Tim Forsyth, *Critical Political Ecology: The Politics of Environmental Science* (New York: Routledge, 2003).

13. Mary Douglas and Aaron Wildavsky, *Risk and Culture: An Essay on the Selection of Technical and Environmental Dangers* (Berkeley: University of California Press, 1992); Pat O'Malley, "Risk and Responsibility," in *Foucault and Political Reason: Liberalism, Neo-liberalism and Rationalities of Government*, ed. Andrew Barry, Thomas Osborne, and Nikolas Rose (London: University College London Press, 1996), 189–207.

14. Jessica Weinkle, "The New Political Importance of the Old Hurricane Risk: A Contextual Approach to Understanding Contemporary Struggles with Hurricane Risk and Insurance," *Journal of Risk Research* 22, no. 3 (2019): 320–333; Jessica Weinkle and Roger Pielke Jr., "The Truthiness about Hurricane Catastrophe Models," *Science, Technology, & Human Values* 42, no. 4 (2017): 547–576.

15. Douglas and Wildavsky, *Risk and Culture*; Mary Douglas, "Risk as a Forensic Resource," *Daedalus* 119, no. 4 (1990): 1–16.

16. A and V zones are further subdivided based on the topography of the land, other features of the area (e.g., AO zones may have areas of high flood velocities), and whether elevations are defined for the area (i.e., AE zones are those with established hydrological elevations). V zones are the areas subject to flooding by the 1-percent-annual-chance flood event *and* additional hazards due to storm-induced velocity wave action, i.e., coastal areas where storm surge will push water over land. "Moderate" or "minimal" flood hazard areas are also shown on the FIRMs and may be labeled Zone B or Zone C, but flood insurance from the NFIP is not available in these zones. In the late 1970s FEMA removed the distinction between B and C zones, but these designations still appear on older maps; see Mark Monmonier, *Cartographies of Danger: Mapping Hazards in America* (Chicago: University of Chicago Press, 1997).

17. Timothy W. Collins, "The Production of Unequal Risk in Hazardscapes: An Explanatory Framework Applied to Disaster at the US–Mexico Border," *Geoforum* 40, no. 4 (2009): 589–601.

18. The technical requirements for making a map, and the process for taking it from draft to effective FIRM, are established at the federal level in FEMA's *Guidelines and Specifications*, developed by the agency's Risk Analysis Division and periodically amended through "Procedural Memoranda." FEMA monitors the mapmaking process through its "Mapping Information Platform" (MIP), which allows its mapping partners "to create, validate, store, track, and update flood data according to FEMA's standards." See Government Accountability Office, *GAO-11-17. FEMA FLOOD MAPS: Some Standards and Processes in Place to Promote Map Accuracy and Outreach, but Opportunities Exist to Address Implementation Challenges* (Washington, DC: Government Accountability Office, 2010), 17.

19. Government Accountability Office, *GAO-11-17. FEMA FLOOD MAPS.*

20. FEMA has three national Production and Technical Services (PTS) contractors; these are private engineering firms working under contract to FEMA, each of which is responsible for a regional portfolio of flood study projects. *GAO-11-17. FEMA FLOOD MAPS.* See also Robert Soden, Leah Sprain, and Leysia Palen, "Thin Grey Lines: Confrontations with Risk on Colorado's Front Range," *Proceedings of the 2017 CHI Conference on Human Factors in Computing Systems*, ACM, May 6–11, 2017, Denver, Colorado: 2042–2053. On privatization and contracting at FEMA more generally, see Gotham, "Disaster, Inc."

21. LiDAR is short for Light Detection and Ranging; it is a remote sensing method that uses light in the form of a pulsed laser to measure ranges of distance to the Earth. LiDAR data is often collected by air, with survey aircraft. These light pulses—combined with other data recorded by the airborne system—generate three-dimensional information about the shape of the Earth and its surface characteristics. A LiDAR instrument principally consists of a laser, a scanner, and a specialized GPS receiver. Topographic LiDAR typically uses a near-infrared laser to map the land, while bathymetric LiDAR uses water-penetrating green light to also measure seafloor and riverbed elevations.

22. Technical Mapping Advisory Council, *Future Conditions Risk Assessment and Modeling* (Washington, DC: Federal Emergency Management Agency, 2016).

23. Stephen Hilgartner, "The Social Construction of Risk Objects," in *Organizations, Uncertainty and Risk*, ed. James F. Short and Lee Clarke (Oxford: Westview Press, 1992), 39–53.

24. Tierney, "Towards a Critical Sociology of Risk"; Niklas Luhmann, *Risk: A Sociological Theory* (New York: A. de Gruyter, 1993); Peter Taylor-Gooby and Jens Zinn, ed., *Risk in Social Science* (Oxford: Oxford University Press, 2006); Michael Power, *Organized Uncertainty* (Oxford: Oxford University Press, 2007); Angela Oels, "Rendering Climate Change Governable by Risk: From Probability to Contingency," *Geoforum* 45 (March 2013): 17–29; Brian Wynne, "Risk and Social Learning: Reification to Engagement," in *Social Theories of Risk*, ed. Sheldon Krimsky and Dominic Golding (London: Praeger, 1992), 275–297; Bridget M. Hutter and Sally Lloyd-Bostock, "Risk, Interest Groups, and the Definition of Crisis: The Case of Volcanic Ash," *British Journal of Sociology* 64, no. 3 (2013):

383–404; Geoffrey C. Bowker and Susan Leigh Star, *Sorting Things Out: Classification and its Consequences* (Cambridge, MA: MIT Press, 2000).

25. Theodore M. Porter, *Trust in Numbers: The Pursuit of Objectivity in Science and Public Life* (Princeton, NJ: Princeton University Press, 1995), 105.

26. Wynne, "Risk and Social Learning"; Tierney, "Towards a Critical Sociology of Risk"; Kristin Shrader-Frechette, *Burying Uncertainty: Risk and the Case Against Geological Disposal of Nuclear Waste* (Berkeley: University of California Press, 1993).

27. Janette Webb, "Making Climate Change Governable: The Case of the UK Climate Change Risk Assessment and Adaptation Planning," *Science and Public Policy* 38, no. 4 (2011): 279–292, 281.

28. Andy Stirling, "How Politics Closes Down Uncertainty," *STEPS Centre* (blog), February 20, 2019, https://steps-centre.org/blog/how-politics-closes-down-uncertainty/.

29. Carol Heimer, *Reactive Risk and Rational Action: Managing Moral Hazard in Insurance Contracts* (Berkeley: University of California Press, 1985); Mitchell Dean, "Risk, Calculable and Incalculable," in *Risk and Sociocultural Theory: New Directions and Perspectives*, ed. Deborah Lupton (Cambridge: Cambridge University Press, 1999), 131–159; Gerda Reith, "Uncertain Times: The Notion of 'Risk' and the Development of Modernity," *Time & Society* 13, nos. 2–3 (2004): 383–402; Bruce G. Carruthers, "From Uncertainty Toward Risk: The Case of Credit Ratings," *Socio-Economic Review* 11, no. 3 (2013): 525–551.

30. James Knighton, Osamu Tsuda, Rebecca Elliott, and M. Todd Walter, "Challenges to Implementing Bottom-Up Flood Risk Decision Analysis Frameworks: How Strong are Social Networks of Flooding Professionals," *Hydrology and Earth System Sciences* 22 (November 2018): 5657–5673.

31. Soden, Sprain, and Palen, "Thin Grey Lines."

32. Technical Mapping Advisory Council, *Future Conditions Risk Assessment and Modeling*.

33. Monmonier, *Cartographies of Danger*, 114.

34. Government Accountability Office, *GAO-11-17. FEMA FLOOD MAPS*, 19.

35. Technical Mapping Advisory Council, *Future Conditions Risk Assessment and Modeling*, 3–4; Government Accountability Office, *GAO-11-17. FEMA FLOOD MAPS*, 10.

36. Government Accountability Office, *GAO-11-17. FEMA FLOOD MAPS*, 10.

37. Liz Koslov, "How Maps Make Time: The Temporal Politics of Life in the Flood Zone," *CITY* 23, nos. 4–5 (2019): 658–672, 662.

38. Kathleen J. Tierney, *The Social Roots of Risk* (Palo Alto, CA: Stanford University Press, 2014).

39. This style of risk classification is a key difference between the NFIP and private insurers, which tend to have instead a large number of relatively homogeneous risk classes. According to the Academy of Actuaries, a professional membership organization for the actuarial profession, the NFIP's broad risk classes, with their attendant insurance rates, "facilitate the operations of the program" and "its unique public policy goals." See Academy of Actuaries, *The National Flood Insurance Program: Past, Present . . . and Future?* (Washington, DC: American Academy of Actuaries, 2011).

40. City Of New York, *PlaNYC: A Stronger, More Resilient New York* (New York: Office of the Mayor, 2013).

41. Department of City Planning, *Coastal Climate Resiliency: Retrofitting Buildings for Flood Risk* (New York: Department of City Planning, 2014), 16.

42. Congressional Budget Office, *The National Flood Insurance Program: Financial Soundness and Affordability* (Washington, DC: Government Printing Office, September 2017).

43. Austin Zeiderman, "Spaces of Uncertainty: Governing Urban Environmental Hazards," in *Modes of Uncertainty: Anthropological Cases*, ed. Limor Samimian-Darash and Paul Rabinow (Chicago: University of Chicago Press, 2015), 182–200; quote on 195.

44. Jameson M. Wetmore, "Distributing Risks and Responsibilities: Flood Hazard Mitigation in New Orleans," *Social Studies of Science* 37, no. 1 (2007): 119–126.

45. James C. Scott, *Seeing Like a State: How Certain Schemes to Improve the Human Condition Have Failed* (New Haven, CT: Yale University Press, 1999); Timothy Mitchell, *Rule of Experts* (Berkeley: University of California Press, 2002).

46. J. B. Harley, "Deconstructing the Map," *Cartographica* 26, no. 2 (1989): 1–20.

47. Academy of Actuaries, *The National Flood Insurance Program*, 10, fn 24.

48. In 1983, the insurance ratings associated with these broader risk classes were also simplified: Zones A1 to A30 were grouped under a single set of rate schedules, and similar changes were made for Zones V1 to V30; see Federal Emergency Management Agency (FEMA), *A Chronology of Major Events affecting the National Flood Insurance Program* (Washington, DC: FEMA, 2005).

49. Federal Emergency Management Agency, *Flood Map Modernization: Mid-Course Adjustment* (Washington, DC: Federal Emergency Management Agency, 2006).

50. Federal Emergency Management Agency, *A Chronology of Major Events*.

51. James Porter and David Demeritt, "Flood-Risk Management, Mapping, and Planning: The Institutional Politics of Decision Support in England," *Environment and Planning A* 44, no. 10 (2012): 2359–2378.

52. Weinkle and Pielke Jr., "The Truthiness about Hurricane Catastrophe Models."

53. U.S. Congress, *Moving Ahead for Progress in the 21st Century Act, Title II: Flood Insurance*, P.L. 112–141, 112th Congress, 2nd sess., 2012.

54. U.S. Senate, Committee on Banking, Housing, and Urban Affairs, *Hearing: Reauthorization of the National Flood Insurance Program, June 9 and June 23, 2011*, 112th Cong., 1st sess. (Washington, DC: Government Printing Office, 2011), 89.

55. Technical Mapping Advisory Council, *Future Conditions Risk Assessment and Modeling*.

56. Hilgartner, "The Social Construction of Risk Objects"; Tierney, "Towards a Critical Sociology of Risk"; Ulrich Beck, "Living in the World Risk Society," *Economy and Society* 35, no. 3 (2006): 329–345; Harriet Bulkeley, "Governing Climate Change: The Politics of Risk Society?," *Transactions of the Institute of British Geographers* 26 (2001): 430–447; Jens Oliver Zinn, "Living in the Anthropocene: Towards a Risk-Taking Society," *Environmental Sociology* 2, no. 4 (2016): 385–394.

57. Pralle, "Drawing Lines"; Monmonier, *Cartographies of Danger*.

58. "Eligible" appeals are appeals from communities or individuals that are based on knowledge or information indicating that the proposed BFEs are scientifically or technically inaccurate and that contain supporting documentation, and are

submitted during the designated ninety-day period. Appeals that do not meet these criteria are "ineligible" appeals or "protests." FEMA does not track information on ineligible appeals and protests; see Government Accountability Office, *GAO-11-17. FEMA FLOOD MAPS*.

59. FEMA may respond to valid community concerns even in the absence of an official challenge; see Pralle, "Drawing Lines."

60. Field notes, October 15, 2014.

61. Miranda Leitsinger, "For Average Joes, Fighting FEMA Flood Maps Isn't Easy or Cheap," *NBC News*, February 20, 2014.

62. Dean, "Risk, Calculable and Incalculable," 150.

63. Wendy Espeland, *The Struggle for Water: Politics, Rationality, and Identity in the American Southwest* (Chicago: University of Chicago Press, 1998).

64. Interview, September 26, 2016. On how risk debates socially construct community identity and culture, see Kevin Fox Gotham, "Coastal Restoration as Contested Terrain: Climate Change and the Political Economy of Risk Reduction in Louisiana," *Sociological Forum* 31, no. S1 (2016): 787–806.

65. Jonathan Simon, "The Emergence of Risk Society: Insurance, Law and the State," *Socialist Review* 95 (1987): 61–89; Jonathan Simon, "The Ideological Effects of Actuarial Practices," *Law and Society Review* 22, no. 4 (1988): 771–800; Daniel Defert, "'Popular Life' and Insurance Technology," in *The Foucault Effect: Studies in Governmentality*, ed. Graham Burchell, Colin Gordon, and Peter Miller (London: Harvester Wheatsheaf, 1991), 211–234.

66. This activation need not work in the direction of trying to make the flood zones smaller. On Staten Island, where residents were trying to qualify for a state-funded buyout, residents wanted to make the flood zones bigger, so that they would be deemed "at risk" enough to qualify. See Liz Koslov, "The Case for Retreat," *Public Culture* 28, no. 2 (2016): 359–387.

67. Mayor's Office of Recovery and Resiliency, *Appeal of FEMA's Preliminary Flood Insurance Rate Maps for New York City* (New York: Office of the Mayor, 2015), 1.

68. Mayor's Office of Recovery and Resiliency, *Appeal of FEMA's Preliminary Flood Insurance Rate Maps*, 2 (emphasis in original).

69. Daniel Sarewitz, "How Science Makes Environmental Controversies Worse," *Environmental Science & Policy* 7, no. 5 (2004): 385–403, 389.

70. Weinkle and Pielke Jr., "The Truthiness about Hurricane Catastrophe Models"; Lakoff and Klinenberg, "Of Risk and Pork."

71. Quoted in Corinne Ramey, "New York Disputes FEMA on Flood Risk," *Wall Street Journal*, August 18, 2005.

72. Federal Emergency Management Agency, "News Release: Mayor De Blasio and FEMA Announce Plan to Revise NYC's Flood Maps," October 17, 2016.

73. Email from FEMA spokesperson to author, November 4, 2016.

74. Webb, "Making Climate Change Governable"; Lee Clarke, *Mission Improbable: Using Fantasy Documents to Tame Disaster* (Chicago: University of Chicago Press, 1999); Sophie Webber, "Performative Vulnerability: Climate Change Adaptation Policies and Financing in Kiribati," *Environment and Planning A* 45, no. 11 (2013): 2717–2733.

75. In moderate- to low-risk zones, "Preferred Risk Policies" (PRP) are available to residential and nonresidential buildings that do not have serious flood loss histories.

Insurance rates on PRP policies are not actuarially derived and are set affordably in order to encourage purchase.

76. Zinn, "Living in the Anthropocene."
77. Federal Emergency Management Agency, "Definitions," last updated August 21, 2018, https://www.fema.gov/national-flood-insurance-program/definitions.
78. Committee on the Affordability of National Flood Insurance Program Premiums, *Affordability of National Flood Insurance Program Premium: Report 1* (Washington, DC: National Academies Press, 2015); Carolyn Kousky and Leonard Shabman, "Pricing Flood Insurance: How and Why the NFIP Differs from a Private Insurance Company," *Resources for the Future Discussion Paper* 14–37 (2014): 1–17.
79. Committee on the Affordability of National Flood Insurance Program Premiums, *Affordability of National Flood Insurance Program Premium: Report 1*, 30–31.
80. Kousky and Shabman "Pricing Flood Insurance."
81. For more details on cross-subsidization, see Carolyn Kousky, "Financing Flood Losses: A Discussion of the National Flood Insurance Program," *Risk Management and Insurance Review* 21, no. 1 (2018): 11–32.
82. Committee on the Affordability of National Flood Insurance Program Premiums, *Affordability of National Flood Insurance Program Premium: Report 1*; Kousky and Shabman, "Pricing Flood Insurance," 9–10.
83. Ericson and Doyle, *Uncertain Business*, 15; also Ericson, Doyle, and Barry, *Insurance as Governance*; Andrea Mennicken and Ebba Sjögren, "Valuation and Calculation at the Margins," *Valuation Studies* 3, no. 1 (2015): 1–7; Pat O'Malley and Alex Roberts, "Governmental Conditions for the Economization of Uncertainty," *Journal of Cultural Economy* 7, no. 3 (2014): 253–272. For more on histories and analyses of actuarialism and its relationship to insurance and risk management more broadly, see Peter L. Bernstein, *Against the Gods: The Remarkable Story of Risk* (New York: Wiley, 1998); Dan Bouk, *How Our Days Became Numbered: Risk and the Rise of the Statistical Individual* (Chicago: University of Chicago Press, 2015); Ian Hacking, *The Taming of Chance* (Cambridge: Cambridge University Press, 1990); Pat O'Malley, *Risk, Uncertainty and Government* (London: The Glass House Press, 2004); JoAnne Yates, *Structuring the Information Age: Life Insurance and Technology in the Twentieth Century* (Baltimore: Johns Hopkins University Press, 2008).
84. Technical Mapping Advisory Council, "Minutes: Technical Mapping Advisory Council Meeting March 10–11, 2015," last updated April 13, 2015, https://www.fema.gov/media-library-data/1429730866544-f8ac3427604286398b658245276be532/TMAC_Meeting_Summary_March_10–11_2015.pdf.
85. Howard Kunreuther and Erwann Michel-Kerjan, *At War with the Weather: Managing Large-Scale Risks in a New Era of Catastrophes* (Cambridge, MA: MIT Press, 2009), 107–108.
86. Wendy Espeland and Mitchell Stevens, "Commensuration as a Social Process," *Annual Review of Sociology* 24 (1998): 313–343.
87. Kousky and Shabman, "Pricing Flood Insurance," 9–10.
88. Property Casualty Insurers Association of America, *True Market-Risk Rates for Flood Insurance* (Des Plaines, IL: Property Casualty Insurers Association of America, 2011).
89. Erwann O. Michel-Kerjan, "Catastrophe Economics: The National Flood Insurance Program," *Journal of Economic Perspectives* 24, no. 4 (Fall 2010): 165–186.

90. Government Accountability Office, *GAO-09-455: Flood Insurance: Opportunities Exist to Improve Oversight of the WYO Program* (Washington, DC: Government Accountability Office, 2009), 10. See also *Government Accountability Office, GAO-09-12: Flood Insurance: FEMA's Rate-Setting Process Warrants Attention* (Washington, DC: Government Accountability Office, 2009); Government Accountability Office, *GAO-10-66: FINANCIAL MANAGEMENT: Improvements Needed in National Flood Insurance Program's Financial Controls and Oversight* (Washington, DC: Government Accountability Office, 2010).

91. Kevin Fox Gotham, "Disaster, Inc." See also Naomi Klein, *The Shock Doctrine: The Rise of Disaster Capitalism* (New York: Henry Holt, 2007); Vincanne Adams, *Markets of Sorrow, Labors of Faith* (Durham, NC: Duke University Press, 2013).

92. Koslov, "How Maps Make Time."

93. Xavier Landes, "How Fair is Actuarial Fairness?," *Journal of Business Ethics* 128, no. 3 (2015): 519–533.

94. Tom Baker, "Containing the Promise of Insurance: Adverse Selection and Risk Classification," *Connecticut Insurance Law Journal* 9, no. 2 (2002): 371–396. As Jens Oliver Zinn notes, economic tools in relation to nature "are likely to further proceed in societal contexts that enjoy broad social support for individual decision-making, rational choice and instrumental rationality, both being crucial for the economic worldview." Zinn, "Living in the Anthropocene," 391.

95. Turo-Kimmo Lehtonen and Jyri Liukko, "The Forms and Limits of Insurance Solidarity," *Journal of Business Ethics* 103 (April 2011): 33–44; Turo-Kimmo Lehtonen and Jyri Liukko, "Producing Solidarity, Inequality, and Exclusion Through Insurance," *Res Publica* 21 (May 2015): 1–15.

96. Kousky and Shabman, "Pricing Flood Insurance."

97. Landes, "How Fair is Actuarial Fairness?"; Lehtonen and Liukko, "The Forms and Limits"; Lehtonen and Liukko, "Producing Solidarity, Inequality, and Exclusion Through Insurance"; Carol Heimer, "Insurers as Moral Actors," in *Risk and Morality*, ed. Richard V. Ericson and Aaron Doyle (Toronto: University of Toronto Press, 2003), 284–316.

98. Tom Baker, "On the Genealogy of Moral Hazard," *Texas Law Review* 75, no. 2 (1996): 237–292.

99. Kousky and Shabman, "Pricing Flood Insurance." For an account of how this cross-subsidization is organized and has changed over time, see Committee on the Affordability of National Flood Insurance Program Premiums, *Affordability of National Flood Insurance Program Premium: Report 1*, 35.

100. Wendy Espeland, *The Struggle for Water*, 25.

101. Lehtonen and Liukko, "The Forms and Limits."

102. Stone, "Beyond Moral Hazard."

103. Baker, "Containing the Promise of Insurance," 379.

104. Beck, "Living in the World Risk Society," 333; see also Ulrich Beck, *Risk Society* (New York: SAGE Publications, 1992); Douglas, "Risk as a Forensic Resource."

105. Sheila Jasanoff, "Ordering Knowledge, Ordering Society," in *States of Knowledge: The Co-Production of Science and Social Order*, ed. Sheila Jasanoff (New York: Routledge, 2004), 13–45; Karin Knorr-Cetina, *Epistemic Cultures: How the Sciences Make Knowledge* (Cambridge, MA: Harvard University Press, 1999); Steven Shapin

and Simon Schaffer, *Leviathan and the Air-Pump: Hobbes, Boyle, and the Experimental Life* (Princeton, NJ: Princeton University Press, 1985).

106. Wynne, "Risk and Social Learning"; Weinkle and Pielke Jr., "The Truthiness about Hurricane Catastrophe Models"; Graham Haughton and Iain White, "Risky Spaces: Creating, Contesting and Communicating Lines on Environmental Hazard Maps," *Transactions of the Institute of British Geographers* 43 (2017): 435–448; Soden, Sprain, and Palen, "Thin Grey Lines."

107. Harriet Bulkeley, "Governing Climate Change: The Politics of Risk Society?," *Transactions of the Institute of British Geographers* 26 (2001): 430–447. Greta Krippner has also shown that the possibilities of claims-making in the credit market in the contemporary United States are forged in line with the way its component technologies relate to group identities and relations of inequality; see Greta Krippner, "Democracy of Credit: Ownership and the Politics of Credit Access in Late Twentieth-Century America," *American Journal of Sociology* 123, no. 1: 1–47.

108. Ian Hacking, "The Looping Effects of Human Kinds," in *Causal Cognition: A Multidisciplinary Debate*, ed. Dan Sperber, David Premack, and Ann James Premack (New York: Oxford University Press, 1995), 351–394.

4. SHIFTING RESPONSIBILITIES FOR LOSS: NATIONAL REFORM OF FLOOD INSURANCE

1. Field notes, October 16, 2013.

2. Brian Steensland, "Cultural Categories and the American Welfare State: The Case of Guaranteed Income Policy," *American Journal of Sociology* 111, no. 5 (2006): 1273–1326; Brian Steensland, *The Failed Welfare Revolution: America's Struggle over Guaranteed Income Policy* (Princeton, NJ: Princeton University Press, 2008); Michael B. Katz, *The Undeserving Poor: From the War on Poverty to the War on Welfare* (New York: Pantheon Books, 1989); Joel F. Handler and Yeheskel Hasenfeld, *The Moral Construction of Poverty: Welfare Reform in America* (Newbury Park, CA: SAGE Publications, 1991); Arthur L. Stinchcombe, "The Functional Theory of Social Insurance," *Politics & Society* 14, no. 4 (1985): 411–430; Gøsta Esping-Andersen, "Power and Distributional Regimes," *Politics & Society* 14, no. 2 (1985): 223–256; Anne Schneider and Helen Ingram, *Deserving and Entitled: Social Constructions and Public Policy* (Albany: State University of New York Press, 2005); Martin Gilens, *Why Americans Hate Welfare: Race, Media and the Politics of Antipoverty Policy* (Chicago: University of Chicago Press, 1999).

3. Joshua Guetzkow, "Beyond Deservingness: Congressional Discourse on Poverty, 1964–1999," *Annals of the American Academy of Political & Social Science* 629 (2010): 173–197.

4. An important exception to this can be found in the work of Michele Landis Dauber, especially in *The Sympathetic State: Disaster Relief and the Origins of the American Welfare State* (Chicago: University of Chicago Press, 2013).

5. Logan Strother, "The National Flood Insurance Program: A Case Study in Policy Failure, Reform, and Retrenchment," *Policy Studies Journal* 46, no. 2 (2016): 452–480.

6. Committee on the Affordability of National Flood Insurance Program Premiums, *Affordability of National Flood Insurance Program Premium: Report 1* (Washington, DC: National Academies Press, 2015), 63.

7. Eli Lehrer, "Strange Bedfellows: SmarterSafer.Org and the Biggert-Waters Act of 2012," *Duke Environmental Law & Policy Forum* 23 (Spring 2013): 351–361. The Center for Climate and Energy Solutions, Ceres, ConservAmerica, Defenders of Wildlife, the Natural Resources Defense Council, and the Nature Conservancy have also been SmarterSafer members at some point.

8. Interview, October 25, 2013.

9. US Congress, House, Subcommittee on Insurance, Housing, and Community Opportunity, *Legislative Proposals to Reform the National Flood Insurance Program, Part I: Hearing before the Subcommittee on Insurance, Housing, and Community Opportunity, House of Representatives*, 112th Cong., 1st sess., 2011, 3. In fact, data constraints limit FEMA's ability to estimate the aggregate costs of subsidies to the program; see Government Accountability Office, *GAO-13-607: FLOOD INSURANCE: More Information Needed on Subsidized Properties* (Washington, DC: Government Accountability Office, 2013).

10. US Congress, House, Subcommittee on Insurance, *Legislative Proposals, Part I*, 7–8, 10.

11. US Congress, House, Subcommittee on Insurance, *Legislative Proposals, Part I*, 27.

12. US Congress, House, Subcommittee on Insurance, *Legislative Proposals, Part I*, 35.

13. US Congress, House, Subcommittee on Insurance, *Legislative Proposals, Part I*, 37, 39.

14. US Congress, House, Subcommittee on Insurance, *Legislative Proposals, Part I*, 69.

15. US Congress, Senate, Subcommittee on Economic Policy of the Committee on Banking, Housing, and Urban Affairs, *Examining the Need for Long-Term Reauthorization and Reform of the National Flood Insurance Program*, 112th Cong., 2nd sess., 2012, 3.

16. US Congress, Senate, Subcommittee on Economic Policy, *Examining the Need*, 103.

17. Josh Dawsey, "The Super Activist That Sandy Made," *Wall Street Journal*, March 23, 2014.

18. For a detailed analysis of how Stop FEMA Now used social media, see Melissa Checker, "Stop FEMA Now: Social Media, Activism and the Sacrificed Citizen," *Geoforum* 79 (February 2017): 124–133.

19. Citizens for Homeowners Insurance Reform in Massachusetts, Facebook Group, accessed January 15, 2019, https://www.facebook.com/CitizensforHomeownersInsuranceReform/; Gulf Coast East Coast Homeowners Hurricane Insurance Coalition, Facebook Group, accessed January 15, 2019, https://www.facebook.com/pg/Gulf-Coast-East-Coast-Homeowners-Hurricane-Insurance-Coalition-259123800865886/about/?ref=page_internal; "Mississippi Homeowners Insurance Bill of Rights," accessed January 15, 2019, http://www.msbillofrights.com/.

20. "Homeowners' Hurricane Insurance Initiative," last updated November 8, 2013, archived website: https://web.archive.org/web/20131108035459/http://www.hhii.us#.

21. Homeowners' Hurricane Insurance Initiative, Facebook post, January 18, 2005, https://www.facebook.com/Homeowners-Hurricane-Insurance-Initiative-332310433663/.

22. Homeowners' Hurricane Insurance Initiative, Facebook post, May 24, 2014, https://www.facebook.com/Homeowners-Hurricane-Insurance-Initiative-3323 10433663/.

23. Interview, October 16, 2013.

24. Interview, October 22, 2013.

25. Committee on the Affordability, *Report 1*; Government Accountability Office, *GAO-13-607: FLOOD INSURANCE*.

26. Interview, October 26, 2013.

27. "Soaring Flood Insurance Rates: Should Congress Step In?" (panel discussion, Columbia Law School, Center for Climate Change Law, New York City, December 4, 2013).

28. Interview, September 26, 2013.

29. Richard M. Mizelle Jr., "Princeville and the Environmental Landscape of Race," *Open Rivers: Rethinking Water, Place and Community* 2 (Spring 2016): 16–28, 17. An E&E News analysis of $31 billion in claims for flood damage paid by the NFIP between January 2010 and August 2019 found that nearly 20 percent of claims dollars were paid in zip codes where at least one-quarter of the residents are black. Those zip codes made up only 13 percent of the U.S. population, suggesting that flooding disproportionately affects neighborhoods with a substantial black population. Thomas Frank, "Flooding Disproportionately Harms Black Neighborhoods," *E&E News*, June 2, 2020; Jess Bidgood, "A Wrenching Decision Where Black History and Floods Intertwine," *New York Times*, December 9, 2016; Keeanga-Yamahtta Taylor, *Race for Profit: How Banks and the Real Estate Industry Undermined Black Homeownership* (Chapel Hill: University of North Carolina Press, 2019); Jacob W. Faber, "Racial Dynamics of Subprime Mortgage Lending at the Peak," *Housing Policy Debate* 23, no. 2 (2013): 328–349; Zachary Paganini, "Underwater: Resilience, Racialized Housing, and the National Flood Insurance Program in Canarsie," *Geoforum* 104 (August 2019): 25–35.

30. Government Accountability Office (GAO), *RED-76-94: Formidable Administrative Problems Challenge Achieving National Flood Insurance Program Objectives* (Washington, DC: Government Accountability Office, 1976); *Oversight of the National Flood Insurance Program: Hearing before the Committee on Banking, Housing, and Urban Affairs of the United States Senate*, 109th Cong., 1st sess. (2005), statement of Robert J. Hunter, Director of Insurance, Consumer Federation of America; Scott Gabriel Knowles and Howard C. Kunreuther, "Troubled Waters: The National Flood Insurance Program in Historical Perspective," *Journal of Policy History* 26, no. 3 (2014): 327–353.

31. Field notes, October 16, 2013.

32. Rachel Cleetus, *Overwhelming Risk: Rethinking Flood Insurance in a World of Rising Seas* (Cambridge, MA: Union of Concerned Scientists, 2013); Rob Moore, "The Changing Climate for Flood Insurance," *NRDC Switchboard*, August 16, 2013.

33. "Soaring Flood Insurance Rates: Should Congress Step In?"

34. Greg Hanscom, "Flood Pressure: Climate Disasters Drown FEMA's Insurance Plans," *Grist*, January 13, 2014, https://grist.org/cities/flood-pressure-how-climate
-disasters-put-femas-flood-insurance-program-underwater/.

35. Interview, October 17, 2013.

36. Michael Eric Dyson, *Come Hell or High Water: Hurricane Katrina and the Color of Disaster* (New York: Basic Civitas Books, 2006); Robert D. Bullard and Beverly Wright, *The Wrong Complexion for Protection: How the Government Response to Disaster Endangers African American Communities* (New York: New York University Press, 2012).

37. Associated Press, "FEMA Sets up Review Process for Sandy Flood Insurance Claims," March 12, 2015.

38. Interview, October 25, 2013.

39. Wall Street Journal Editorial Board, "Editorial: Flooding Taxpayers Again: A Bipartisan Caucus Wants to Keep Subsidies Flowing to the 1%," *Wall Street Journal*, December 1, 2013.

40. Fieldnotes, October 16, 2013.

41. Roger Gendron, remarks at Rockaway, New York Stop FEMA Now rally, September 28, 2013.

42. Eric Ulrich, remarks at Rockaway, New York Stop FEMA Now rally, September 28, 2013.

43. Palmer Doyle, Open letter on Stop FEMA Now Facebook page, accessed February 27, 2014, https://www.facebook.com/StopFemaNow/photos/a.120204218150455 .21829.120198111484399/256475421190000/.

44. Interview, September 26, 2013.

45. Interview, October 16, 2013.

46. Bill Dedman, "Meet the Flood Insurance 'Robin Hood' Who Saves Condo Owners Millions," *NBC News*, February 19, 2014; Miranda Leitsinger, "For Average Joes, Fighting FEMA Flood Maps Isn't Easy or Cheap," *NBC News*, February 20, 2014.

47. Government Accountability Office, *GAO-13-607: FLOOD INSURANCE*, 12, 22. The Congressional Budget Office also found, in 2007, that many subsidized properties had high values (in coastal areas more attributable to the value of the land than to the value of the structures that occupy it), though the analyzed sample wasn't statistically random so it cautioned against extrapolating results nationwide. See Congressional Budget Office, *Value of Properties in the National Flood Insurance Program* (Washington, DC: Congressional Budget Office, 2007).

48. "Rep. Waters, Author of Flood Reform Act, Calls for Delay in Implementation," *Insurance Journal*, September 30, 2013, http://www.insurancejournal.com/news /national/2013/09/30/306602.htm. As Logan Strother notes, however, the Congressional record from before Biggert-Waters' passage indicates that members of Congress surely did know what was coming: "In short, there can be little doubt that members of Congress, both those in favor of the reforms, and those opposed, were fully aware that premiums would rise. Nor were they unaware that some citizens would be displeased by this disruption of the status quo. As such, the claim that Grimm-Waters [the Homeowner Flood Insurance Affordability Act] was simply an attempt to address unintended consequences of the reform package is suspect." Strother, "The National Flood Insurance Program," 23.

49. Committee on the Affordability, *Report 1*.

50. Field notes, March 27, 2014.

51. Committee on the Affordability of National Flood Insurance Program Premiums, *Affordability of National Flood Insurance Program Premiums—Report 2* (Washington, DC: National Academies Press, 2015), 4.

52. Small Business Administration loans for repair and rebuilding, however, are means-tested and must be repaid.

53. Committee on the Affordability, *Report 1*.

54. Calculated according to policyholders' income. The range captures eligibility thresholds of 80 and 140 percent of area median income, thresholds commonly used in Department of Housing and Urban Development and other government programs; see Government Accountability Office, *GAO-16-190: National Flood Insurance Program: Options for Providing Affordability Assistance* (Washington, DC: Government Accountability Office, 2016). An April 2017 GAO study of NFIP reform further recommended that Congress consider (1) funding such an assistance program through appropriation rather than discounted premiums; (2) making any assistance temporary; (3) allowing assistance to be used for the purchase of private policies; (4) prioritizing investments in mitigation over premium assistance where feasible; and (5) prioritizing mitigation loans over mitigation grants. See Government Accountability Office, *GAO-17-425: Flood Insurance: Comprehensive Reform Could Improve Solvency and Enhance Resilience* (Washington, DC: Government Accountability Office, 2017).

55. Dauber, *The Sympathetic State*, 13.

56. Barbara Kiviat, "The Moral Limits of Predictive Practices: The Case of Credit-Based Insurance Scores," *American Sociological Review* 84, no. 6 (2019): 1134–1158; see also Deborah A. Stone, "Causal Stories and the Formation of Policy Agendas," *Political Science Quarterly* 104, no. 2 (1989): 281–300; Marion Fourcade and Kieran Healy, "Seeing Like a Market," *Socio-Economic Review* 15, no. 1 (2017): 9–29.

57. Daniel Hirschman and Elizabeth Popp Berman, "Do Economists Make Policies? On the Political Effects of Economics," *Socio-Economic Review* 12, no. 4 (2014): 779–811.

58. Keith Hall, Congressional Budget Office, to Jeb Hensarling, Chairman, US House Financial Services Committee, April 19, 2017, *Re: Preliminary Results from CBO's Analysis of the National Flood Insurance Program*, https://www.cbo.gov/system /files/115th-congress-2017–2018/reports/52638-nfipletter.pdf.

59. David Moss, "Courting Disaster? The Transformation of Federal Disaster Policy since 1803," in *The Financing of Catastrophe Risk*, ed. Kenneth A. Froot (Chicago: University of Chicago Press, 1999), 307–362; Adelle Thomas and Robin Leichenko, "Adaptation Through Insurance: Lessons from the NFIP," *International Journal of Climate Change Strategies and Management* 3, no. 3 (2011): 250–263; Committee on the Affordability, *Report 1*.

60. Christopher Flavelle, "Climate Advocates Cheer Trump Policy Shift on Flood Insurance," *Bloomberg News*, March 18, 2019; "NFIP Transformation and Risk Rating 2.0," Federal Emergency Management Agency, last updated November 15, 2019, https://www.fema.gov/nfiptransformation.

5. FLOODPLAIN FUTURES: TRAJECTORIES OF LOSS

1. Kasia Paprocki, "All That Is Solid Melts into the Bay: Anticipatory Ruination and Climate Change Adaptation," *Antipode*, 51, no. 1 (2019): 295–315; Kasia Paprocki, "Threatening Dystopias: Development and Adaptation Regimes in Bangladesh,"

Annals of the American Association of Geographers 108, no. 4 (2018): 955–973; Sarah Knuth, "'All that is Solid . . . ': Climate Change and the Lifetime of Cities," *City* 24, nos. 1–2 (2020): 65–75.

2. Jesse M. Keenan, Thomas Hill, and Anurag Gumber, "Climate Gentrification: From Theory to Empiricism in Miami-Dade County, Florida," *Environmental Research Letters* 13, no. 5 (2018): 054001.

3. Steven A. McAlpine and Jeremy R. Porter, "Estimating Recent Local Impacts of Sea-Level Rise on Current Real-Estate Losses: A Housing Market Case Study in Miami-Dade, Florida," *Population Research and Policy Review* 37, no. 6 (2018): 871–895.

4. First Street Foundation, *As the Seas Have Been Rising, Tri-State Home Values Have Been Sinking*, last updated August 23, 2018, https://assets.floodiq.com/2018/08/17a e78f7df2f7fd3176e3f63aac94e20-As-the-seas-have-been-rising-Tri-State-home -values-have-been-sinking.pdf.

5. The researchers define "similar" as: properties in the same zip code, sold in the same month, in the same 200-foot band of distance to the coast, with similar elevation, number of bedrooms, property, and owner type. The analysis combines Zillow and National Oceanic and Atmospheric Administration data to define "exposed" properties as those that would be inundated at highest tide with a six-foot global average sea level rise. Asaf Bernstein, Matthew Gustafson, and Ryan Lewis, "Disaster on the Horizon: The Price Effect of Sea Level Rise," *Journal of Financial Economics* 134, no. 2 (2019): 253–272.

6. Note that these home prices have to be interpreted, in some areas in particular, as measures of highly uneven recovery from the housing crisis that began in 2007. Ian Urbina, "Perils of Climate Change Could Swamp Coastal Real Estate," *New York Times*, November 24, 2016.

7. The authors interpret this as evidence of an "information signal" from the maps rather a "price signal" from the premiums. However, as my own findings in chapter 2 suggest, these are difficult to disentangle in practice. See Matthew Gibson and Jamie T. Mullins, "Climate Risk and Beliefs in New York Floodplains," *Journal of the Association of Environmental and Resource Economists* (forthcoming). See also Francesc Ortega City and Suleyman Taspinar, "Rising Sea Levels and Sinking Property Values: The Effects of Hurricane Sandy on New York's Housing Market," Social Science Research Network Working Paper, March 29, 2018, http://dx.doi.org/10.2139/ssrn.3074762.

8. Lloyd Dixon, Noreen Clancy, Benjamin M. Miller, Sue Hoegberg, Michael M. Lewis, Bruce Bender, Samara Ebinger, Mel Hodges, Gayle M. Syck, Caroline Nagy, and Scott R. Choquette, *The Cost and Affordability of Flood Insurance in New York City* (Santa Monica, CA: RAND Corporation, 2017), 86–87. This is not just a flood story. Another 2018 Attom Data Solutions analysis on home prices and sales across 3,397 U.S. cities found that between 2007 and 2017, average home prices in areas facing the lowest risk of not only flooding, but also hurricanes and wildfires, have far outpaced those with the greatest risk. While home prices increased generally (7.3 percent over the ten-year period) across these cities, that overall rise masks the fact that prices for homes at high or very high risk of natural hazards have dropped; see Christopher Flavelle and Allison McCartney, "Climate Change May Already Be Hitting the Housing Market," *Bloomberg*, June 18, 2018.

9. Yi Qiang, "Disparities of Population Exposed to Flood Hazards in the United States," *Journal of Environmental Management* 232 (February 2019): 295–304; Virginia Eubanks, "My Drowned City Is a Harbinger of Climate Slums to Come," *The Nation*, August 29, 2016.

10. James Knighton, personal communication, February 4, 2020. Based on all available policy records from 2009 through February 3, 2020. Data available here: https://www.fema.gov/media-library/assets/documents/180376. FEMA deems a "primary residence" to be a single family building, condominium unit, apartment unit, or unit within a cooperative building that will be lived in by the policyholder or the policyholder's spouse for 1) more than 50 percent of the 365 calendar days following the current policy effective date; or 2) 50 percent or less of the 365 calendar days following the current policy effective date if the policyholder has only one residence and does not lease that residence to another party or use it as rental or income property at any time during the policy term. A policyholder and the policyholder's spouse may not collectively have more than one primary residence.

11. Natural Resources Defense Council, "Seeking Higher Ground," Issue Brief, July 2017, https://www.nrdc.org/sites/default/files/climate-smart-flood-insurance-ib.pdf.

12. Federal Emergency Management Agency, *An Affordability Framework for the National Flood Insurance Program* (Washington, DC: Federal Emergency Management Agency, April 17, 2018), 11. States where income is greater inside an SFHA, at statistically significant levels, are: South Carolina, Alaska, North Dakota, Maine, Florida, and Louisiana.

13. Federal Emergency Management Agency, *An Affordability Framework*, 13, 6.

14. Zip codes where household incomes have declined since 2016 also have relatively high hurricane insurance costs. Taylor also finds that these particularly vulnerable housing geographies are far more likely to be nonwhite, where residents may face compounding historical legacies of housing discrimination that have made home ownership difficult and expensive. See Zac J. Taylor, "The Real Estate Risk Fix: Insurance-Linked Securitization in the Florida Metropolis" (PhD diss., University of Leeds, 2018).

15. Earthea Nance, "Exploring the Impacts of Flood Insurance Reform on Vulnerable Communities," *International Journal of Disaster Risk Reduction* 13 (September 2015): 20–36.

16. Ajita Atreya and Jeffrey Czajkowski, "Is Flood Risk Universally Sufficient to Offset the Strong Desire to Live Near the Water," Working Paper, 2014–09 (November 26, 2014), Risk Management and Decision Processes Center, The Wharton School of the University of Pennsylvania, https://pdfs.semanticscholar.org/b93d/4222e323030561a31ebef116726dbc69ca54.pdf.

17. Freddie Mac, Economic & Housing Research Group, *Life's a Beach*, April 26, 2016, http://www.freddiemac.com/research/insight/20160426_lifes_a_beach.html.

18. Jesse M. Keenan and Jacob T. Bradt, "Underwaterwriting: From Theory to Empiricism in Regional Mortgage Markets in the U.S.," *Climatic Change* (June 2020), https://doi.org/10.1007/s10584-020-02734-1.

19. Urbina, "Perils of Climate Change."

20. Molly Peterson, "What Happens When You Buy a House in a Disaster Zone—And No One Told You?" *The Guardian*, September 25, 2018; Urbina, "Perils of Climate Change."

21. Abigail Darlington, "Little-Known Federal Law Keeps Buyers from Finding Out If a Home Routinely Floods," *The Post and Courier*, August 9, 2018.

22. Bernstein, Gustafson, and Lewis, "Disaster on the Horizon."

23. For more on this political and cultural context, see Debbie Becher, *Private Property and Public Power* (New York: Oxford University Press, 2014).

24. Zac J. Taylor, "The Real Estate Risk Fix: Residential Insurance-Linked Securitization in the Florida Metropolis," *Environment and Planning A: Economy and Space* (2020): 1–19.

25. Ian Gray, "Catastrophe Merchants: The Uncertain Convergence of Climate Data and Risk Analytics in Estimating Disaster Loss," *Economy and Society* (forthcoming); Jessica Weinkle and Roger Pielke Jr., "The Truthiness about Hurricane Catastrophe Models," *Science, Technology, & Human Values* 42, no. 4 (2017): 547–576.

26. Jessica Weinkle, "A Public Policy Evaluation of Florida's Citizens Property Insurance Corporation," *Journal of Insurance Regulation* 34, no. 1 (2015): 1–34, 1; also Martin F. Grace and Robert W. Klein, "The Perfect Storm: Hurricanes, Insurance, and Regulation," *Risk Management and Insurance Review* 12, no. 1 (2009): 81–124.

27. Ashley Dawson, *Extreme Cities: The Peril and Promise of Urban Life in the Age of Climate Change* (New York: Verso, 2017).

28. Prashant Gopal, "Distressed Investors Are Already Buying Houston Homes for 40 Cents on the Dollar," *Bloomberg*, October 12, 2017; Simon Romero, "Houston Speculators Make a Fast Buck From Storm's Misery," *New York Times*, March 23, 2018; David Hunn and Matt Dempsey, "Who's Buying Harvey-Flooded Homes in Houston? Mostly Investors," *Houston Chronicle*, May 10, 2018; Audra D. S. Burch, "Brutal Choice in Houston: Sell Home at a Loss or Face New Floods," *New York Times*, March 30, 2018.

29. Keenan, Hill, and Gumber, "Climate Gentrification"; Carolyn Beeler, "Miami Residents Fear 'Climate Gentrification' As Investors Seek Higher Ground," *Public Radio International*, December 19, 2017.

30. Keenan, Hill, and Gumber, "Climate Gentrification."

31. Stefanos Chen, "New Buildings Rise in Flood Zones," *New York Times*, July 6, 2018; Sarah Knuth, "'All that is Solid . . . ,'" 71.

32. Keenan, Hill, and Gumber, "Climate Gentrification"; Melissa Checker, "Wiped Out by the 'Greenwave': Environmental Gentrification and the Paradoxical Politics Of Urban Sustainability," *City and Society* 23, no. 2 (2011): 2l0–229; Kenneth A. Gould and Tammy L. Lewis, *Green Gentrification: Urban Sustainability and the Struggle for Environmental Justice* (New York: Routledge, 2017).

33. Jennifer L. Rice, Daniel Aldana Cohen, Joshua Long, and Jason R. Jurjevich, "Contradictions of the Climate-Friendly City: New Perspectives on Eco-Gentrification and Housing Justice," *International Journal of Urban and Regional Research* 44, no. 1 (2020): 145–165.

34. Stephen Collier and Savannah Cox, "Governing Urban Resilience: Insurance and the Techno-politics of Climate Risk," Working Paper.

35. For a critical account of the climate refugee narrative, see Carol Farbotko and Heather Lazarus, "The First Climate Refugees? Contesting Global Narratives of Climate Change in Tuvalu," *Global Environmental Change* 22, no. 2 (2012): 382–390.

36. Oliver Milman, "'We're Moving to Higher Ground': America's Era of Climate Mass Migration Is Here," *The Guardian*, September 24, 2018. See also Orrin H. Pilkey,

Linda Pilkey-Jarvis, and Keith C. Pilkey, *Retreat from a Rising Sea: Hard Choices in an Age of Climate Change* (New York: Columbia University Press, 2017).

37. Elizabeth Rush, *Rising: Dispatches from the New American Shore* (Minneapolis: Milkweed Editions, 2018); Coral Davenport and Campbell Robertson, "Resettling the First American 'Climate Refugees,'" *New York Times*, May 2, 2016.

38. Christopher Flavelle, "Trump Administration Presses Cities to Evict Homeowners from Flood Zones," *New York Times*, March 11, 2020.

39. Liz Koslov, "The Case for Retreat," *Public Culture* 28, no. 2 (2016): 359–387, 375; Liz Koslov, "Avoiding Climate Change: 'Agnostic Adaptation' and the Politics of Public Silence," *Annals of the Association of American Geographers* 109, no. 2 (2019): 568–580, 7.

40. Koslov, "Avoiding Climate Change."

41. Kevin Loughran and James R. Elliott, "Residential Buyouts as Environmental Mobility: Examining Where Homeowners Move to Illuminate Social Inequities in Climate Adaptation," *Population and Environment* 41, no. 1 (2019): 52–70.

42. Katharine J. Mach, Caroline M. Kraan, Miyuki Hino, A.R. Siders, Erica M. Johnston, and Christopher B. Field, "Managed Retreat Through Voluntary Buyouts of Flood-Prone Properties," *Science Advances* 5, no. 10 (2019): 1–9.

43. Anna Weber and Rob Moore, "Going Under: Long Wait Times for Post-Flood Buyouts Leave Homeowners Underwater," Natural Resources Defense Council, September 2019.

44. Elizabeth Marino, *Fierce Climate Sacred Ground* (University of Alaska Press, 2015); Elizabeth Marino, "Adaptation Privilege and Voluntary Buyouts: Perspectives on Ethnocentrism in Sea Level Rise Relocation and Retreat Policies in the U.S.," *Global Environmental Change* 49 (2018): 10–13; Duff Wilson, "The Village that Must Move, but Can't," *Reuters*, November 24, 2014.

45. Collier and Cox, "Governing Urban Resilience."

46. Lori Mack, "New Haven Gets High Rating For Coastal Resiliency Efforts," *WNPR*, September 26, 2017.

47. Chris Rotolo, "Flood Insurance Break for Sea Bright," *Two River Times*, May 4, 2018.

48. Taylor, "The Real Estate Risk Fix."

49. Ryan McNeill, Deborah J. Nelson, and Duff Wilson, "As the Seas Rise, a Slow-Motion Disaster Gnaws at America's Shores," *Reuters*, September 4, 2014.

50. Kevin Sack and John Schwartz, "Left to Louisiana's Tides, a Village Fights For Time," *New York Times*, February 24, 2018.

51. Another emergent model of federal financing is competition-based: after Hurricane Sandy, the U.S. Department of Housing and Urban Development announced a regional resilience competition called "Rebuild By Design," for which teams of designers, engineers, and architects were invited to propose innovative proposals for "regionally scalable but locally contextual solutions that increase resilience in the region." Cost-benefit analysis played a major role in defining the attractiveness of different project proposals. See Stephen J. Collier, Savannah Cox, and Kevin Grove, "Rebuilding By Design in Post-Sandy New York," *Limn* 7, July 2016, https://limn.it/articles/rebuilding-by-design-in-post-sandy-new-york/.

52. Localize Labs, "Localize.city Finds 12 Percent of New Units Are Being Built on City's Riskiest Land," July 6, 2018, http://labs.localize.city/developers-keep-flockin

g-to-flood-zones-localize-city-finds-12-percent-of-new-units-are-being-built-on-citys-riskiest-land/; Localize used FEMA's 2015 Preliminary Flood Insurance Rate Map and Department of Buildings permit data. The analysis looks at construction of multi-family buildings (with four or more units) in the city's 100-year-flood zone.

53. Climate Central, "Ocean at the Door: New Homes and the Rising Sea," November 13, 2018, http://www.climatecentral.org/news/ocean-at-the-door-new-homes-in-harms-way-zillow-analysis-21953.

54. Jeremy Pais and James R. Elliott, "Places as Recovery Machines: Vulnerability and Neighborhood Change After Major Hurricanes," *Social Forces* 86, no. 4 (2008): 1415–1453.

55. James R. Elliott and Matthew Thomas Clement, "Natural Hazards and Local Development: The Successive Nature of Landscape Transformation in the United States," *Social Forces* 96, no. 2 (2017): 851–876; Kevin Fox Gotham and Miriam Greenberg, *Crisis Cities: Disaster and Redevelopment in New York and New Orleans* (New York: Oxford University Press, 2014); Miriam Greenberg, "The Disaster inside the Disaster: Hurricane Sandy and Post-crisis Redevelopment," *New Labor Forum* 23, no. 1 (2014): 44–52; Naomi Klein, *The Shock Doctrine: The Rise of Disaster Capitalism* (New York: Picador, 2008).

56. Jeff Goodell, *The Water Will Come: Rising Seas, Sinking Cities, and the Remaking of the Civilized World* (New York: Little, Brown, 2017).

57. Taylor, "The Real Estate Risk Fix: Insurance-Linked Securitization"; see also Urbina, "Perils of Climate Change."

58. Taylor, "The Real Estate Risk Fix: Residential Insurance-Linked Securitization"; Zac J. Taylor and Jessica L. Weinkle, "The Riskscapes of Re/insurance," *Cambridge Journal of Regions, Economy and Society* (forthcoming); Leigh Johnson, "Catastrophic Fixes: Cyclical Devaluation and Accumulation Through Climate Change Impacts," *Environment and Planning A* 47, no. 12 (2015): 2503–2521; Leigh Johnson, "Geographies of Securitized Catastrophe Risk," *Economic Geography* 90, no. 2 (2014): 155–185.

CONCLUSION: WHAT DO WE HAVE TO LOSE?

1. Kate Lyons, Sam Levin, Matthew Weaver and Jamiles Lartey, "Five Dead in Tropical Storm as Flooding and Surges Continue—As It Happened," *The Guardian*, September 15, 2018; Oliver Laughland, Adam Gabbatt, and Khushbu Shah, "Carolinas Face Catastrophic Flooding as Florence Breaks Rainfall Records," *The Guardian*, September 15, 2018.

2. Molly Peterson, "What Happens When You Buy a House in a Disaster Zone—And No One Told You?," *The Guardian*, September 25, 2018.

3. Carolyn Kousky and Leonard Shabman, *The Realities of Federal Disaster Aid: The Case of Floods* (Washington, DC: Resources for the Future, 2012). Though FEMA can provide up to $34,000 per household in individual assistance disaster aid, the average amount paid out individually to homeowners in Hurricane Harvey was just over $8,900; in Irma and Maria, it was approximately $2,100 and $3,400,

respectively. See Margaret A. Walls and Danae Hernandez Cortez, "Recovering from Disasters: Evaluating FEMA's Housing Assistance Program in the 2017 Hurricane Season," Wharton Risk Management and Decision Processes Center, University of Pennsylvania, September 24, 2018, https://riskcenter.wharton.upenn.edu /resilience-lab-notes/recovering-from-disasters-evaluating-femas-housing -assistance-program-in-the-2017-hurricane-season/.

4. Vivien Gornitz, Michael Oppenheimer, Robert Kopp, Philip Orton, Maya Buchanan, Ning Lin, Radley Horton, and Daniel Bader, "New York City Panel on Climate Change 2019 Report, Chapter 3: Sea Level Rise," *Annals of the New York Academy of Sciences* 1439, no. 1 (2019): 71–94.

5. Richard Ericson and Aaron Doyle, *Uncertain Business: Risk, Insurance and the Limits of Knowledge* (Toronto: University of Toronto Press, 2004); Evan Mills, "Insurance in a Climate of Change," *Science* 309, no. 5737 (2005): 1040–1044; Paula Jarzabkowski, Rebecca Bednarek, and Paul Spee, *Making a Market for Acts of God* (Oxford: Oxford University Press, 2015).

6. Kevin Grove, "Insuring 'Our Common Future?' Dangerous Climate Change and the Biopolitics Of Environmental Security," *Geopolitics* 15, no. 3 (2010): 536–563; Kevin Grove, "Preempting the Next Disaster: Catastrophe Insurance and the Financialization of Disaster Management," *Security Dialogue* 43, no. 2 (2012): 139–155; Leigh Johnson, "Catastrophe Bonds and Financial Risk: Securing Capital and Rule Through Contingency," *Geoforum* 45 (March 2013): 30–40; Leigh Johnson, "Index Insurance and the Articulation of Risk-Bearing Subjects," *Environment & Planning A* 45, no. 11 (2013): 2663–2681; Leigh Johnson, "Catastrophic Fixes: Cyclical Devaluation and Accumulation Through Climate Change Impacts," *Environment and Planning A* 47, no. 12 (2015): 2503–2521; Isabelle Hualt and Hélène Rainelli-Weiss, "A Market for Weather Risk? Conflicting Metrics, Attempts at Compromise, and Limits to Commensuration," *Organization Studies* 32, no. 10 (2011): 1395–1419; Stephen J. Collier, "Enacting Catastrophe: Preparedness, Insurance, Budgetary Rationalization," *Economy and Society* 37, no. 2 (2008): 224–250; Philip Bougen, "Catastrophe Risk," *Economy and Society* 32 (2003): 253–274; Luis Lobo-Guerrero, *Insuring Security: Biopolitics, Security, and Risk* (Abingdon, UK: Routledge, 2011); JoAnne Linnerooth-Bayer, Swenja Surminski, Laurens M. Bouwer, Ilan Noy, and Reinhard Mechler, "Insurance as a Response to Loss and Damage?," in *Loss and Damage from Climate Change*, ed. Reinhard Mechler, Laurens M. Bouwer, Thomas Schinko, and Swenja Surminski (Boston: Springer, 2019), 483–512; Christopher Flavelle and Katherine Chiglinksy, "Quick Cash, Few Questions: Insurers Pitch Wild Storms Protection," *Bloomberg*, April 4, 2019.

7. Jonathan Salem Baskin, "While Politicians Debate, Munich Re Innovates," *Forbes*, September 10, 2015; Megan Rowling, "Insurance Gains Clout As Climate Change Solution for the Poor," *Reuters*, June 19, 2015; Brian Chappatta, "The Catastrophe Bond Business Is Booming," *Bloomberg*, September 11, 2018.

8. Turo-Kimmo Lehtonen, "Objectifying Climate Change: Weather-Related Catastrophes as Risks and Opportunities for Reinsurance," *Political Theory* 45, no. 1 (2017): 32–51, 33.

9. Arthur Neslen, "Climate Change Could Make Insurance Too Expensive for Ordinary People—Report," *The Guardian*, March 21, 2019.

10. Mitchell Dean, "Risk, Calculable and Incalculable," in *Risk and Sociocultural Theory: New Directions and Perspectives*, ed. Deborah Lupton (Cambridge: Cambridge University Press, 1999), 131–159, 138.

11. Wendy Espeland, *The Struggle for Water: Politics, Rationality, and Identity in the American Southwest* (Chicago: University of Chicago Press, 1998), xiii; Wendy Espeland and Mitchell Stevens, "Commensuration as a Social Process," *Annual Review of Sociology* 24 (1998): 313–343; Marion Fourcade, "Cents and Sensibility: Economic Valuation and the Nature of 'Nature,'" *American Journal of Sociology* 116, no. 6 (2011): 1721–1777; Viviana Zelizer, *Pricing the Priceless Child: The Changing Social Value of Children* (New York: Basic Books, 1985).

12. Didier Fassin, ed., *At the Heart of the State: The Moral World of Institutions* (London: Pluto Press, 2015), 9.

13. "Number of New, Renewed, and Non-Renewed Residential Dwelling Policies in Moderate to Very High Fire Risk ZIP Codes Based on CalFire's State Responsibility Area Map," California Department of Insurance, accessed February 13, 2020, http://www.insurance.ca.gov/0400-news/0100-press-releases/2019/upload/nr063_nonrenewaldatahighfirerisk.pdf.

14. Colin Dwyer, "Footing the Bill For Climate Change: 'By The End Of The Day, Someone Has To Pay," *National Public Radio*, September 20, 2018. Similar outcomes have been reported in Puerto Rico in the aftermath of Hurricane Maria in 2017. Two insurers went out of business and over a billion dollars of claims were still unpaid over two years later; see Frances Robles and Patricia Mazzei, "After Disasters, Puerto Ricans Are Left With $1.6 Billion in Unpaid Insurance Claims," *New York Times*, February 6, 2020.

15. Johnson, "Catastrophic Fixes"; Paula Jarzabkowski, Rebecca Bednarek, Konstantinos Chalkias, and Eugenia Cacciatori, "Exploring Inter-Organizational Paradoxes: Methodological Lessons from a Study of a Grand Challenge," *Strategic Organization* 17, no. 1 (2019): 120–132.

16. Alexis C. Madrigal, "Kim Kardashian's Private Firefighters Expose America's Fault Lines," *The Atlantic*, November 14, 2018. For more on the rise of private firefighting offered by insurance companies, see McKenzie Funk, *Windfall: The Booming Business of Global Warming* (New York: Penguin, 2014).

17. Richard Ericson, Dean Barry, and Aaron Doyle, "The Moral Hazards of Neo-Liberalism: Lessons from the Private Insurance Industry," *Economy and Society* 29, no. 4 (2000): 532–558; Liz McFall, "Is Digital Disruption the End of Health Insurance? Some Thoughts on the Devising of Risk," *Economic Sociology: The European Electronic Newsletter* 17, no. 1 (2015): 32–44.

18. Tom Baker and Jonathan Simon, *Embracing Risk: The Changing Culture of Insurance and Responsibility* (Chicago: University of Chicago Press, 2002), 3; Suzanne Mettler, *The Submerged State: How Invisible Government Policies Undermine American Democracy* (Chicago: University of Chicago Press, 2011).

19. Jacob S. Hacker, *The Great Risk Shift: The Assault on American Jobs, Families, Health Care, and Retirement* (Oxford: Oxford University Press, 2006), 6; Jacob S. Hacker, "Privatizing Risk without Privatizing the Welfare State: The Hidden Politics of Social Policy Retrenchment in the United States," *American Political Science Review* 98, no. 2 (2004): 243–260; Jacob S. Hacker and Anne O'Leary, *Shared*

Responsibility, Shared Risk: Government, Markets, and Social Policy in the Twenty-First Century (Oxford: Oxford University Press, 2012).

20. Baker and Simon, *Embracing Risk*, 6.

21. Craig Calhoun, "The Privatization of Risk," *Public Culture* 18, no. 2 (2006): 257–263; Marianne Cooper, *Cut Adrift: Families in Insecure Times* (Berkeley: University of California Press, 2014); Margaret Somers, *Genealogies of Citizenship: Markets, Statelessness, and the Right to Have Rights* (Cambridge: Cambridge University Press, 2008); Joshua Guetzkow, "Beyond Deservingness: Congressional Discourse on Poverty, 1964–1999," *Annals of the American Academy of Political & Social Science* 629 (2010): 173–197; Martha McCluskey, "Rhetoric of Risk and the Redistribution of Social Insurance," in *Embracing Risk: The Changing Culture of Insurance and Responsibility*, ed. Tom Baker and Jonathan Simon (Chicago: University of Chicago Press, 2002), 146–170; Lyle Scruggs, "The Generosity of Social Insurance, 1971–2002," *Oxford Review of Economic Policy* 22, no. 3 (2006): 349–364; Peter Taylor-Gooby, "Does Risk Society Erode Welfare State Solidarity?" *Policy & Politics* 39, no. 2 (2011): 147–161.

22. Eric Klinenberg, *Palaces for the People: How Social Infrastructure Can Help Fight Inequality, Polarization, and the Decline of Civic Life* (New York: Penguin, 2018).

23. Earthea Nance, "Exploring the Impacts of Flood Insurance Reform on Vulnerable Communities," *International Journal of Disaster Risk Reduction* 13 (September 2015): 20–36. On the intersection of austerity and climate change, see Naomi Klein, *This Changes Everything* (New York: Simon and Schuster, 2015).

24. Miriam Greenberg, "What On Earth Is Sustainable? Toward Critical Sustainability Studies," *BOOM: A Journal of California* 3, no. 4 (2013), 54.

25. Mettler, *The Submerged State*, 19.

26. This can result in what Liz Koslov examines as "agnostic adaptation," following Katrina Fischer Kuh; see Liz Koslov, "Avoiding Climate Change: 'Agnostic Adaptation' and the Politics of Public Silence," *Annals of the Association of American Geographers* (2019); Katrina Fischer Kuh, "Agnostic Adaptation," *Environmental Law Reporter* 45, no. 1 (2015): 10027–10048.

27. Paul Pierson, "Public Policies as Institutions," in *Rethinking Political Institutions: The Art of the State*, ed. Ian Shapiro, Stephen Skowronek, and Daniel Galvin (New York, New York University Press, 2006), 114–131, 116; Paul Pierson, "When Effect Becomes Cause: Policy Feedback and Political Change," *World Politics* 45, no. 4 (1993): 595–628.

28. David Garland, "The Rise of Risk," in *Risk and Morality*, ed. Richard V. Ericson and Aaron Doyle (Toronto: University of Toronto Press, 2003), 48–86, 62. See also Deborah Stone, "Beyond Moral Hazard: Insurance as Moral Opportunity," in *Embracing Risk: The Changing Culture of Insurance and Responsibility*, ed. Tom Baker and Jonathan Simon (Chicago: University of Chicago Press, 2002), 52–79; Mitchell Dean, "Risk, Calculable and Incalculable," in *Risk and Sociocultural Theory: New Directions and Perspectives*, ed. Deborah Lupton (Cambridge: Cambridge University Press, 1999), 131–159.

29. Ulrich Beck, "Living in the World Risk Society," *Economy and Society* 35, no. 3 (2006): 329–345, 339. Ulrich Beck, "Remapping Social Inequalities in an Age of

Climate Change: For a Cosmopolitan Renewal of Sociology," *Global Networks* 10, no. 2 (2010): 165–181.

30. For an examination of these efforts in the wake of Hurricane Sandy, see Ashley Dawson, *Extreme Cities: The Peril and Promise of Urban Life in the Age of Climate Change* (New York: Verso, 2017), chap. 6.

31. That Stop FEMA Now focused in this way aligns with some more general findings from Brian McCabe's study of homeowners' civic engagement. Contrary to the "ideology of homeownership" that holds that homeownership brings civic benefits from increased engagement in building communities and strengthening citizenship, McCabe shows that homeowners are not more likely than otherwise similar long-term residents to participate in civic life and, when they do, he argues that they engage in an exclusionary form of politics, out of an interest in protecting property values, that draws and enforces boundaries between homeowners and renters. Brian McCabe, *No Place Like Home: Wealth, Community, and the Politics of Homeownership* (New York: Oxford University Press, 2016).

32. Christopher Robbins, "Gentrified Aquarium: De Blasio's Streetcar and the Tale of Two Waterfronts," *Village Voice*, September 13, 2016; Make the Road New York (MRNY), *Treading Water: Renters in Post-Sandy New York City* (New York: MRNY, 2014). For a detailed demographic analysis of the effects of Hurricane Sandy, see Jacob William Faber, "Superstorm Sandy and the Demographics of Flood Risk in New York City," *Human Ecology* 43 (June 2015): 363–378.

33. Junia Howell and James R. Elliott, "Damages Done: The Longitudinal Impacts of Natural Hazards on Wealth Inequality in the United States," *Social Problems* 66, no. 3 (2019), 465. See also Jessica Schultz and James R. Elliott, "Natural Disasters and Local Demographic Change in the United States," *Population & Environment* 34, no. 3: 293–312; Kevin Fox Gotham, "Racialization and Rescaling: Post-Katrina Rebuilding and the Louisiana Road Home Program," *International Journal of Urban and Regional Research* 38, no. 3 (2014): 773–790; Kevin Fox Gotham and Miriam Greenberg, *Crisis Cities: Disaster and Redevelopment in New York and New Orleans* (New York: Oxford University Press, 2014); James R. Elliott and Jeremy Pais, "Race, Class, and Hurricane Katrina: Social Differences in Human Responses to Disaster," *Social Science Research* 35, no. 2 (2006): 295–321; Jeremy Pais and James R. Elliott, "Places as Recovery Machines: Vulnerability and Neighborhood Change after Major Hurricanes," *Social Forces* 86, no. 4 (2008): 1415–1453.

34. Lawrence J. Vale, "The Ideological Origins of Affordable Homeownership Efforts," in *Chasing the American Dream: New Perspectives on Affordable Homeownership*, ed. William M. Rohe and Harry L. Watson (Ithaca, NY: Cornell University Press, 2007), 15–40.

35. Sarah Quinn, *American Bonds: How Credit Markets Shaped a Nation* (Princeton, NJ: Princeton University Press, 2019); Christopher Howard, *The Welfare State Nobody Knows: Debunking Myths about U.S. Social Policy* (Princeton, NJ: Princeton University Press, 2006); Isaac Martin, *The Permanent Tax Revolt: How the Property Tax Transformed American Politics* (Stanford, CA: Stanford University Press, 2008); Mettler, *The Submerged State*.

36. Stephen Collier and Savannah Cox, "Governing Urban Resilience: Insurance and the Techno-politics of Climate Risk," Working Paper.

37. Liz Koslov, "Agnostic Adaptation," 4.

38. Tom Baker, "On the Genealogy of Moral Hazard," *Texas Law Review* 75, no. 2 (1996): 237–292; see also Margaret R. Somers and Fred Block, "From Poverty to Perversity: Ideas, Markets, and Institutions Over 200 Years of Welfare Debate," *American Sociological Review* 70 (April 2005): 260–287.

39. Dean, "Risk, Calculable and Incalculable," 145; Turo-Kimmo Lehtonen and Ine Van Hoyweghen, "Insurance and the Economization of Uncertainty," *Journal of Cultural Economy* 7, no. 4 (2014): 532–540.

40. Deborah Stone, "Beyond Moral Hazard: Insurance as Moral Opportunity," in *Embracing Risk: The Changing Culture of Insurance and Responsibility*, ed. Tom Baker and Jonathan Simon (Chicago: University of Chicago Press, 2002), 52–79, 53.

41. Stone, "Beyond Moral Hazard," 74.

42. National Oceanic and Atmospheric Administration, "Spring Flooding Summary 2019," accessed February 7, 2020, https://www.weather.gov/dvn/summary_Spring Flooding_2019.

43. AECOM, *The Impact of Climate Change and Population Growth on the National Flood Insurance Program Through 2100* (Washington, DC: Federal Emergency Management Agency, June 2013). See also Adelle Thomas and Robin Leichenko, "Adaptation Through Insurance: Lessons from the NFIP," *International Journal of Climate Change Strategies and Management* 3, no. 3 (2011): 250–263.

44. R. Dean Hardy, Richard A. Milligan, and Nik Heynen, "Racial Coastal Formation: The Environmental Injustice of Colorblind Adaptation Planning for Sea-Level Rise," *Geoforum* 87 (December 2017): 62–72; Earthea Nance, "Exploring the Impacts of Flood Insurance Reform."

45. John O'Neill and Martin O'Neill, *Social Justice and the Future of Flood Insurance* (York, UK: Joseph Rowntree Foundation, 2012).

46. Mettler, *The Submerged State.*

47. Janette Webb, "Making Climate Change Governable: The Case of the UK Climate Change Risk Assessment and Adaptation Planning," *Science and Public Policy* 38, no. 4 (2011): 279–292; John Urry, *Climate Change and Society* (Cambridge: Polity Press, 2011).

48. Brian Wynne, "Risk and Social Learning: Reification to Engagement," in *Social Theories of Risk*, ed. Sheldon Krimsky and Dominic Golding (London: Praeger, 1992), 275–297, 283. See also Deborah Lupton, "Risk as Moral Danger: The Social and Political Functions of Risk Discourse in Public Health," *International Journal of Health Services* 23, no. 3 (1993): 425–435.

49. Charles Perrow, *Normal Accidents* (Princeton, NJ: Princeton University Press, 1999), 355.

50. Sheila Jasanoff, "A New Climate for Society," *Theory, Culture & Society* 27, nos. 2–3 (2010): 233–253, 248.

METHODOLOGICAL APPENDIX

1. Michèle Lamont and Ann Swidler, "Methodological Pluralism and the Possibilities and Limits of Interviewing," *Qualitative Sociology* 37, no. 2 (2014): 153–171; Colin Jerolmack and Shamus Khan, "Talk Is Cheap: Ethnography and the Attitudinal Fallacy," *Sociological Methods & Research* 43, no. 2 (2014): 178–209.

2. Kristin Luker, *Salsa Dancing into the Social Sciences: Research in an Age of Info-Glut* (Cambridge, MA: Harvard University Press, 2008).

3. Michèle Lamont and Patricia White, *Workshop on Interdisciplinary Standards for Systematic Qualitative Research* (Washington, DC: National Science Foundation, 2007).

4. Karl N. Llewellyn and E. Adamson Hoebel, *The Cheyenne Way: Conflict and Case Law in Primitive Jurisprudence* (New York: William S. Hein and Co., 1941); Matthew Desmond, "Relational Ethnography," *Theory and Society* 43 (September 2014): 547–579, 555; Viviana A. Zelizer, "How I Became a Relational Economic Sociologist and What Does That Mean?" *Politics & Society* 40, no. 2 (2012): 145–174.

5. Adele Clarke, Carrie Friese, and Rachel Washburn, *Situational Analysis: Grounded Theory After the Postmodern Turn*, 2nd ed. (Thousand Oaks, CA: SAGE Publications, 2005). Examples that have inspired me in economic sociology and studies of insurance include: Paula Jarzabkowski, Rebecca Bednarek, and Paul Spee, *Making a Market for Acts of God* (Oxford: Oxford University Press, 2015); Timothy Mitchell, "The Properties of Markets," in *Do Economists Make Markets? On the Performativity of Economics*, ed. Donald MacKenzie, Fabien Muniesa, and Lucia Siu (Princeton, NJ: Princeton University Press, 2007), 244–275; José Ossandón, "Reassembling and Cutting the Social with Health Insurance," *Journal of Cultural Economy* 7, no. 3 (2014): 291–307; Ine Van Hoyweghen, "Taming the Wild Life of Genes by Law? Genes Reconfiguring Solidarity in Private Insurance," *New Genetics and Society* 29, no. 4 (2010): 431–455.

6. Eugene McCann and Kevin Ward, "Assembling Urbanism: Following Policies and 'Studying Through' the Sites and Situations of Policymaking," *Environment and Planning A* 44, no. 1 (2012): 42–51; Colin McFarlane, "Translocal Assemblages: Space, Power and Social Movements," *Geoforum* 40 (July 2009): 561–567.

7. Jacob S. Hacker and Paul Pierson, "After the 'Master Theory': Downs, Schattschneider, and the Rebirth of Policy-Focused Analysis," *Perspectives on Politics* 12, no. 3 (2014): 643–662, 643.

8. Mario Small, "How Many Cases Do I Need? On the Science and Logic of Case Selection in Field-Based Research," *Ethnography* 10, no. 1 (2009): 5–38.

9. Brian Wynne, "Misunderstood Misunderstanding: Social Identities and the Public Uptake of Science," *Public Understanding of Science* 1, no. 3 (1992): 281–304; see also Howard Becker, "The Epistemology of Qualitative Research," in *Ethnography and Human Development: Context and Meaning in Social Inquiry*, ed. Richard Jessor, Anne Colby, and Richard A. Shweder (Chicago: University of Chicago Press, 1996), 53–70.

10. Small, "How Many Cases."

11. Robert S. Weiss, *Learning from Strangers: The Art and Method of Qualitative Interview Studies* (New York: The Free Press, 1994).

12. Michael Burawoy, "For Public Sociology," *American Sociological Review* 70, no. 1 (2005): 4–28.

13. Rebecca Elliott and Elizabeth Rush, "Stormy Waters: The Fight Over New York City's Flood Maps," *Harper's Monthly*, June 2017.

INDEX